A Level Politics
Study and Revision Notes

A comprehensive set of notes on global politics in accordance with the Edexcel A Level Politics specification, complete with comparisons and tables.

Pearson Edexcel Level 3 Advanced GCE in Politics (9PL0)

Global Politics

Authored by: Percival Fletcher

Global Politics

Overview

We live in a complex world with significant challenges, including global terrorism, poverty, economic instability, weapons proliferation, failing states and environmental degradation. These challenges require global co-operation if they are to be resolved. Global politics gives students an opportunity to develop an understanding of the local, national, international and global dimensions of political activity. It also gives them the opportunity to explore the political issues that affect all of us. Students will gain understanding of abstract political concepts through grounding them in contemporary real-world examples and case studies that will develop an international awareness and knowledge of multiple perspectives. Global politics encourages discussion and debate and requires students to study and present different global perspectives, as well as interpreting competing and contestable claims. The key mainstream perspectives on global politics are liberalism and realism, and students will be expected to understand how these perspectives are applied throughout all elements of the global politics content.

- Taken from A Level Politics Specification available at https://qualifications.pearson.com/content/dam/pdf/A%20Level/Politics/2017/Specification%20and%20sample%20assessments/A-level-Politics-Specification.pdf

Table of Contents

GLOBALISATION

Globalisation is defined by Held et al. (1999) as "the widening, intensifying, speeding up and growing impact of world-wide interconnectedness." Globalisation is not a single process, but a complex of them working in uneven tandem:

- **Cultural globalisation**
- **Political globalisation**
- **Economic globalisation**

This unit explores a number of key questions about globalisation:

- Is it a phenomenon (something that naturally happens) or a policy (something which must be consciously implemented and pursued)?
- Is globalisation synonymous with 'Westernisation' or 'Americanisation'?
- Is globalisation really happening, or has its extent/scale been overexaggerated?
- Can globalisation be reversed or controlled; is this already happening?
- Is globalisation a positive development; and for who?

The historical perspective

There have always been historical global flows...

- ***Of cultures and religions:***
  When people move, they bring with them new cultural and religious ideas. Even when people do not physically move en masse, these cultural and religious ideas can still be transmitted by individuals or small groups, or via texts, artworks and physical objects. Examples of this include the spread of Greek culture in the ancient world through the Macedonian Empire, reflected in the Ptolemaic dynasty of Egypt and Greco-Buddhist sculptures in India; and the spread of Christianity from Palestine across the Mediterranean between the 1st and 4th centuries

- *Of peoples and nations:*
  Peoples and 'nations' have moved across the planet for millennia. By migrating, they reshape demographics, form relationships and fundamentally change the regions they live in. Examples of this include the Bantu migrations in sub-Saharan Africa between the 10th century BC and the 17th century AD; the Arab migrations between the 6-8th centuries across the Middle East and North Africa; and the Turkic migrations between the 11th-15th centuries that displaced the local Greek population from Anatolia, in what is now modern-day Turkey

- *Of trade and economy:*
  The story of trade and economic integration (whether cooperative or enforced) is almost as old as written history. States, kingdoms and political entities have always exchanged goods and services with each other. Examples of this include the ancient Silk Roads linking Han China and the Roman Empire, which never directly interacted but traded extensively indirectly through intermediaries in Persia and India; and the British Raj, which was foremost a commercial endeavour seeking to extract wealth, agricultural resources and labour from India and transfer it to the British homeland

- *Of political centralisation:*
  On regional, continental and global scales, it seems that over millennia, nations and states have been drawn together into blocs and alliances of increasing magnitude. This far precedes the onset of the 'modern' world, and like economic flows, can be both voluntary and enforced. Examples of this include the Roman Empire, which evolved from a small polity on the Italian peninsula into the dominant force across the Mediterranean, implementing a codified system of laws and political directives; and the Haudenosaunee or 'Iroquois' Native American confederacy in what is now the north-eastern United States, which saw six separate tribes join together into a formidable political and military union which resisted French expansion

All of this begs the question; **what makes 'globalisation' today any different?** Surely it is just our perception of a historical norm which has been happening for centuries and millennia.

According to some theories, there *is* nothing different about globalisation; it is merely a continuation of these previous global flows, and there is no special 'interdependence' or 'interaction' in the modern-day sense. This is called the sceptical position, and usually reflects realist views of IR, since it maintains that states remain unitary, sovereign, self-contained actors.

According to others, the distinguishing aspect of modern globalisation is the intensity of the process – both in pace and scape. Although there is disagreement over whether globalisation will end in a completely unified world (the hyperglobalist position) or whether it has limits (the transformationalist position), many theorists believe that modern globalisation is changing the world at an unprecedented rate. These usually reflect liberal views of IR, since it proposes that states are not fully unitary, and that sovereignty is not absolute but conditional on interactions with other states

The engines of globalisation

We can identify three 'engines' of modern globalisation:

Communication:

- Technology has had a huge impact on modern communication. Virtually instantaneous communication is now available to billions of people through the Internet, smartphones, and cheap computing power. This is true even in states which are not economically developed, like India, where apps like WhatsApp allow for the rapid dissemination of information (and tacky good morning messages)
- The cost of Internet usage has fallen precipitously in the last three decades, driven by better fibre-optic and satellite technology, and private companies compete to provide services. In 1990, only 2.6 million people had access to the Internet – today, the global total is approximately 4 billion (a growth of 154,000%)
- Through social media, the average degree of social separation between two randomly chosen people *anywhere in the world* on Facebook is 4.5
- Communication not only allows for the maintenance of worldwide social networks, but for the greater availability of news and information which arguably aids in the process of democratisation in states where official media is tightly regulated
- Communication has led to a vastly more globalised world, albeit not always for 'good' purposes. The Arab Spring protests in the Middle East have largely been organised through Twitter and global pressure on dictators was increased by viral clips of army and police atrocities; but social media has also been used by ISIS to transmit its brutal propaganda executions and recruit new followers

Transport:

- Like communication, modern technology means that the speed of transport has hugely reduced in recent decades. In 1800, it would have taken over two months for a ship to cross the Atlantic from the UK to New York; steam power slashed this in half by the 1840s; today, oil/gas engines mean a ship can make the

journey in less than four days; a plane can make the journey in about five hours in good conditions
- As well as transport becoming faster, it has become cheaper due to the availability of new technology and competing private companies (e.g. airlines). It is no longer prohibitive for individuals to travel frequently or to move goods *en-masse* across the world. In 1956, the largest cargo ships could carry approximately 80 cargo containers. The largest 'Post New Panamax' ships today can carry approximately 18,000 containers
- Goods can be produced in one part of the world and shipped to another in a matter of days; most flowers you see in UK supermarkets have been grown in East African countries like Kenya and Tanzania, freshly cut, and shipped over to the UK

Migration:

- As discussed above, the low cost of travel has meant that migration is generally available to a much larger share of the human race than it ever has been before
- The cost of staying in contact with one's home country is also a lot lower, because of cheap communications, which reinforces connections between 'host' and 'home' countries instead of individuals merely moving to a new country and completely losing links with their former home, as may have happened even in the early 1900s
- Economic booms encourage workers to move to countries with higher economic development or big infrastructure programmes, in pursuit of a better life. This is not always the case – Gulf States like Qatar and the UAE are tremendously wealthy because of oil, and have encouraged Indian and Nepali workers to migrate to the Gulf to work in construction in appalling conditions. Well over 50% of the total Gulf population is composed of Indian migrants
- Many Western states also have increasing migrant populations; the British NHS for example has tens of thousands of staff with Indian, Filipino, Irish, Polish and Portuguese nationality

All of these engines of globalisation are interlinked – e.g. better communications and transport encourages migration. We can separate them for the purposes of definition, but they are closely tied together. As well as being **causes** of globalisation, they are also **outcomes** of it. A world with more integrated flows of goods, people, ideas, etc. is one in which people have a greater desire to travel, to consume 'exotic' foreign goods, and to communicate more widely; as well as providing the pool of talent and innovation to create new technologies and drive the process further forwards. 49% of the UK's largest companies, for example, were founded by immigrants (compared to 14% of the UK population who are immigrants).

Many people would argue that this process:

Advances in communication, transport and migration → economic, cultural and political integration → advances in communication, transport and migration ad infinitum

: is effectively unbreakable and that globalisation is a **self-sustaining** and inevitable process. This reflects the liberal view in increasing institutional cooperation. Others would argue that there are genuine roadblocks that mean that this is a process which can be stopped, or even put into reverse. The current coronavirus pandemic is one such example; although communication has intensified, transport and migration have stalled. One could argue that states are becoming more isolated and detached from each other, and even that some states are choosing to purposefully distance themselves from other states which are seen as public health risks (e.g. China). This reflects the realist view that any cooperation and interdependence is ultimately superficial and temporary.

CULTURAL GLOBALISATION

Cultural globalisation is the 'flattening out' of differences in culture between different nation-states. Cultural **heterogeneity** is therefore replaced by cultural **homogeneity**, and the globe as a whole will move towards a **monoculture**. A 'culture' can be very broadly defined as the "ideas, customs and social behaviours of a given group". Cultural globalisation can be seen in many areas of life:

- Music, film and television
- Food and drink
- Consumption of brands
- Political and religious beliefs

Advantages and disadvantages of cultural globalisation

As discussed in the previous section, cultural globalisation is generally enabled by technological advances that have led to increased communication; migration; and transport. There are many identifiable advantages and disadvantages of cultural globalisation, outlined below.

Advantages of cultural globalisation	Disadvantages of cultural globalisation
Spread of liberal democracy: States will theoretically move towards a common ground on political ideas, including things like human rights, individualism, democracy and liberalism. For example, when the Berlin Wall came down and the Soviet Union collapsed in the early 1990s, these cultural ideas about politics spread rapidly into Eastern Europe. More recently, huge pro-democracy protests have been seen in Iraq; Chile; and Hong Kong, to name a few. This can be seen as	Westernisation/Americanisation: Cultural globalisation can be seen as an unequal process – not cultures blending together and sharing their 'best parts', but of a dominant culture being imposed over all others. Historically, this dominant culture has been Western, or more specifically Western culture, in the late 20th/21st century because of the West's imperial and then economic dominance. Western beauty standards, consumption patterns, media and values have therefore

good for individuals (better civil liberties), for states (more meritocratic government is probably more efficient) and for international relations (the liberal theory that democracy engenders peace)	become ubiquitous worldwide, displacing other cultures. However, there is no reason that this will always be the case – a future imperial/economic giant (China?) might take over this dominant role
Cultural co-existence: Cultural globalisation means there is an increased possibility of co-existence and peace between cultures – this is especially important in a modern multicultural society when many states no longer correlate neatly with a 'cultural nation' and coexistence is vital. Exposure to a variety of lives, beliefs and behaviours enriches the human experience – London, New York, Singapore or any other diverse city is a good example of this. Cultural globalisation is correlated with 'tolerance'; if we map the % of Brexit vote with % of UK constituency that is foreign-born and observe a negative correlation [i.e the more exposure to foreigners, the less pro-Leave an area]	**Disproportionate role of TNCs:** Transnational corporations play a disproportionate role in cultural globalisation, as they are usually the vehicle by which elements of culture are transmitted across the globe either physically or digitally on an unprecedented scale, e.g. sports teams, music styles, food and drink, etc. This has two impacts which have been critiqued – (i) it tends to reinforce Western cultural dominance, since most powerful TNCs are based in the West; and (ii) it may lead to 'cultural appropriation', where meaningful elements of non-Western cultures are made profitable for Western TNCs (e.g. Sioux eagle-feather headdresses; hadith; Holi; etc.)

A third, more complex, critique of cultural globalisation is outlined below; along with a counter-criticism. The **'Clash of Civilizations'** is a book written by Samuel Huntington (which is named for the central thesis of the book, deeply critical of cultural globalisation). He argues that the world is divided into a number of cultural civilisations – Western, Islamic, Chinese, Orthodox, Latino, African, etc. These civilisations all have their own unique sets of defining values, e.g.:

- **Western:** Individualism, liberty, rationalism, secularism, rights
- **Sinic [Chinese]:** Order, hierarchy, patriotism, loyalty, authority

- **Islamic:** Islam, social conservatism, social morality, political traditionalism

Huntington argues that 'civilisational' identity is becoming more important in the modern world. This is because (as he argues):

1. Differences between civilisations are fundamental and based on history, language, culture, tradition and **most importantly, religion**

2. The world is becoming a 'smaller' place **due to technological advancements in communication** which intensifies civilisational consciousness – people are therefore more aware of differences between 'them' and 'others'

3. People are separated from 'local' or 'regional' identities due to economic and social change – civilisational religious identity tends to replace this

4. This process is accelerated by the overwhelming power of the liberal Western world, which runs into the desire of non-Western civilisations to shape a distinct future for themselves

He notes that clashes will happen along geographic **fault-lines** between civilisations, where they border one another; or where a civilisation tries to impose its values on another, leading to an inevitable backlash. According to Huntington, the majority of modern conflicts can be understood through this paradigm, for example:

- The EU clashing with Russia, especially in Ukraine **(Western v Orthodox civilisation)**
- Hostilities between India and Pakistan **(Hindu v Islamic civilisation)**
- Islamist terrorism, e.g. 9/11 and 7/7, right-wing supremacist terrorism, e.g. the neo-Nazi Christchurch shooting, and the 'War on Terror' in Afghanistan, Iraq and the Middle East more broadly **(Western v Islamic civilisation)**
- Trump's racism against Hispanic immigrants **(Western v Latino civilisation)**
- The Chinese programme of genocidal suppression in Xinjiang **(Sinic v Islamic civilisation)**

In Huntington's view, therefore, civilisations are bound to **'clash'** since they are incommensurable, inherently distinct, and mutually incompatible. Cultural globalisation is in his view a recipe for accelerating civilisational conflict, so he is deeply critical of it. This generally fits in with the realist view of nation-states (or civilisation-states?) fiercely defending their sovereignty and protecting their interests in a zero-sum battle for power.

It is worth considering some key counter-arguments to Huntington's thesis, though it may seem superficially attractive:

1. What Huntington calls innate, inherent civilisational values are in fact very flexible and change over time. Democracy, liberalism and secularism have only been 'Western' values since the late 1700s at the earliest (full suffrage in the UK wasn't until the 1920s)

2. Most conflicts in the world tend to be between members of the same 'civilisation' rather than between 'civilisations' – so Huntington's theory doesn't seem to be empirically supported

3. The concept of a 'civilisation' is far too broad and brushes over significant differences of identity; for example, Iran and Saudi Arabia are both lumped into an 'Islamic civilisation'

4. The existence of reasonably stable multicultural societies (e.g. London!) is testament to the fact that it is possible for 'civilisations' to coexist and even recombine in new ways

The sustainability of cultural globalisation

The case for sustainability: Cultural globalisation is a phenomenon enabled by new modes of technology, transport and the unprecedented movement of people across the globe. People are becoming more 'global' citizens, demanding foods, experiences, products, music, etc. from more varied sources. The cult success of K-Pop in the West; Starbucks and McDonalds in Asia; the popularity of European footballing teams in Africa; and the globalisation of media consumption through online platforms like Netflix all attest to this. It is not possible for states to stem the flow of cultural globalisations – once exposed to the richness of opportunities and consumption, individual citizens would simply not accept the state taking all of this away. On top of this, political culture is becoming increasingly globalised in the form of the spread of liberal democracy. Pro-democratic protests across the world from Chile to Iraq to Hong Kong to Thailand to Nigeria show that a single global political culture is slowly evolving, even though it may face some setbacks. Cultural globalisation is therefore inevitable and irreversible on the world stage.

The case against sustainability: Cultural globalisation is a phenomenon enabled by a relative minority in global terms. There is a small elite which benefit from and appreciate multicultural tastes, but most people across the world want to retain a traditional, conservative national identity. This can be seen in the manifestation of political parties, processes and figures from around the world; Brexit and Farage in the UK; Trump in the USA; Bolsonaro in Brazil; the AKP and Erdogan in Turkey; Xi Jinping in China; Narendra Modi in India, and so on. All of these parties and individuals campaign on a message of the state reinforcing sovereignty and imposing a national identity, and rejecting cultural influences from beyond the borders of the nation-state. They have implemented programmes to encourage traditional practises and purify the nation-state of 'foreign influences'. The globalisation of political culture is also questionable; the crushing of pro-democratic movements in the Arab Spring (Syria, Saudi Arabia) and in China (Hong Kong) suggests that there is nothing inevitable about cultural globalisation. Sovereign states have always had the power, and now the will, to stop it.

POLITICAL GLOBALISATION

Political globalisation is the process of increasing cooperation and coordination between national governments through the creation of global political institutions. These can deal with a variety of issues – economics, climate change, conflict resolution, human rights, etc. It can also involve the creation of non-state global political institutions. Together, these represent a move towards **global governance.** This is different to historical forms of inter-state coordination, because modern political globalisation is now **institutionalised** and **multilateral**.

There are two main manifestations of political globalisation:

Intergovernmental organisations (IGOs): IGOs are established **between states**. They have increased exponentially in number over the last 150 years, and especially since the mid-1940s (after WWII, to prevent the recurrence of another destructive global conflict). They continued to grow in number throughout the latter half of the 20th century as states began to identify more global challenges and issues that required inter-state cooperation. Examples of IGOs are the United Nations; the EU; the IPCC (Intergovernmental Panel on Climate Change).

Nongovernmental organisations (NGOs): Nongovernmental organisations (NGOs) are those that are established to deal with global issues but that **do not principally involve states**. When referring to NGOs, we usually are referring to non-state and non-profit organisations, rather than for-profit organisations like corporations. Examples of NGOs include Amnesty International (human rights); Greenpeace (environmental) and Medicins sans Frontieres (conflict alleviation). It is currently estimated that there around 6000 NGOs in the world, depending on the precise definition used.

Advantages and disadvantages of political globalisation

As discussed in the previous section, political globalisation is generally enabled by technological advances that have led to increased communication; migration; and transport. There are many identifiable advantages and disadvantages of political globalisation, outlined below.

Advantages of political globalisation	Disadvantages of political globalisation

Dealing with global problems (IGOs): Many problems in the modern world are global problems and cannot be solved by a single state in isolation – for example climate change and terrorism (which are inherently cross-border issues) and workers' rights (since a lack of cooperation would simply lead to a race to the bottom to maximise economic profitability). Intergovernmental organisations are therefore vital. The United Nations Framework Convention on Climate Change (UNFCCC) was the basis for the Paris Agreement (2015) limiting global greenhouse emissions; Interpol is vital for cracking down on international criminal networks; the EU has begun to implement more stringent directives on workers' rights and labour laws	'Loss' of sovereignty: A frequent complaint of nation-states is that globalisation sees effective decision-making power transferred to global political institutions (IGOs and NGOs), undermining the principle of state sovereignty – since they may be *compelled* to accept certain decisions. The fear is that this is a slippery slope to the complete loss of power in the long-run. This is the argument expressed by many populists with reference to the institutions that they are part of; Viktor Orban (Hungary) and the Law and Justice Party (Poland) are both very critical of the EU, arguing that it undermines their ability to preserve their national identity, implement strict anti-immigration and socially conservative (abortion, homosexuality, etc.) laws within their own borders
Dealing with global problems (NGOs): Much like domestic pressure groups in the UK, NGOs are an important element of political globalisation, since they can provide expertise on particular issues or attention towards otherwise sidelined issues. NGOs can directly influence/solve certain issues where they do not violate state sovereignty, e.g. Oxfam's programmes to increase access to clean water; or they can put pressure on state governments to	Domination by larger states: Another potential downside of political globalisation is that ostensibly 'global' institutions do not provide equitable solutions – they are dominated by more powerful states, who used political globalisation to extend and entrench their influence. Examples of this include Russia's use of their position on the Permanent 5 (P5) of the UN Security Council to veto action against their ally, Assad, in Syria; or by the USA to veto resolutions

change their policies, e.g. Amnesty International's very successful campaign for the abolition for the death penalty across much of the world; or Greenpeace and the WWF's (Worldwide Wildlife Foundation) campaigns for better ecological protections	critical of Israel. Another example was Meng Hongwei's presidency of Interpol (2016), where he abused his position to issue 'red notice' international criminal warrants against pro-democracy Chinese activists in exile, e.g. Wei Jingsheng (Switzerland)

The sustainability of political globalisation

The case for sustainability: Since the end of WWII, political globalisation has been on a steady upwards trajectory. The number of intergovernmental institutions has proliferated at an exponential rate as states recognise the challenges of the modern world – terrorism, climate change, etc. – that can be dealt with only in conjunction. We can see that the general pattern is for states to want to join these intergovernmental institutions and partnerships to make common policy decisions – there are currently several EU candidates (Serbia, Montenegro, Macedonia and Albania) in the Balkans; and two potential candidates (Kosovo and Bosnia). Even where a state moves away from political globalisation, sub-units and actors within the state still tend towards cooperation – Governor Brown of California, for example, signed a separate deal with China to work on climate change despite Trump's withdrawal from the Paris Climate Agreement. Given that California accounts for 13% of the US economy, this is not insignificant! The strength of political globalisation can also be seen in the endurance of the United Nations. Even where states are unhappy with most other states (e.g. North Korea), they still do not seek to leave the UN – no state ever has (contrary to the pre-WWII League of Nations, which was abandoned by Germany, Japan and the Soviet Union). States fundamentally recognise the value of cooperation and dialogue – political globalisation is therefore irreversible.

The case against sustainability: What we have seen in the past decade is a concerted move away from political globalisation and towards states reclaiming national political sovereignty – the ability to make their own policy decisions without the interference of other states or institutions. This has been reflected prominently in the West, with Trump's threats to withdraw from NATO and his withdrawal from the Paris Climate

Agreement; in Brexit, with the UK detaching itself from the EU; and in other nationalist movements across Europe which seek 'independence' from the European Union. Intergovernmental institutions, though they may continue to exist, are becoming increasingly hamstrung by the rise of belligerent states which do not wish to cooperate with common decision-making and want to double-down on the principles of state sovereignty. This can be seen through Russia's militarism in Syria and China's genocide in Xinjiang and their refusal to allow the UN to discuss these issues collectively. States are also still clearly more powerful than NGOs and can bar them from performing their functions – e.g. Israel's banning of Amnesty International from the West Bank – this again limits the scope of political globalisation. Political globalisation is in terminal decline – it is a comforting illusion behind which the realist truth of state sovereignty persists.

ECONOMIC GLOBALISATION

Economic globalisation can be defined as the increasing integration of national and regional economies. In practise, this means an intensification of cross-border flows of:

- Goods
- Capital
- Services
- Technology
- Information
- Labour

Previously, global integration of national and regional economics was hindered by technological limitations – an inability to **communicate** and **transport** goods/services in large quantities or at appropriate speeds to stop the deterioration of perishable products. Economic globalisation has a long history, but has been recently accelerated and increased in scope due to:

1. **Air travel:** Allowing corporations/businesses to operate across states and continents due to rapid travel of individuals for business meetings, etc., as well as the rapid transit of goods

2. **Container ships:** Most goods are moved around the world via container ships, the largest of which can carry upwards of 15,000 containers (each around 6x2x2 metres in size)

3. **The Internet:** This allows for ease of communication, enhancing cross-border economic activity, and has even led to the development today of entirely new corporate ecosystems with Internet-based services (e.g. Amazon) and extended supply chains

4. **Reduced migration barriers:** This allows for talent, innovation and labour to flow freely across borders, and contributes to the growth of transnational corporations with branches or different stages of a production line in different countries

5. **Reduced tariffs:** The reduction of 'tax' on the trade of goods/services between states has incentivised companies to seek further consumer markets and

resources abroad

6. **Deregulation of financial markets:** This has enabled currencies and stocks to be traded more freely, again enhancing the growth of large transnational corporations

All of these things are to some extent under the control of states, since **sovereign** states can implement **financial** barriers, **physical** barriers to the movement of goods/people, and even **virtual** barriers on the Internet through censorship.

A brief history of economic globalisation

Bretton Woods system (1944): As WWII drew to a close, the 'Bretton Woods' economic system was designed to prevent a reoccurrence of the circumstance that led to pre-war economic catastrophe. The system was focused on fixed exchange rates and regulations to encourage trade between countries. The Marshall Plan for massive reconstruction investment in Europe was also carried out by the USA. This led to a boom in economic growth and employment in the West

Oil Crisis and Bretton Woods II (1973): The oil crisis and the collapse of fixed exchange rates led to floating exchange rates. This led to greater competition between national economies and a growth in transnational corporations investing and operating across nation-states

'Opening' of China (1970-1990s): After the fall of Mao Zedong as his 'Cultural Revolution' floundered in chaos, successive Chinese leaders began liberalising China's economy (though not its politics) and encouraging foreign investment and Chinese exports

Collapse of communism (1990s): The collapse of Communism in the Soviet Union and Eastern Europe opened up new markets and investment opportunities, and new pools of labour and resources for the international, globalised market

Advantages and disadvantages of economic globalisation

As discussed in the previous section, economic globalisation is generally enabled by technological advances that have led to increased communication; migration; and transport. There are many identifiable advantages and disadvantages of economic globalisation, outlined below.

Advantages of economic globalisation	Disadvantages of economic globalisation
Greater quality of goods/services: Economic globalisation means that there is a significant rise in trade between nation-states. This will lead to a greater availability and quality of goods (physical items), because they can be sourced from across the world. This is the case for individual products (e.g. tropical fruits in British supermarkets) or composite products, where different components may be made in different countries (e.g. steel in China, transistors in Taiwan, electronics in India, from rare earth minerals mined in Congo, etc.). They will also be generally cheaper because of comparative advantage – states produce what they can at the lowest opportunity cost and then trade with each other. Economic globalisation has demonstrably brought down costs for foods, electronics, manufactured goods, clothes, etc.	Rising inequality within states: Although globalisation has raised the GDP of developing states as a whole, the spread of wealth *within* states has been very uneven. In developing states, the statistical evidence suggests economic globalisation benefits mainly male and urban populations. In developed states, 'modern' sectors of the economy will flourish but areas which formerly relied heavily on manufacturing, e.g. the north of England or the 'Rust Belt' in the USA are likely to suffer because of the outsourcing of jobs to developing countries with cheaper labour costs and less regulations, e.g. China and India.
This is also true for services, especially in more developed nation-states. The more integrated movement of global labour helps to	Contagion of instability: Although globalisation leads to a more integrated global economy, offering more opportunities and wealth, it also means economic problems are more contagious – i.e. they will spread more rapidly across the world, as states are more interdependent and have interconnected banking systems.

fill gaps in the labour market (e.g. the shortfall of doctors and nurses in the NHS) of developed countries and spawns further innovation and wealth.	Examples include the Asian Financial Crisis (1997), the bursting of the 'Dot-Com' bubble (2001) and the Financial Crisis (2008)
Reduction in global poverty: Economic globalisation means that transnational corporations often shift or outsource many aspects of their manufacturing or production to the developing world. This provides more job opportunities, improves infrastructure and generates wealth. For example, virtually all of Vietnamese workers employed by TNCs are in the top 20% of the country's earners (even though they are underpaid and work long hours by Western standards). As well as the economic opportunities provided by integration into a global economy, advances in knowledge and technology can be lowered in price and rapidly transmitted to the developing world in a globalised economy, 'skipping over' earlier stages of technological development that developed countries have passed through. For example, mobile phones and the internet have led to a massive growth in	Ecological destruction: Economic globalisation has created something approximating a global capitalist economy. Because capitalism is driven by the profit motive, corporations often (i) move production to companies with lax environmental regulations (e.g. strip-mining cobalt in the Congo, polluting the local water supply) and/or (ii) extract resources at an unsustainable rate (e.g. 60% of Amazonian deforestation is for the purpose of cattle ranches). As a result of greenhouse gases generated by industry, climate change raises global temperatures and damages the environment as a whole (rising sea levels, desertification, tropical storms etc.)
	Corporate threat to democratic sovereignty: In developing states, powerful states can take advantage of lax environmental and labour laws and 'pay off' a ruling elite to maintain this, e.g. Central American 'banana republics'. In developed

online banking in sub-Saharan Africa, which in turn has reduced poverty in rural areas. Economic globalisation via the Internet is quantitatively different from former types of economic integration, since it provides instantaneous global connections. As a result of the globalised economy, every state is significantly better off in terms of GDP per capita and life expectancy compared to the early 1900s (see bubble-graph below)	states, the 'military-industrial complex' is a phenomenon where corporations lobby for and encourage military action abroad, so they can reap profit by selling expensive weapons (e.g. Lockheed Martin, Blackwater, and the Iraq War (2003)). In all states, data harvested by social media giants can be used to sway elections and referendums, and to boost divisive content (e.g. right-wing nationalism) for more engagement and ad revenue.

The sustainability of economic globalisation

The case for sustainability: The march of the globalised world economy has been unstoppable since the end of WWII. It began with the West; it spread to China under Deng Xiaoping's economic reforms; and then to Eastern Europe and Russia with the end of the Cold War. There is now nearly nowhere on the planet which is untouched by the interconnected global flows of goods, services, labour and ideas. The transnational corporations that exist today strengthen and reaffirm this links on a daily basis, with their supply chains stretching across multiple countries and continents. Economic globalisation is effectively inevitable and irreversible; since every state benefits from it, and cannot maintain current standards of living without it, it is difficult to see how or why a state would detach itself from this mutually beneficial process. Even where we states attempting to do so, we can simultaneously see how this is either impossible or self-defeating. For example, Brexit was conceived partially as a process of removing the UK from the EU's economic structures and common market, and re-instating a position of national economic sovereignty. Nevertheless, the UK cannot avoid participation in the global economy – it must still strike new trade deals with states like the USA and

India, who will in turn make their own demands; e.g. the lowering of food safety standards, and an increase in the volume of permitted visas respectively. As another example, when Trump imposed tariffs on China, this resulted in a collapse in the US agricultural industry, for which China is a major export market – the US then had to spend $28 billion bailing out American farmers, and Trump eventually ended the trade war and returned to the status quo. It is now functionally impossible for any state to operate and flourish outside the globalised economy.

The case against sustainability: Economic globalisation seems to have been on an unrelenting trajectory for the last half-century, but the interconnectedness of the global economy has caused some serious issues which will lead to its possible fracturing over the next few decades. We can already see some of the precursors of this in Brexit and Trumpism. In addition, the dominance of China in the global economy is a cause for worry for many other states because it means that China has a great deal of leverage over other states, e.g. the pressure it has placed on Pakistan and Turkey to not speak out on the issue of the Uighur genocide in Xinjiang, despite the fact that they are both Muslim states and very vocal on other issues of 'Muslim rights', e.g. the Charlie Hebdo cartoons in France and the Israel-Palestine conflict. Combined with China's role as the originator of coronavirus, this could lead to an attempt to disentangle the global economy in the coming decades and reduce China's role as the 'factory of the world'. Given environmental concerns about the impact of a globalised economy, a 'throw-away' culture of mass production of cheap goods which break down quickly, and the carbon footprint of extended supply chains, it is also possible that states will move towards more self-contained national economies with a reduced ecological impact (thereby moving away from a global economy that is as integrated as it currently is).

GLOBALISATION, STATES AND INTERNATIONAL LAW

N.B. The content of this section will be covered in much more depth in Unit 3.3. (Global Governance in Human Rights and Environmental Issues). This is just a brief summary to understand how globalisation has impacted international law

What is 'international law'?

Typically speaking, we define law as a set of rules with the following characteristics:

- Universal jurisdiction (it applies over all other customs and belief systems)
- It is compulsory and coercive (it must be followed, with the threat of punishment)
- It has a 'public quality' (everyone knows broadly what it is and buys into it)
- It often embodies moral claims (in terms of what is 'good' or 'bad')

This is how law operates on a domestic scale, but as we shall see, international 'law' is quite different.

International law as an **institution** (a body of rules and practises) began to emerge in the 16th and 17th centuries in Europe through a number of different post-conflict treaties:

- *Augsburg (1555):* Different territories in Europe could freely choose their own religion
- *Westphalia* **(1648):** Principle of state sovereignty
- *Utrecht (1713):* The idea of sovereignty explicitly linked to a defined territorial border

A man called **Hugo Grotius** was key to the development of early international law, focusing specifically on the conditions for a just war and the rights of different states in relation to each other.

In summary, the key thrust of international law before the 20th century was the notion of Westphalian sovereignty – each nation-state should be able to determine its own laws. International law was primarily concerned with **non-interference** in the affairs of other states. **'Just wars'** could still occur as a last resort, proportionate, defensive action against the aggression of another state.

25

However, in the first half of the 20th century (1900s), there were numerous atrocities which challenged the Westphalian concept of international law as an **amoral** institution which should primarily preserve unquestioned state sovereignty. These included the mass casualties of WWII, specifically the Holocaust carried out by Nazi Germany against Jews, Romani, homosexuals, disabled people and Slavs; and Imperial Japan's extensive litany of civilian murders, industrial-scale rape and horrific human experimentation in their occupation of China and Korea. Theoretically speaking, these were all legally valid under the Westphalian model as they happened within territory that was under the sovereign jurisdiction of Germany and Japan at the time.

What began to emerge after WWII, therefore, was the development of a concept of **human rights** and a **universalised** or **globalised** standard of international law – a common standard of behaviour and rights which all states should follow, and which theoretically was 'higher' than the principle of state sovereignty. The institutions founded in the aftermath of WWII (like the United Nations) were the foundation of what we recognise today as 'international law'.

Comparing domestic and international law

Individuals are compelled to follow domestic law because the state is sovereign and has an apparatus of coercion to enforce it (the police, the courts, prison, etc.) International law is much more like a set of norms and rules which have developed by consensus and cannot be 'imposed' in the same way, since states are the sovereign actors in the international arena. This begs the question – why do sovereign states follow international law if there is no global sovereign to impose them?

1. **Common rules are mutually beneficial:** This is the English School explanation – that having a common set of rules provides order and stability, and this is mutually beneficial for all states because it enables them to make decisions in a more predictable context, leading to more reliably good outcomes. E.g. if all states stuck to trade treaties they signed, then it would be more likely that states would want to negotiate trade treaties

2. **Conferral of legitimacy and 'soft power':** Following international law, established by more powerful states, can provide global legitimacy, status and improve the standing of states which previously did not respect human rights or otherwise violated international treaties. In turn, this is a route to better

relations and the benefits of trade, interaction, etc. For example, in 2003, Colonel Gaddafi (the Libyan leader) announced that it would dismantle its nuclear weapons programme (which was in violation of the Non Proliferation Treaty) in order to secure better relations with European states, e.g. the UK under Tony Blair at the time

3. **Genuine moral belief in international law:** Some states may just be genuinely committed to the ideals of humanitarianism and liberal human rights, and follow international law for that reason, e.g. Canada or Germany

4. **Fear of isolation and punishment:** Although there is no global sovereign to enforce international law, a coalition or body of states might band together to 'punish' a state if it egregiously violates international law and is seen as a threat to other states, e.g. an Arab-American-European coalition against Iraq in 1991 after it invaded Kuwait. Otherwise, a state that does not follow international law might become a pariah (outcast), damaging its ability to trade and interact with other states (this is shown in the example above regarding Gaddafi's renouncing of nuclear weapons and international terrorism – e.g. the Lockerbie bombing and the Berlin discotheque bombing)

Humanitarian intervention

Although there is no 'world army' to uphold international law in the sense of human rights, since the 1990s a concept of **humanitarian intervention** has emerged in which a state/states intervene in another state, in which genocide, war crimes or crimes against humanity are taking place. The point of the intervention is not to extend a state's strategic or economic power, but to reduce suffering.

Examples of 'successful' humanitarian interventions include:

- **Kurdistan region of Iraq (1991):** NATO established a 'no-fly zone' over the Kurdistan region of Iraq in the aftermath of the Gulf War to prevent Saddam Hussein launching a chemical-weapons genocide against the Kurds, as he had attempted in the 1980s

- **NATO in Kosovo (1999):** NATO intervened in a Balkans conflict, where the majority Muslim-Albanian population of Kosovo was under risk of genocide from the Serbian state from which they sought independence. NATO bombed key Serbian military and political buildings in order to force Serbia to recognise Kosovan independence. (In the aftermath of this, many Kosovans named their child 'Tony Blair' in recognition of the UK's role)

- **Sierra Leone (2000):** The UK intervened in the Sierra Leonean Civil War, bringing an end to many years of brutal fighting and helping to establish a stable parliamentary democracy

Humanitarian intervention therefore has the capacity to save thousands, or even millions of lives. It is generally seen as a positive development in a **liberal** framework of global political understanding, since it involves cooperation between states to apply a universalist moral framework; and further notes that state sovereignty is no longer absolute, but this is to the benefit of individual citizens.

There are, however, some critiques of humanitarian intervention:

1. **Violates state sovereignty:** Humanitarian intervention violates the established Westphalian norm of non-intervention and inviolable state borders, and in turn threatens order – since if states feel like borders are no longer meaningful, they may begin to adopt a position of military adventurism (e.g. Turkey expanding into northern Syria, under the guise of 'humanitarian intervention' but really to push back Kurdish populations who they see as a threat, because of Kurdish separatism in south-east Turkey)

2. **Goes beyond just war as 'self-defence':** Just war is generally defined as a war in 'self-defence'; humanitarian intervention is about 'defending others'. This provides a potentially unlimited justification for war, since there will always be some group, somewhere in the world to defend. Not only does it allow for an unlimited justification which may be abused, but it imposes *obligations* on other states to intervene – who should take responsibility?

3. **Goes beyond just war as 'last resort':** Just war is generally defined as a war in 'last resort', but to prevent a genocide or large scale loss of life, pre-emptive force must be used before mass killings take place. Again, this provides a potentially unlimited justification for war, since the proposal and rationale for war is inherently counter-factual

4. **Assumption of universal human rights:** Some would argue that human rights (democracy, freedom of speech, freedom of religion, etc.) are not really 'universal' concepts, but are Western-specific concepts – and that the imposition of these through humanitarian intervention is equivalent to Western cultural imperialism. This was a common critique of the rationale for the wars in Afghanistan and Iraq; and has also been deployed by China to warn against interference in Xinjiang

5. **No guarantee of improvement:** Practically speaking, there is no guarantee that intervention will improve the 'situation on the ground' in terms of securing human rights – several interventions have made things demonstrably worse, e.g. NATO intervention in Afghanistan (2001-present) and in Libya (2011). In the case of the latter, the overthrow of Gaddafi and the lack of a coherent follow-up plan meant that the country quickly devolved into warring factions, including ISIS, other warlords, rogue military officials, etc.

6. **Window-dressing for imperialism:** 'Humanitarianism' may be used to give a veneer of legitimacy to wars of conquest or imperialism against nation-states. It is specifically alleged this is used by Western powers to maintain their hegemony (dominance), e.g. the war in Iraq (2003) launched by the USA, in violation of UN resolutions declaring it illegal

These are all **realist** objections to humanitarian intervention, since it is seen as damaging state sovereignty; the underpinning cornerstone of any meaningful international order. It is difficult to see how humanitarian intervention can be squared with state sovereignty, since it explicitly places the importance of globalised and universal human rights above the sovereign will of states to dictate policy within their own borders. There have been some attempts to 'square the circle' and make human rights compatible with state sovereignty. One of these is the concept of **R2P (Responsibility to Protect)** which was formulated as a doctrine by Canada and adopted by the UN in 2005. In essence, it argues:

- States *are* sovereign as per the Westphalian model
- Sovereignty is conditional on following certain responsibilities
- These include protecting one's citizens (actively and passively)

- If a state does not uphold this responsibility, either through direct persecution (e.g. genocide) or inaction (e.g. not dealing with a famine amongst a specific ethnic group) then other states may conduct a humanitarian intervention

Despite all of the above, it is not necessarily the case that interventions will always occur. Non-intervention in **Syria, Yemen** and **Xinjiang** despite mass casualties (because of the objections of Russia, the USA and China respectively) suggest that the globalisation of law through humanitarian intervention is limited by the state that it targets. Major world powers, or their clients/allies, cannot be effectively targeted in humanitarian interventions – this seems to be a limitation of globalised law.

International courts and tribunals

Another challenge posed by globalised international law to state sovereignty is the role of international courts. The **International Criminal Court** was established in 2002 by the Rome Statute and is based in the Netherlands. States who have ratified the Rome Statute are subject to the Court's jurisdiction, and leaders/individuals from those states can be prosecuted for genocide, war crimes or crimes against humanity – the definition of these crimes are part of the Rome Statute. This would reflect a **liberal** view of increasingly international and supranational global governance

However, many key countries including the USA, Russia, China, Israel, India, Saudi Arabia and Iran – have either **not signed up**, **not ratified** or have **withdrawn their signature from** the Rome Statute. The jurisdiction of the ICC does not extend to them. This is problematic, because most of the states which have not signed up to the Rome Statue account for the majority of the world's egregious human rights abuses. This again seems to suggest the challenge posed by globalised law to state sovereignty in the form of international courts is limited. This would reflect the **realist** view that state sovereignty is not fundamentally challenged by global legal institutions.

THE DEATH OF GLOBALISATION?

De-globalisation is the concept that globalisation can be put into reverse, either through active pursuit of policies of national sovereignty by states, or simply as a 'natural' phenomenon, reversing the artifice of globalisation to a pre-existing equilibrium. This can be seen in the sub-concepts of:

- **Political de-globalisation:** States withdrawing from international organisations and pushing their own interests to the detriment of institutional cooperation
- **Economic de-globalisation:** States attempting to disentangle their economies from other economies and restrict the flow of goods, services and people across borders
- **Cultural de-globalisation:** States rejecting the maxim of cultural homogeneity and seeking to preserve a distinct national-cultural identity

Why does de-globalisation happen?

A slowdown or reversal of globalisation is historically triggered by a major catastrophe which makes individuals in nation-states around the world feel (perhaps fairly) that globalisation has not been a 'fair deal' for them, and that they would do better 'on their own'. This reflects **realist** ideas that any cooperation or integration between states is at best temporary, and eventually states will return to a position of self-contained sovereign units.

In the 1930s-40s, for example, this catastrophe was the Great Depression, which:

- Pushed the 'democratic' Western powers; Britain, France and the USA; into isolationism
- Lead to the growth of virulent expansionist autocracies in Germany, Italy and Japan

Today, the catastrophe which seems to have triggered the modern wave of so-called de-globalisation is the Financial Crisis of 2008 and its worldwide repercussions, although each country and region has its own unique circumstances, individual figures, political parties, etc.

The key question we have to answer here is – "Is de-globalisation happening? If so, on what scale?" The information below helps to answer that question, although there is no clear-cut conclusion.

The de-globalisation of the West?

The right-wing de-globalisation of the West in favour of a set of policies focused on maintaining the economic, political and cultural sovereignty of nation-states can be seen in:

The USA: The election of Trump as President in 2016 was based on an explicitly 'America First' platform, disengaging with global partnerships and institutions. This included criticisms of NATO (alleging the USA was paying 'too much' towards European defence); NAFTA (alleging the USA was being flooded by cheap Canadian and Mexican imports); and trade with China (accusing them, somewhat fairly, of being currency fixers and less fairly, of stealing American jobs). More generally, Trump argued for the recreation of an 'American' identity. Despite losing the 2020 election, Trump still received over 70 million votes (more than he did in 2016). During his presidency, Trump:

- Withdrew the USA from the Paris Climate Agreement to reduce carbon emissions
- Imposed a slew of tariffs on Chinese industry which reduced Chinese imports by 30%
- Banned immigration from a range of Middle Eastern countries (the 'Muslim Ban')
- Restricted immigration from Central America by adopting a severe anti-migrant policy on the Mexican border, separating children from their parents and interring them in detention camps
- Supported white nationalist voices in the USA opposing cultural integration and admixture

The UK: The Brexit vote seemed to indicate that the UK was opposed to globalisation in the sense of political, economic and cultural unity with Europe. The Conservative Party, currently led by Boris Johnson, has tended towards the pursuit of a 'hard' or 'No Deal' Brexit, in which we leave both the political structures of the EU and the economic customs union/single market. This has been largely driven by the European Research Group (ERG) faction within the Conservative Party. There has also been a recent tendency in the UK towards a glorification of Empire, figures such as Churchill, and the key ingredients of a cultural-national British identity

Europe: Across Europe, there seems to be a resurgence of nationalism. Parties whose platforms can be defined as 'right-wing nationalist' dominate in many countries – the most notable of these are:

- Jobbik and Fidesz (Hungary)
- The Freedom Party (Austria)
- Alternativ fur Deutschland – the AfD (Germany)
- The Front National (France)
- The Five Star League (Italy)

All of these governing parties (as majorities or in coalition partners) have expressed a deep antipathy towards receiving Middle Eastern immigrants, characterising them as a threat to conservative, white, Christian European identity. Many of them are also opposed to the EU in its current state, claiming that it disadvantages less wealthy states. It could also be argued that France, under the leadership of Emmanuel Macron, is currently undergoing a process of cultural nationalism vis-à-vis trying to cut religion, particularly Islam, out of the public sphere of life.

However, all of the above should be balanced by some caveats...

1. Donald Trump only won the 2016 election because of the quirk of the Electoral College – he actually received 3 million votes less than Clinton. He also lost the 2020 election to Joe Biden, suggesting that his brand of nationalist populism is becoming less popular

2. Polling in the UK seems to indicate that most Britons are now *against* Brexit. In addition to this, even though Brexit may be seen as an act of de-globalisation, its proponents see it as a way to *further* globalise Britain's economy by giving it the ability to strike independent deals with countries like India, China and the USA (regardless of whether this is actually possible)

3. Electoral and polling evidence suggests many nationalist parties have become slightly less popular recently. A particularly spectacular collapse is that of the Golden Dawn neo-fascist party in Greece, where 13 major party leaders were recently jailed on supremacist terror charges in Athens, the Greek capital

N.B. The case for de-globalisation is not purely a right-wing one. Many left-wing politicians in the West have called for de-globalisation, arguing that globalisation has had a negative impact in their countries. This is because globalisation has established a worldwide capitalist economy, and the shift of manufacturing to the developing world, where regulations are lax and labour is cheap, has decimated many traditional 'working-class' regions of developed states. Both Corbyn and Sanders (runner-up in the 2016 and 2020 Democratic primaries in the USA) have called for less economic globalisation, although they have not necessarily been critical of cultural globalisation. They have also embraced the notion of political globalisation (states cooperating to establish a common good).

The champions of globalisation

At the same time, several states and organisations have emphasised the global nature of challenges faced by the modern world and sought to keep liberal, Western-led globalisation alive. In the West, this movement has been prominent represented by Emmanuel Macron (France), Angela Merkel (Germany) and Justin Trudeau (Canada). All of these leaders have:

- Advocated policies to continue membership of and respect for international organisations such as the United Nations, International Criminal Court, and European Union
- Promoted international free trade and low tariffs (Canada and the EU negotiated a trade deal)
- Argued against isolationist policies and taken in refugees (Merkel took 1 million Syrian refugees into Germany despite heavy domestic criticism; Canada offered to take 1000 Rohingya from the Myanmar genocide)
- Taken the lead on climate change policy, with independent proposals for carbon emission reductions (EU 45% 2030 target)

Again, there are some caveats...

1. There is no guarantee that these politicians, or their parties, will be indefinitely elected. Macron in particular seems under siege from centre-right parties and the 'Gilet Jaunes' (Yellow Jacket) protests, which seem to reflect a generally traditionalist, 'France-first' approach to politics and a rejection of global internationalism

2. It is unclear whether these states alone can maintain the momentum of globalisation without the leadership of the USA. With Biden winning the presidency in 2020, this seems more likely, but 70 million people still voted for Trump and it is not beyond the realm of possibility that another anti-globalist president (or an anti-globalist Senate) is elected in the USA

Chinese-led globalisation

One might argue that although the West seems to be in retreat from the principles of globalised foreign policy, other states – primarily Xi Jinping's China – are fully committed to a globalised world and will move to fill the vacuum, taking the lead in promoting globalisation.

China is deeply committed to the ideals of economic globalisation, because it has allowed China to become a leading world power by becoming the 'factory of the world'. The booming economic power of China has in turn allowed it to project Chinese influence and power across vast swathes of the planet. China is currently undertaking what is called either the **Silk Roads**; the **One Belt, One Road;** or the **Belt and Road Initiative (BRI).** This is a development strategy involving infrastructure developments across Europe, Asia and Africa. The BRI involves:

- The construction of ports, roads, railways, and airports
- $1 trillion ($1,000,000,000,000,000) of projected spending
- $210 billion ($210,000,000,000) of current spending
- Control of 10% of major European ports

Most of the BRI's construction is carried out by Chinese companies, using materials produced by Chinese industry, which has significantly boosted the Chinese economy. The advantage of the BRI is that it will enable a much greater volume of trade across Afro-Eurasia and increase the interconnectedness of economies. In this way, China is becoming the spearhead for a new wave of economic globalisation.

However, critics of the BRI point out that China spends in order to intentionally lock other countries into a debt cycle, which then makes them dependent on China. This allows China to then leverage the debt for territorial concessions (for example, Malaysia, Sri Lanka and Pakistan have all ceded control of key naval bases in exchange for debt write-offs) or diplomatic concessions (Tajikistan, Pakistan and Kazakhstan have all been very quiet about Uighur persecution). China also uses the BRI to project 'Chinese Confucian' values of loyalty, order and patriotism, seeking to undermine liberal democracy and spread its own political values. More broadly, China's expansion of cultural influence can be seen through:

- The 2008 Beijing Olympics
- Threatening to stop airing NBA games in China after the executive of the Houston Rockets tweeted in support of pro-democratic protestors in Hong Kong (2019)
- Threatening to stop airing Arsenal games in China after Mesut Ozil, an Arsenal player, tweeted in support of the Uighur people (2019)

Some may argue, therefore, that even though the Western/American-led era of globalisation may be drawing to a close, it is merely being replaced by an era of Chinese-led globalisation, with 'Chinese values' becoming the dominant paradigm and China as the heart of the global economy. Indeed, one may go further and say that globalisation itself is an inevitability – the only question is which world power is dominant in shaping the narrative and globalisation's political and cultural contours.

On the other hand, it could be said that China's autocratic values and the focus on suppressing democracy, free speech and 'liberal human rights' means that a Chinese-globalised world could never be as globalised as one which embraces liberal values, since the prioritisation of state sovereignty and non-interference as a principle of the Chinese Communist Party (CCP) means that global integration will always be limited.

Technology: the 'Pandora's Box'?

Although political globalisation remains dominated by state actors, economic globalisation and cultural globalisation is driven massively by technology and transnational corporations. This includes things like the Internet, block-chain, social media, online banking, 3-D printing (estimated to be commercially viable within decades), and smartphones.

States *are* able to somewhat restrict economic and cultural globalisation my throwing up virtual and physical barriers to the transmission of goods, services, ideas and people. However, the rapid growth of digital technology makes it harder for states to regulate and restrict economic and cultural globalisation, since virtual barriers are more easily circumvented by physical ones. Even in states with strict censorship regimes, e.g. the 'Great Firewall of China', cheap or free VPNs can be used to access material which is forbidden by the state. Recent protests, e.g. in Thailand against the monarchy and military government – criticism of which is disallowed in formal printed and television media; have been largely catalysed and organised via social media and the digital ecosystem, allowing ideas of political culture, liberal democracy, etc. to spread more easily. Some may therefore argue that given advances in digital technology, globalisation is now irreversible.

Conversely, it should be noted that digital technologies can be just as easily utilised by the state to reinforce cultural and political nationalism, and reject globalised notions of culture, politics, law and human rights. For example in Myanmar, researchers have demonstrated that the government utilised Facebook to spread hate and dehumanise the Muslim Rohingya minority in Rakhine state; organise genocidal actions; and then spread disinformation to cover up the extent of the violence. This could be seen as a particularly violent rejection of cultural globalism, enabled by digital technology.

The impact of the coronavirus pandemic

In many ways, the coronavirus pandemic (2019-present) could be seen as something which has started hammering the nails into the coffin of globalisation. There have been many far deadlier pandemics in the past, but this is the first pandemic in a truly globalised and interconnected world.

- As states struggle to bring the pandemic under control, many have imposed travel restrictions which at their height accounted for approximately a 40% reduction in air traffic

- The imposition of national lockdowns also collapsed many corporate supply chains. This has hit 'manufacturing' countries like Bangladesh especially hard, since their economies are heavily reliant on the export of cheap textile-related goods in the global economy

- The slowdown in economic activity has also hit oil-producing countries hard, since less economic activity means less demand for energy and therefore oil; it has also struck countries that rely on foreign aid, e.g. Yemen

- Many states have expressed anger at China's initial actions in 'covering up' the pandemic in December 2019, and scepticism of the World Health Organisation (WHO), a UN branch, for naively believing China's initial assertions that the virus was not airborne or very contagious. Many states have considered bringing manufacturing back 'in-house' to reduce dependence on China, given their role in the origin of the pandemic

It remains to be seen whether coronavirus will fundamentally reshape or cut back the processes of globalisation that have taken place over the past few decades; or whether it is just a minor blip along the road to a fully globalised and integrated world.

PERSPECTIVES ON GLOBALISATION

These perspectives should not be learned in isolation, but be critically assessed with reference to the information above and integrated as explanatory frameworks into your conclusions.

The hyperglobalist perspective: Hyperglobalists believe that globalisation is inevitable as a consequence of advances in technology, and that humankind is entering a new and unprecedented age of interconnectivity and interdependence. Eventually, the world will become borderless and nation-states will cease to be relevant as we will have a single monocultural global nation; a single interlinked global economy; and a single global political sovereign

The sceptical perspective: Sceptics see much of globalisation as a myth and argue that the so-called integrated global economy does not exist. In reality, regional, national and local economies are more significant. Cultural homogenisation is also limited in scope and will face an inevitable backlash. Sceptics further argue that international trade and capital flows are not new phenomena – they have been happening for millennia, and what is happening today is nothing new or special.

The transformationalist perspective: Transformationalists occupy a middle ground between hyperglobalisers and sceptics. They acknowledge that significant changes have occurred due to globalisation, but that they have not fundamentally changed the Westphalian system of sovereign states. Interconnectedness has increasing in breadth, intensity and speed. The governments of individual nation-states are perhaps becoming less important, but this is because they voluntarily submit to the process of globalisation, recognising that it is in both mutual and individual states' interests. They can equally voluntarily reverse this integration.

REALIST AND LIBERAL FRAMEWORKS (3.6)

Realism	Liberalism
Globalisation is not a new process – it is a continuation of former flows of capital, goods, people and services before the 'modern' era	Globalisation is a qualitatively new process – the speed of interconnectivity and interdependence is something unprecedented
'Globalisation' does not overturn the primary of the nation-state as the key unit of global politics; the sovereign state remains more powerful and important than IGOs, NGOs and TNCs; and retains absolute control over economic and cultural policy within their borders	Globalisation has not made the nation-state redundant, but it has meant that both IGOs, NGOs and TNCs have grown in influence – nation-states cannot ignore them altogether. States no longer have 'absolute' sovereign control over economic and cultural policy
'Globalisation' is not truly cooperative, but involves some states extending their power by dominating institutions/processes; and other less powerful states suffering in this zero-sum game	Globalisation is a truly cooperative process in which all states are mutually benefited; even smaller states extend their power and gains by participation in institutions and processes
Globalisation has not really increased interdependence between states – however, it has provided an 'excuse' or rationale for powerful states to interference in the affairs of others and violate their sovereignty. In this sense 'globalisation' has been destabilising	Globalisation has increased interdependence between states – this is a positive development, because it encourages cooperation and working together to solve global issues such as climate change, terrorism, genocide, etc. States can no longer act effectively in isolation

GLOBAL GOVERNANCE

Governance is all of the processes of governing (making and enforcing laws/policy/conventions), whether this is undertaken by:
- **A government(s)**
- **A market or network**
- **A social/religious group**

over any social system – a family, tribe, formal or informal organisation, a territory or multiple territories; and whether this is done through:
- **Laws**
- **Norms**
- **Language**

In this way, **governance** differs from **government.** 'The government' as the classically-conceived sovereign political entity is one way of executing 'governance', but 'governance' is a broader concept which may be carried out by actors other than 'governments'. Consequently, **global governance** is different from the idea of a **world government.** A 'world government' requires a single political sovereign for the planet, whereas it is possible for 'governance' to be carried out on a global scale between a coalition of nation-states and non-state actors, even if there is no single world sovereign.

In this unit, we will explore institutions/mechanisms of 'political' and 'economic' global governance – those elements of global governance that primarily concern political and economic issues. However, it is not possible to completely disentangle the two; they are separated for reasons of analytical ease, rather than because they are qualitatively distinct categories.

POLITICAL GLOBAL GOVERNANCE

The United Nations

The most important institution of global governance is the **United Nations (UN).** The United Nations was founded in 1945 as WWII drew to a close. Prior to this, the world had faced what some call a 'long war' spanning three decades.

- **1914-1918:** WWI was fought, involving all major global nation-states. Many saw the roots of this conflict as a battle for international and colonial influence between Germany and Britain. Between 18-20 million people, both civilians and soldiers, were killed or died as a result of starvation, pandemics, etc. resulting from wartime conditions

- **1919:** The 'League of Nations' was founded at the Paris Peace Conference with the aim of preventing future wars. The leading members were France, Britain, Japan and Italy. Three powerful states did not participate in the League – the Soviet Union was excluded because it was Communist; Germany was excluded as a punishment for starting WWI; and the USA did not join, because although the League was President Wilson's idea, the American Senate refused to ratify the Treaty of Versailles

- **1929:** The 'Wall Street Crash' in the USA triggered a global economic disaster

- **1931:** Japan invaded Manchuria, a resource-rich province in northern China. The League of Nations did not take effective action and Japan left the League after being criticised

- **1935:** Fascist Italy invaded Abyssinia (Ethiopia). Again, the League refused to take action

- **1939:** Germany annexed Czechoslovakia, after annexing Austria and parts of Czechoslovakia the previous year. The League again refused to take action. Germany then invaded Poland, triggering the Second World War. Over 60 million people died (3% of the global population at the time), making it by some distance the bloodiest conflict in human history

- **1945:** WWII came to an end with the defeat of the Axis (Japan, Germany, Italy)

The United Nations was therefore conceived of as a replacement for the League of Nations as an instrument of global governance and the prevention of horrific wars; one that would hopefully be more effective than the League of Nations in doing so. The **United Nations Charter**, the founding document of the UN makes clear its foundational aims with reference to the events discussed above. The preamble states:

"WE THE PEOPLES OF THE UNITED NATIONS DETERMINED; to save succeeding generations from the scourge of war, which twice in our lifetime has brought untold sorrow to mankind, and; to reaffirm faith in fundamental human rights, in the dignity and worth of the human person, in the equal rights of men and women and of nations large and small, and; to establish conditions under which justice and respect for the obligations arising from treaties and other sources of international law can be maintained, and; to promote social progress and better standards of life in larger freedom..."

Article I of the UN Charter makes clear that the maintenance of international peace and security; the development of friendly international relations; and cooperation on global issues are the key aims of the UN.
Article 2 reaffirms the principle of state sovereignty and emphasises that international disputes should be solved by peaceful means, not the threat or the use of force. However, it does also acknowledge that force can be used "in the common interest".

A brief history of the United Nations
Before looking at the structures and efficacy of the UN as it exists today, it is worth briefly examining some key changes in the UN's structure over time.

- **1945:** The UN was founded. The five members of the Security Council (discussed below) were the USA, the Soviet Union, the UK, France and China

- **1947:** The Cold War was underway by this point. This was a global geopolitical rivalry between the two main superpowers at the time – the authoritarian-

Communist Soviet Union and the (nominally democratic)-capitalist USA. Both attempted to 'convert' other states to their ideological banner, either by economic influence or the use of force

- **1949:** The Chinese Civil War (which started in the late 1920s, paused between 1936-1945 when Japan invaded China, and resumed when Japan was defeated in 1945) came to an end. It was won by Mao Zedong's Communist faction, which assumed control over mainland China as the 'People's Republic of China'. Meanwhile, the Nationalist faction, led by Jiang Jieshi, fled to the island of Taiwan and continued governing as the 'Republic of China', claiming authority over Taiwan *and* the mainland (but really only exercising authority in Taiwan). The US successfully insisted, against Soviet protests, that the Republic of China be defined as the 'real' China and should retain 'China's' seat on the UN Security Council and in the UN. The US hoped that one day, the Nationalist government could retake the mainland

- **1950:** The Soviet Union briefly boycotted the UN over the China issue

- **1960-1970:** The decolonisation of European empires in Africa, Asia and the Caribbean led to a large number of newly-created, predominantly African states joining the UN. In 1964, under the leadership of Algeria, the 'Group of 77' was formed – a coalition of developing states which wanted to advance their interests in the UN. As a result, the UN began to shift its focus away from conflict resolution and peacekeeping and towards social, economic, education and health development programmes

- **1971:** By 1971, it was clear that the Nationalists were not going to retake the Chinese mainland, and that the Communist regime was there to stay. The PRC governed over significantly more people and territory than the ROC and had a much larger economy and military forces. Consequently, the UN voted to officially recognise the Communist PRC as the 'real' China and give them the 'Chinese' seat on the UN Security Council, whilst the US-backed Nationalist ROC was expelled from the UN. As a result, Taiwan is still today a technically unrecognised state

- **1975:** The UN passed a resolution declaring that Zionism was equivalent to racism, against US protests. This demonstrated the growing power of African and Asian countries in the UN

- **1989:** The USA and the USSR declared the Cold War over. Paradoxically, in the two decades preceding this (1970s and 1980s), despite the Soviet Union's progressive military and economic decline, it was at its most powerful relative to the US in the UN. This was because they could rely on the votes/backing of the newly-recognised Communist China, and an increasing number of pro-Communist decolonised states

- **1991:** The Soviet Union collapsed and was dissolved into 15 republics. Russia was given the Soviet Union's seat on the Security Council. Between 1991 and 2001, the UN intervened in as many conflicts as it did between 1951 and 1991. This is because between 1951 and 1991, the Cold War rivalry between the Soviet Union and the USA prevented consensus on many issues. With the collapse of the USSR, the US was left as the sole, dominant global superpower and was able to more effectively impose its will onto the UN since it faced no serious geopolitical opponents in shaping consensus in the Security Council

Structures of the United Nations
The UN has five active 'organs' – the Security Council; General Assembly; Economic and Social Council (ECOSOC); the International Court of Justice (ICJ) and the Secretariat. We will look at each of these in turn and consider their strengths and weaknesses as instruments of global governance. In doing so, it is important to consider a range of criteria:
- How **effective** is the institution at achieving its aims and implementing its policies?
- How **democratic** is the decision-making of the institution?
- How **legitimate** is the institution considered to be amongst nation-states?

The Security Council

The Security Council's role is the protection of international peace and security. The **resolutions** (decisions) of the Security Council are **binding** on all UN member states, something which is not true of the decisions of other UN institutions. Where necessary, the Security Council's decisions are enforced by UN peacekeepers – soldiers which are provided voluntarily by UN member states. The UNSC also recommends candidates for the position of UN Secretary-General; and nation-states for membership of the UN.

The Security Council is based in New York. It is composed of five permanent members (the P5) – the USA, Russia, China, UK and France; and ten non-permanent members who are elected for two-year terms by the General Assembly, with the intention of giving representation to different areas of the globe (3 from Africa, 3 from Asia-Pacific, 2 from Eastern Europe, 2 from Latin America and the Caribbean, and 5 from Europe/North America). Security Council resolutions are passed if **9 out of 15** members vote for them. However, if any of the P5 vote against a resolution (even if all other Security Council members vote for it), this is considered to be a **veto** and the resolution does not pass.

Strengths of the UNSC	Weaknesses of the UNSC
Represents the realities of power: The distribution of seats in the UNSC does not represent population or states, but it does accurately represent the distribution of economic, military and political power across the globe. Western states have a third of the seats because of the disproportionate power of the West; Africa has a fifth, because as of yet, there are no superpowers in Africa. Additionally, the P5 is distinguished by their possession of nuclear weapons (only	Unrepresentative composition: A third of the UNSC's members are from Western countries despite representing only about a seventh of the global population. Meanwhile, Asia (representing 59% of the global population) has only a fifth of the total seats. This discrepancy is even more evident within the P5 specifically – three of the five states there are 'Western democracies' (UK, USA, France) and a fourth is also a European non-democracy (Russia). This has led to criticisms of the UNSC

four states outside the P5 – India, Pakistan, Israel and North Korea also have them). Having the most powerful states as the P5 of the UNSC means that when the UNSC has to execute an intervention or peacekeeping operation, it is more likely to succeed because it is backed by the weight of global power (unlike the League of Nations, which the USA and Soviets did not participate in, contributing to its inefficacy)	as a "pillar of global apartheid" (Titus Alexander) and having an "illogical, unjust and undemocratic structure" (Ayatollah Khamenei). This also means that the UNSC may selectively intervene in conflicts which are relevant to their interests, whilst disregarding others (e.g. assisting oil-rich Kuwait in 1991 when Saddam Hussein invaded, but largely ignoring the Rwandan Genocide of 1994, in which 1 million people perished)
Can act collaboratively: The UNSC has proven itself to be capable of collaborate to authorise peacekeeping operations which have been successful in many instances. A recent success was UNSC Resolution 1528 (all states voted for, none abstained or against) which authorised a peacekeeping operation in Cote d'Ivoire after a damaging civil war which saw 3,000 killed and 300,000 refugees. The nearly-12,000 deployed peacekeepers disarmed nearly 70,000 combatants and reintegrated them into society; oversaw two peaceful elections; the return of 250,000 refugees; and decreased intercommunal conflicts by 80% by 2017	Internal rivalries cripple efficacy: Because of the operation of the P5 veto within the UNSC, anything which contradicts the core national interests of one of the P5 members will be vetoed, or withdrawn under threat of a veto. This is especially the case if one of the P5 feels a resolution may 'advantage' another one of the P5 members relative to themselves. Recently, the veto has been exercised by (i) the USA, to prevent resolutions against Israel – a key Middle Eastern ally; (ii) Russia, to prevent resolutions against Bashar Assad in Syria – a key Middle Eastern ally; and (iii) threatened by China with regards to the Uighur issue in Xinjiang

Represents collective security: The UNSC represents the principle of collective security – that an attack on any state should be considered as an attack on the global order of sovereignty and peace; and that this should be dealt with by all states acting in concert. An example of this is the 1990s Gulf War, where Iraq invaded the neighbouring oil-rich state of Kuwait and was repelled by a coalition force authorised by the UNSC. Since the end of WWII, there have been 111 military conflicts worldwide, but only 9 of these have involved a state invading another, perhaps suggesting that the UNSC has been successful in promoting collective security	Difficult to reform: The P5 is difficult to reform. Members of the P5 would veto any attempt to expand the permanent members of the UNSC since this would dilute their own power – this effectively makes it impossible to add or remove permanent members. Given that the contours of global politics have changed significantly since 1945, there are many states which feel like they should be permanent members (e.g. the 'G4' - Germany, Japan, India, Brazil), and have no viable route to achieving this. A realist framework of power-seeking, amoral states operating in a zero-sum game seems to explain this behaviour

The General Assembly

The General Assembly, like the UNSC, is also based in New York. All **193** UN member states have a delegation of three representatives, who collectively cast a single vote on resolutions. There are two observer states (Palestine and the Vatican) who can participate in debates but not vote. Each member state has one vote, regardless of population. Votes are decided by a **simple majority** (50% of votes cast), or in the cases of issues deemed to be 'important', such as the UN budget; the expulsion of member states; and recommendations on peace/security – by a **supermajority** (66% of votes cast).

The General Assembly may debate and vote on any issue. They specifically have the power to elect the officers of the UN (including the Secretary General; and the non-permanent members of the UNSC) and to vote on the admission, suspension and expulsion of states from the UN. The General Assembly is able to pass recommendations on global issues, but unlike the resolutions of the UNSC, the General Assembly's resolutions are **non-binding.**

Strengths of the General Assembly	Weaknesses of the General Assembly
Global forum: The General Assembly is a global forum for the solving of global issues. As some have argued, "if it did not exist, it would have to be invented" – given how unique and vital it is as a space in which problems affecting multiple countries can be discussed. An example of this is the currently ongoing 31st UN General Assembly special session on the coronavirus pandemic, where state representatives are gathering to discuss how to tackle the economic, social and political fallout of the virus, especially on vulnerable people. For this reason, no state has ever permanently withdrawn from the Assembly (and only one did so briefly – Indonesia in 1965-66)	Represents states, not people: The General Assembly represents states, not people. Every state gets a single vote, regardless of population size. It is possible (but unlikely) for states representing only 5% of the global population to pass a vote on an important issue (66% of states), because the global population is so unevenly distributed – this may be seen as undemocratic. Furthermore, because the UN is based on the principle of state sovereignty, the concerns of oppressed minorities *within* states, e.g. the Rohingya in Myanmar; the Uighurs in China; LGBT people in Chechnya, Russia; are overlooked because state governments debate and vote based on their overarching interests
Equal representation: The Assembly provides one vote per state regardless of population size or military/economic/political power. This encourages participation from smaller states and ensures their voices can be heard. For many	'Rewards' dictatorship: The Assembly gives one vote per state, and it is the duty of the state government to decide who they want to send as delegates to the Assembly and how to instruct them to vote. This could be seen as 'rewarding' dictatorship,

smaller states, the UN is their principal outlet for foreign policy and influence. It means that within the body of the General Assembly, it is not possible for more powerful states to veto resolutions, and they are often outvoted by developing or non-hegemonic states. For example, the Group of 77 (which now has 134 members!) was instrumental in passing resolutions against the apartheid regime in South Africa; and supporting initiatives towards global disarmament and demilitarisation	because an autocratic state gets to cast a vote in the UN on behalf of all of their citizens, regardless of whether or not the citizens have democratically consented to their rule, and regardless of what their citizens think. Because all states are treated as of equivalent value, despotic regimes can play a key role in shaping global policy, e.g. Saudi leadership of the UN Human Rights Commission (a sub-body of the Assembly) in 2015, despite beheading more people than ISIS in that year
Promotes dialogue: The General Assembly promotes dialogue between nation-states and reduces the chance of conflict. By providing an outlet for verbal, diplomatic sparring it allows state representatives to vent their frustrations, concerns and put forward their interests in a constructive and non-violent manner. Even where it may seem that the dialogue is not constructive (e.g. Khrushchev banging his shoe on a table whilst denouncing the Filipino delegate as a "toady of American imperialism" in 1960; or Gaddafi's rambling 100 minute speech in	Merely a 'talking shop': The Assembly does not have the power to make binding resolutions – these must also be approved by the UNSC to take effect. Therefore, many would criticise the Assembly as a 'talking shop' where the same issues are debated over and over again without any progress. For example, Israel has been condemned in 45 resolutions (45.9% of state-specific resolutions) for activities such as illegal settlement-building in occupied Palestinian territories, and the occupation of the Golan Heights (Syria). Similar resolutions are passed every year, yet there have been no

2009), it is better than war. In addition, it is clear that although the General Assembly cannot prevent every conflict, the number of inter-state wars has fallen dramatically since 1945 – it does appear that dialogue has superseded violence	moves towards peace in the region. Additionally, Kofi Annan (a former UN Secretary-General) criticised the Assembly for passing watered-down resolutions reflecting "the lowest common denominator of widely different opinions."

The International Court of Justice

The ICJ, unlike most other organs of the UN, is not based in New York but in the Hague, in the Netherlands. It is composed of **fifteen judges** elected for **nine-year terms** by the General Assembly and the Security Council, with the distribution of seats fixed for different regions of the world. The court reaches judgements by a **simple majority** (8/15).

The role of the ICJ is to settle legal disputes between UN member states and to give advisory legal opinions to UN agencies who request them. It will only make judgements on contentious cases if they are between states, and if all the states involved agree to abide by its ruling. If this is the case, the ruling of the ICJ are considered binding and the UNSC can enforce them. The advisory opinions are not binding, but widely respected and often followed regardless.

Strengths of the ICJ	Weaknesses of the ICJ
Upholds 'international law': The ICJ is the principal institution which upholds the globalised concept of 'international law' which should apply to all states and actors. The concept of 'international law' requires an 'international court' to arbitrate disputes between states according to established principles and conventions. This involves conflict resolution, but also the	Jurisdiction is conditional: The ICJ's jurisdiction only applies when both states have agreed to abide by a ruling. E.g. in 2018, Iran filed a lawsuit against the USA as a result of the imposition of sanctions on Iran by Trump's administration, who claimed that Iran was developing nuclear weapons. Iran argued this violated the 1955 Treaty of Amity between the USA and Iran. The ICJ ruled in

regulation of things like applying the UN Convention on the Law of the Sea (UNCLOS) which concerns maritime boundaries and responsibilities. In 2002, the ICJ ruled on a case delimiting the continental shelf between Nigeria/ Cameroon	Iran's favour and issued an interim order for the USA to lift sanctions on 'humanitarian goods and civil aviation'. The USA simply refused and withdrew from the Treaty of Amity, pointing out that they had not agreed to ICJ jurisdiction
Genuine neutrality: The fifteen ICJ judges are required to be independent and neutral by Articles 16-18 of the ICJ Statute. Judges are not allowed to hold any other judicial or legal post in any state, or to act as counsel in a professional capacity to prevent conflicts of interest. If a case involves the state of a judge on the ICJ, then the other state involved may select an additional 'ad hoc' judge to prevent any possible biases in judgement. The representation of multiple states of varying levels of power (the current President of the ICJ is Abdulqawi Yusuf, a Somalian) means that most states perceive the Court as genuinely neutral and are willing to submit cases to it for arbitration. For example, Bolivia petitioned the ICJ to hear a case against Chile (landlocked Bolivia had lost all of its coastal territory to Chile in 1883 in a war, and wanted it back so it could have access to the Pacific	Unenforceable rulings: As well as the ICJ's jurisdiction being conditional, there are no formal mechanisms for the enforcement of its rulings. It is often the case that rulings against powerful states go unenforced, because there is no collective consensus in the UNSC for doing so. Examples of the ICJ being unable to enforce rulings against major states include (i) in 1986, where the ICJ ruled that the USA's support of right-wing death squads and militias (the 'Contras') against the Communist Nicaraguan government was illegal, and the US simply ignored this; (ii) in 2014, where the ICJ ruled in favour of Australia and New Zealand, that Japan could not conduct whaling in Antarctic waters because it was not for the claimed 'scientific' purposes, but Japan continued anyway; and (iii) in 2016, where the ICJ ruled in the Philippines' favour that China did not have an absolute right to sovereignty

Ocean). The ICJ rejected Bolivia's claim, and Bolivia accepted the judgement as one made by a neutral body	over the South China Sea, and China continued building naval bases in the region and asserting its military power
Gives states a way to 'back down': Nation-states may not want to back down in disagreements because it would imply a loss of prestige and respect. ICJ rulings provide a way for states to draw back from the brink of conflict without 'losing face'. For example, Preah Vihear is a 900 year old Hindu temple on the Thai-Cambodian border. Cambodia claimed the temple on the basis that it was built by the Khmer (ancient Cambodian) Empire, whereas Thailand claimed it on the basis of the French-drawn border in the early 1900s. Both agreed to ICJ arbitration in 1962, which awarded the temple to Cambodia; and reaffirmed the ruling in 2013. This effectively defused nationalist tensions over the temple which could have led to a full-blown war in the region	Inability to solve intra-state conflicts: The ICJ can only solve conflicts or disputes *between* states (inter-state). It does not have the jurisdiction, in any circumstances, to rule on issues *within* states (intra-state). This renders it powerless to deal with many global disputes and conflicts, the majority of which are today intra-state rather than inter-state conflicts. E.g.: • Civil wars/disputes of secession and independence (the Kurds in Iraq, Syria and Turkey; Catalan independence from Spain; China's suppression of democratic protests in Hong Kong) • Any intra-state genocide (Myanmar; China; Sudan; Bosnia) • Human rights abuses (Iran; Russia)

ECOSOC (the Economic and Social Council)

ECOSOC, like the General Assembly and UNSC is based in New York. It has 54 member states elected by the General Assembly for three-year terms, with fixed numbers of seats for different areas of the planet. The President of ECOSOC is elected for a one-year term (currently this is the Pakistani diplomat Munir Akram) and by convention is one from one of the smaller or mid-ranking powers on the Council. ECOSOC meets for a seven-week session every July and for a shorter meeting every April with the World Bank and IMF.

The role of ECOSOC is to discuss international economic and social problems and formulate policy recommendations for individual UN member states and the UN as a whole. ECOSOC coordinates the activities of a number of United Nations:

- **Functional commissions** (e.g. the UN Commission on Narcotic Drugs; the UN Commission on the Status of Women)
- **Regional commissions** (e.g. the UN Economic Commission for Europe)
- **Special agencies** (e.g. the International Labour Organisation; the International Monetary Fund; The World Bank; the World Health Organisation)

It would be impossible to list all of the strengths and weaknesses of ECOSOC as a whole, since it oversees so many diverse projects and sub-agencies. Instead, we will examine the work of the WHO (World Health Organisation), a special agency of which ECOSOC is the 'parent agency' as a specific case study which illustrates many of the general strengths and weaknesses of ECOSOC.

Strengths of the WHO	Weaknesses of the WHO
The WHO gives the important global issue of health and mortality reduction a specific policy forum to be addressed and tackled. As a result, the world has made huge strides towards fighting diseases, controlling epidemics and improving all-round healthcare. Particular areas of focus for the WHO are viruses/bacteria with extremely high mortality rates, such as malaria, tuberculosis and AIDS, as well as dealing with antibiotic-resistant	The WHO is chronically underfunded, which limits its efficacy. Currently, it has a budget of $4.2bn (by comparison, the US annual military budget is over $700bn). Much of this funding is on a voluntary rather than a compulsory basis, including from private donors in addition to UN states (Bill Gates currently provides 9.4% of the funding for the WHO through his foundation). There are allegations of inefficiency and 'politicisation' in the WHO. In the

'superbugs' like MRSA. Two historical successes of the WHO are (i) The eradication of smallpox through a concerted vaccination and education programme (the latter largely focused on convincing people that vaccines were safe and effective); and (ii) The eradication of polio in all but three countries (Pakistan, Nigeria and Afghanistan – it has persisted here in rural areas because of suspicion of vaccine programmes, and attacks on WHO health workers)

Child (59% reduction) and maternal (44% reduction) mortality have also fallen significantly across the world, as a result of the WHO's concerted health initiatives.

This is symptomatic of the wider success ECOSOC has found in tackling socio-economic issues and moving towards the Millennium Development Goals (2000-2015) and the Sustainable Development Goals (2016-2030)

2013-2015 Ebola epidemic in West Africa (resulting in 11,000+ deaths), the WHO was criticised for staff incompetency; excessive bureaucracy; and a lack of reliable information that made the epidemic worse than it could have been. It was alleged that the WHO did not intervene as quickly as they should have because they were worried about resistance from West African states and the risk of a creating a panic by declaring an emergency. In the context of the 2019-present coronavirus pandemic, the WHO (especially the current Director, Tedros Ghebreysus), were criticised for broadcasting unverified Chinese claims in January 2020 that the virus was not airborne (it is). This led to Trump withdrawing funding from the WHO.

The WHO is similar to other ECOSOC agencies in that it cannot impose binding directives on member states and must do most of the 'heavy lifting' itself, whilst being severely underfunded

Other UN organs

There are two other UN organs which are not on the specification but are worth briefly mentioning:

1. **The Secretariat:** This is the 'civil service' of the UN. 44,000 international civil servants work for the Secretariat across a range of departments and based in many different states. They produce reports which inform the discussions of other institutions of the UN and which carry a great deal of weight in influencing world opinion. The leader of the Secretariat is the 'Secretary-General', who directs its operation; notifies the UNSC of matters they believe are threatening to world peace; and carry out a lot of behind-the-scenes diplomacy. The General-Secretary (currently Antonio Guterres) is the chief administrative officer of the UN and is often seen as the public face of the UN

2. **The Trusteeship Council:** The Trusteeship Council was established to ensure that 'trust territories' – regions which had been under the administration of the League of Nations, or colonies taken for the defeated Axis powers of WWII – were administered in the interests of their inhabitants, with a long-term view to self-determination. The Trusteeship Council has been inactive since 1994, when the last trust territory, Palau (a Pacific island-nation), became an independent state and joined the UN

The North Atlantic Treaty Organisation (NATO)

The Cold War era (1949-1990)

The second institution of global political governance is the North Atlantic Treaty Organisation (NATO). This was formed in **1949** by the **North Atlantic Treaty.** Arguably the most important clause of the treaty is **Article 5**, which commits all members to:

- Consider an armed attack on one member state as an attack on them all

- Consult together when any one member state considers itself to be threatened

NATO was created in the context of the Cold War. It was effectively a commitment by the USA to protect the democratic-capitalist nations of Western Europe against any attack by the Soviet Union. At the time, the USSR had by some distance the largest army in the world and no combination of Western European states would have been able to resist it had it chosen to invade. NATO represented a **volte-face** (reversal of policy) from the USA's isolationism of the 1920s and 30s, where it had remained disinterested in European affairs whilst Hitler built up the strength of Nazi Germany and began to conquer neighbouring states, eventually triggering WWII in 1939 by invading Poland. The North Atlantic Treaty was effectively a commitment from the USA that it would not make the 'same mistake' with the Soviet Union and would act decisively to prevent the spread of totalitarianism.

Shades of blue were part of NATO; shades of red were part of the rival Warsaw Pact

NATO was, and is still, governed by the **North Atlantic Council (NAC)** in Brussels, Belgium, which meets at least weekly. Its meetings are chaired by the **Secretary General** of NATO, who is by convention always a European diplomat. Each NATO member state has a Permanent Representative on the NAC. There is no formal 'voting' process; decisions are only made if they are unanimous, which effectively means every member has a veto. Since 1951, NATO has had a single integrated military command structure. This means that in NATO operations, officers from the armed forces of one state may give orders to officers from the armed forces of another. The **Supreme Commander of the Allied Forces in Europe (SACEUR)** was and is still at the top of this integrated command structure – by convention, this is always an American general. The balance between political leadership of NATO (European) and military leadership (American) contributes to the perception amongst member-states that it is an equitable institution in the common interest, rather than one which is simply a vehicle for the extension of American hegemony.

The USA was responsible for the overwhelming bulk of NATO military spending throughout the Cold War era. Successive American governments sought to persuade their European partners to spend more on defence, with little success. Nonetheless, the American political establishment recognised that its commitment to NATO was in its wider strategic interest (despite the fact it was footing a disproportionate percentage of the bill) because a Soviet takeover of Western Europe had the potential to strengthen the USSR enormously and tip the balance of the Cold War in the Soviets' favour.

During the Cold War, NATO never actually carried out action; nor did it deploy any military forces. Instead, it effectively acted as a **deterrent** – preventing war in Europe by making the outcome for the Soviets so unpalatable and destructive as to be unthinkable. In **1955** (as a response to West Germany's integration into NATO), the Soviet Union and the Communist states of Eastern Europe founded the **Warsaw Pact,** a defensive alliance similar to NATO but for the Communist world. The two rival organisations established what realists would describe as a **'balance of power'** – since both blocs had vast military forces and were backed by nuclear-armed superpowers (the USA and the USSR), neither wished to risk conflict because of the impossibility of a predictable, positive outcome. Conflict therefore became irrational and it did not happen.

NATO membership evolved to a minimal degree during the 20th century:

- The founding members of NATO were the USA; Canada; the UK; France; Italy; Portugal; Belgium; the Netherlands; Luxemburg; Denmark; Norway and Iceland

- Greece and Turkey joined NATO in 1952

- West Germany joined in 1955, after being allowed to remilitarise (both West and East Germany had been forced to demilitarise in the aftermath of WWII)

- France, under the leadership of de Gaulle, withdrew its forces from NATO control, because he wanted France to have a larger role in decision-making. Nevertheless, they agreed that they would commit their forces (under a French flag) if West-East hostilities broke out

- Greece left in 1974 as a result of the Turkish invasion of Cyprus (which had an ethnic Greek majority and a Turkish minority), but re-joined in 1980

- Spain joined in 1982 after the end of Franco's totalitarian dictatorship

Most NATO member-states were democratic throughout the Cold War era, with the exception of:

- **Portugal:** Fascist dictatorship under Salazar until 1974

- **Greece:** Ruled by a dictatorship for a brief period between 1967 and 1974

- **Turkey:** Underwent a number of periods of military rule

These member-states were admitted despite their lack of democracy because they were seen as crucial to the maintenance of Western European security. All three, despite having authoritarian regimes, were committed to the principle of capitalism. Turkey and Greece were especially important for Mediterranean security and for their proximity to the Black Sea and Soviet territory. Nevertheless, there was a general expectation in NATO that states should be liberal-democracies, and this was encouraged by its membership.

The post-Cold War era (1990-present)

Following the end of the Cold War and the dissolution of the Soviet Union, NATO's existential rationale had been removed since there was no longer a threat of Communist invasion. As a result NATO began to change in a number of ways.

1. <u>Humanitarian deployments:</u>

NATO has begun to deploy its forces to achieve humanitarian goals (the protection of human rights and the prevention of genocides and war crimes).

The first major interventions were in the **Bosnian War** of 1992-1995 and the **Kosovo War** in 1999. In both cases, as the **Yugoslav** state collapsed into smaller ethno-states, the Serbian majority attempted to commit genocide against Muslim minorities in Bosnia and Kosovo respectively. NATO bombed Serbian military positions and key buildings in the Serbian capital, **Belgrade**, to force Serbia to recognise the autonomy and independence of Bosnia and Kosovo. NATO also provided 60,000 peacekeepers for the post-conflict UN reconstruction of Bosnia. The airstrikes on Serbia were criticised by some observers as unwarranted warmongering, despite averting genocide, for causing the death of around 500 Serb civilians (and 3 Chinese citizens who were killed when NATO accidentally bombed the Chinese embassy in Belgrade). The rationale for interventions were given by resolutions passed by the **UN General Assembly**; but similar resolutions had been vetoed in the **UN Security Council** by Russia and China, which brought into question the legitimacy of the intervention.

NATO also conducted a humanitarian intervention in Libya in 2011 to enforce **UNSC Resolution 1973**, which approved a **no-fly zone** over Libya. The reason for this was that in the context of the Libyan Civil War, **Gaddafi**, the Libyan leader, had vowed to destroy **Benghazi** (the rebel capital) with his air force, which would have caused hundreds of thousands of civilian casualties. NATO crippled Gaddafi's military and air force with surgical air strikes against Libyan air bases, tanks and vehicles. There were no ground troops committed to the conflict by NATO. The immediate intervention was effective in preventing the destruction of Benghazi. Eventually, the NATO bombing campaign allowed the rebel forces to advance on the capital, Tripoli; Gaddafi was captured and killed at Sirte two months later. The NATO intervention was criticised for '**mission drift'** – moving from protecting civilians to the overthrow of Gaddafi, and the destabilisation of Libya through the removal of a functioning sovereign government.

Between 2009 and 2016, NATO also conducted **Operation Ocean Shield** – an anti-piracy naval operation off the Horn of Africa to reduce Somali piracy. In this, it was very successful.

2. Expansion:

Since the end of the Cold War, NATO has also expanded its membership further eastwards.

In 1990, East Germany reunified with West Germany and became part of NATO as a united Germany with the consent of Mikhail Gorbachev, the last leader of the Soviet Union. An unspoken part of this agreement was that NATO would not seek to expand further. Since then, many states which were formerly part of the **Warsaw Pact** (the Czech Republic, Hungary, Poland, Bulgaria, Romania, Slovakia, Albania, Slovenia, Croatia and Montenegro) or former **constituent republics of the USSR** (Estonia, Latvia and Lithuania) have joined NATO. In addition, Georgia has been officially named as an aspiring member of NATO and promised future membership; and Ukraine's future incorporation has also been discussed. Both Georgia and Ukraine were formerly Soviet republics. Anti-ballistic missiles have been stationed in Eastern Europe and Turkey. The Russian government under Putin, and Russian public opinion, regards NATO expansion into the Soviet Union's former sphere of influence as a thinly-veiled military threat to Russia. This is partially the reason for the following conflicts which have been described as part of a 'new Cold War' between Russia and the Western world:

- **Georgia:** The Russo-Georgian War (2008) which saw the Russian army assist separatists in Abkhazia and South Ossetia to break away from Georgia as nominally independent states

- **Ukraine:** The Russian annexation of Crimea from Ukraine in 2014, and the ongoing conflict in the Donbass region (including the provinces of Luhansk and Donetsk) of eastern Ukraine, in which Russia is covertly and not-so-covertly aiding the pro-Russian separatists. This was the sphere of conflict in which Malaysian Airlines flight MH17 was accidentally shot down

- **UK:** Although there has been no outright conflict between the UK and Russia, Russia has clearly begun to 'test' and aggressively probe the stability and unity of NATO by conducting aggressive acts such as the 2006 assassination of Alexander Litvinenko and 2018 attempted assassination of Sergei Skripal in UK territory, both defectors from the Russian secret services. Livtinenko was poisoned by radioactive polonium in his tea; Skripal was targeted with Novichok, an advanced chemical nerve-agent

Tensions are also rising between Russia and NATO in the **Baltic states** (and former Soviet republics) of Estonia, Lithuania and Russia, where some regions of those states have expressed pro-Russian separatist or pro-independence stances.

3. The invocation of Article V

Following the 9/11 attacks – in which the terrorist group Al-Qaeda flew two planes into the World Trade Centre, a third into the Pentagon and failed to crash a fourth into the Capitol Building – collectively resulting in nearly 3,000 casualties – Article V was invoked for the first and only time. The USA argued that this represented an attack on the USA, and that since there was solid intelligence to show that bin Laden, the leader of Al-Qaeda, was sheltering in Afghanistan, that NATO should assist the US in a war in Afghanistan to capture him. The US invaded Afghanistan and overthrew the radical-Islamist Taliban government, but failed to capture bin Laden (who fled across the border into Pakistan). Since then, NATO troops have played a key part in combating the Taliban **insurgency** (rebellion) and training Afghan policemen and troops. The NATO presence in Afghanistan has been dramatically reduced since the initial invasion, but it still exists.

However, NATO suffered many casualties – 2,000 for the USA and 400 for the UK alone – in the pursuit of this conflict, and has not really achieved its aim of creating stability in Afghanistan. The Taliban still dominate large swathes of the more mountainous, tribal regions of Afghanistan. In addition, there have been many civilian deaths, especially caused by indiscriminate **drone strikes.** A particularly egregious example was the drone bombing of a wedding in 2008 after it was mistaken for a Taliban meeting. NATO's conduct in Afghanistan after the invocation of Article V has raised questions about whether it has global legitimacy and whether it should be allowed to operate beyond 'defensive' parameters. It has been described as becoming a **neo-imperialist** organisation to serve Western interests, rather than serving its initial purpose of self-defence.

Limitations on NATO's effectiveness

Despite NATO's proven, technologically-advanced capabilities in military action; and its vast expenditure (accounting for the bulk of global military spending) there are some things which may limit NATO's current effectiveness and operation.

1. Vulnerability to creeping expansion:

Article V of NATO can be invoked when a member state faces an "armed attack". A unanimous decision is then required in order for a collective security response to be initiated. However, it is questionable whether Article V could be effectively invoked in the case of **'creeping expansion'.** In the invasion of Crimea, a peninsula in southern Ukraine (not a NATO member!), Russia did not simply invade as in a conventional war, but:

- Manufactured a crises where Russian minorities in Crimea were 'threatened' by Ukraine

- Sent in **'little green men'**, non-uniformed Russian troops, to pose as pro-Russian Ukrainian rebels and to seize control of key parts of the local infrastructure – government buildings, airports, seaports, roads, railroad hubs etc.

- Stepped in with official Russian troops to 'restore order' in neighbouring Ukraine, claiming they were not acting in an expansionist matter, but to prevent harm to Russian minorities

- Oversaw a referendum in which the self-declared 'Republic of Crimea' voted to join Russia

- Used cyber-warfare and disinformation to obscure the facts listed above

This **hybrid warfare** (a mixture of disinformation, internal destabilisation and conventional warfare) makes it very difficult to apply Article V – a defence against "armed attack." If similar tactics were pursued by Russia in the NATO-member Baltic states of Estonia, Lithuania and Latvia (which have Russian minorities of 24.8%, 5.8% and 26.2% respectively), there is concern that NATO would not intervene unless there was concrete evidence of aggressive Russian involvement. This problem is exacerbated by the necessity of unanimous decision-making; whilst the Baltic states might want a quick response, states further away from Russia may not feel the immediacy of the threat. By then, it might be too late to meaningfully intervene. Article V was designed to deal with causes of obvious, naked aggression – but it is much harder to deploy it in the case of creeping expansion.

2. American isolationism:

NATO is over-reliant on the military power of the USA, and is dominated by the USA. In 2006, NATO agreed that member states spend at least 2% of their GDP on military expenditure to 'spread the burden' of defence equitably amongst member states. Based on 2019 statistics, only 9 member-states (the USA, the UK, Estonia, Latvia, Lithuania, Poland, Romania, Bulgaria and Greece) meet this threshold. Some states, e.g. Spain and Belgium are below 1% of GDP.

President Trump threatened to withdraw the USA from NATO and to shift 12,000 American troops out of Germany, saying "we don't want to be suckers anymore", arguing with some justification that the US was bearing a disproportionate financial burden with regards to NATO. Given the dependence on the USA, which accounts for 70% of total spending on defence amongst NATO governments, American **isolationism** would be catastrophic for NATO's efficacy.

Some EU leaders, like Macron and Merkel, have mooted the creation of an 'EU Army' to replace NATO if the US withdrew from it, but this would require significant tax increases and would face many political obstacles from EU member-states concerned with the impact on their sovereignty. In summary, if the USA became more isolationist, then NATO would fail. The threat of the USA withdrawing from NATO may be significantly reduced under President Biden.

3. Potential internal rivalries:

Some rivalries have become apparent within the NATO bloc, which may harm its ability to act effectively as a cohesive whole (given the need for unanimous decision-making). The serious current flashpoint is tension between Turkey and the 'Western' NATO states. Turkey has always been something of an outlier within the organisation, given that it is not 'European' or 'Western', and that its commitment to liberal democracy has always been superficial. However, it was included in NATO because it was directly to the south of the Soviet Union (and now Russia), and was therefore a critical juncture for security and the stationing of troops/missiles.

Under Erdogan, Turkey has moved in a more authoritarian direction in the pursuit of a **'neo-Ottomanist'** foreign policy of expansion and regional dominance in the Middle East. The Turkish invasion of the Kurdish regions of northern Syria from 2016 onwards, conducted in three separate operations (Euphrates Shield; Olive Branch; Peace Spring) has seen over 1000 settlements in northern Syria occupied and administered by the Turkish army and allied military forces. The ethnic cleansing of the Kurds from these areas, who are key regional allies of many NATO countries in the war against ISIS, led to criticism of Turkey within NATO and discussions of suspending arms sales to Turkey. In response, Erdogan has floated the idea of withdrawing from NATO and also bought an advanced S-400 missile-defence system from Russia. Turkey's withdrawal from NATO would dramatically undermine NATO's ability to put pressure on Russia in the Caucasus, Black Sea and Middle East.

NATO – a summary

The strengths and weaknesses of NATO as an institution of global political governance are outlined below; 'paired' together so they can be more conveniently evaluated. The relevant evidence is briefly summarised but you should make sure that you can outline them in detail in an explanation using the information above.

Strengths of NATO	Weaknesses of NATO
Prevented the Cold War from going 'hot' - Balance of power between USA/USSR - Involvement of the USA crucial - No interstate conflicts in Europe!	Arguably, has triggered conflict with Russia - Provocation via membership expansion - Security dilemma → retaliation - Ukraine, Georgia, poisonings, Baltics?
Effective humanitarian role since the 1990s - Bosnia/Kosovo genocides - Libyan Civil War intervention - Operation Ocean Shield - Afghanistan?	Imperialist, illegitimate, destabilising wars - Bosnia/Kosovo genocides - Libyan Civil War intervention - Afghanistan? - Neo-imperialism/Western hegemony
Ideologically and politically close-knit - Liberal democracies, pro-capitalist - Essentially 'Western' in nature - Unanimity of decision-making	Serious and growing internal divisions - USA isolationism and funding disputes - Growing Turkey-Western rift

	- Vulnerability to creeping expansion

ECONOMIC GLOBAL GOVERNANCE

In the second part of Unit 3.2, we will look at institutions and key concepts of global economic governance. First, we will look at 5 key institutions – the IMF, World Bank, World Trade Organisation, G7 and G20. Secondly, we will look at different theories of poverty and global economics; and a key recent event (the 2008 Financial Crisis) which these institutions attempted to tackle. These theories/the 2008 Financial Crisis case study will enable us to make more thorough and reasoned judgements on the strengths and weaknesses of the 5 institutions.

The International Monetary Fund (IMF)

The IMF was formed in 1945 as a result of the **Bretton Woods Conference** with the aim of (i) assisting recovery from the Great Depression and World War II (which many saw as having been fundamentally caused by the economic dislocation caused by the Depression); and (ii) preventing future international economic crises. Initially, the main function of the IMF was to oversee the system of **fixed exchange rates** between currencies, which was believed to provide global economic stability. This system ended in 1971, when President Nixon **'floated the dollar'** – breaking away from a system of fixed exchange rates and allowing currency exchange rates to be determined by the market.

Since then, the main aims of the IMF have been:

1. **Financial assistance to states:** When governments face **balance of payments** crises or find themselves in serious debt, then the IMF provides a last resort to 'bail out' struggling states. The money for these loans comes from a pool which is funded collectively by member states, through a quota system proportional to their wealth (i.e. richer states pay more in). IMF loans are made on the basis of 'conditionality' – which means that the IMF will typically insist that the borrower-state engage in specific economic reforms (these are discussed in

67

more detail further in the notes). *This was an aim of the IMF from the beginning.*

2. **Surveillance of the global economy:** The IMF publishes annual reports on the economies of its member-states and recommends improvements to their economic policies to ensure long-term stability. *The IMF adopted this approach in the 1970s as a way of guiding the world economy in the 'right direction' without fixed exchange rates.*

The IMF is based in Washington DC, the American capital. It is technically a special agency of the UN under the sub-jurisdiction of ECOSOC. The IMF is run by two bodies:

- **Board of Governors:** Each member state of the IMF has a representative on the Board of Governors, which meets annually to discuss the decisions of the Executive Board (it has always approved them, so this is something of a formality). Practically every state in the world is a member of the IMF, with the exception of some very small states (East Timor, Liechtenstein, Monaco, the Vatican); strongly Communist states (North Korea, Cuba); and Taiwan, whose membership has been blocked by China. The Board of Governors also elects 16 of the 24 directors on the Executive Board

- **Executive Board:** There are 24 directors on the Executive Board, which is the central decision-making body of the IMF. There are 8 permanent members – the USA, China, Russia, Japan, Germany, France, the UK and Saudi Arabia. The remaining 16 are elected by the Board of Governors, with a fixed number of seats per area of the globe. The Executive Board is led by the Managing Director – currently Kristalina Georgieva, a renowned Bulgarian economist. Traditionally the IMF is led by a European economist; in 2011, the BRIC nations (Brazil, Russia, India, China) issued a statement calling for this convention to be overturned

For a major decision to pass in the Executive Board, it requires **85%** of votes. However, not all states have an equal vote share – this is proportional to a state's quota of IMF funding (i.e. how big its economy is and how much it pays in). Presently, the USA has **16.52%** of votes (followed by Japan and China at around 6%). This effectively means that the USA has a veto over IMF policy, since the absence of its votes would make it impossible to hit the 85% threshold. In 2017, the IMF implemented reforms (which were passed in 2010) to extend the voting power of major developing economies, like China, and cut 'advanced European' seats on the Executive Board by 2 as a result of the changing contours of the global economy. Nevertheless, the USA still retains a 'veto' share of overall votes.

Strengths of the IMF	Weaknesses of the IMF
Promotion of economic stability: The IMF does seem to have been effective in promoting global economic stability. In the 1950s and 60s, OECD (developed) state economies grew at a steady rate of 4-5% annually. The IMF has also played a key role in staving off the total collapse of and restabilising large economies, which would have disastrous regional and global consequences. For example, in the wake of the 2008 Financial Crisis, the IMF played a key role in 'bailing out' Greece, Cyprus, Ireland, Portugal and Spain. Loans to Greece alone totalled $146 billion over three years	Overly influenced by the West: The IMF has been criticised as an institution which is overly influenced by the West in general and the USA specifically. The IMF requires 85% of votes to make a decision, and since the USA has 17% this effectively gives the USA a veto. The IMF is based in the American capital, Washington DC and is led by a European, which again has given rise to allegations that the institution is overly influenced by Western interests and makes global policy to benefit Western states rather than to advance financial stability and the global economy as a whole
Adaptability to global changes: The IMF has shown itself to be adaptable and flexible in many ways to deal with the changing international context. For example: • 1971: When Nixon 'floated' the dollar and the system of fixed exchange rates ended, the IMF	Neoliberal economics: The IMF fundamentally follows a programme of neoliberal economics. The simplified core principles of this are: • A belief in national 'free markets' (minimal government intervention) as the best way to generate wealth

began publishing recommendations on economic policy to 'guide' the world economy in the absence of fixed exchange rates

- 1990: After the fall of the Soviet Union and Communism, and the transition of Eastern Europe to capitalism, the IMF refocused on debt reduction and economic development

- 2008: After the 2008 Financial Crisis, the IMF increased its role in surveying the global economy and warning member-states about potentially hazardous debt burdens

- 2010: As a result of the changing contours of the global economy, the IMF agreed to increase the voting quotas of Brazil, Russia, India and China (implemented in 2017)

- In practise, this means lower taxes, less regulation and less welfare spending
- Privatised industry being better than nationalised, state-controlled industry
- Global free trade with minimal tariffs and restrictions being good for all states

IMF loans always involve conditionalities, or certain criteria that the recipient-state must fulfil in order to receive the loan. Often, these take the form of structural adjustment programmes (SAPs), which require the recipient-state to reform their economies along the lines of neo-liberal economic theory. In several states, this has been demonstrably damaging. Studies (the below is not exhaustive) have shown a clear link between states accepting IMF loans/SAPs and:

- A rise in tuberculosis due to healthcare cuts (Eastern Europe in the 1990s)
- Youth unemployment (Greece, 2010s)
- Corporate political influence (Jamaica)

The World Bank

The World Bank was also formed in 1945 as a result of the Bretton Woods Conference. However, where the IMF is designed for general economic stability and rescuing states from debt crises, the World Bank is specifically geared towards **poverty reduction** by providing loans to states which cannot borrow from 'commercial' banks (because they cannot afford the interest rates; or the commercial bank will not lend to them, because they think the chance of non-repayment is too high). Therefore, whilst both developed and developing states may 'benefit' from the IMF, the World Bank is almost always discussed in relation to developing/middle-income states only.

Until the late 1960s... the World Bank would only lend money for infrastructure projects (e.g. ports, railways, power stations, etc.), since the successful completion of such projects would guarantee income that would enable the borrower-state to repay their loan to the World Bank.

From 1974... under the leadership of American diplomat Robert McNamara, the World Bank began to prioritise meeting the basic needs of people in the developing world by providing much larger loans and loaning money to pay for social services (e.g. education, healthcare) as well as infrastructure. Consequently, the amount of debt owed by developing states to the World Bank grew significantly.

From the 1980s... the World Bank has prioritised lending to developing states to help them achieve economic growth that would allow them to repay their existing debt to the World Bank. Like the IMF, it has insisted that these developing states accept **structural adjustment programmes** (SAPs) and reform their economic policies along the lines of free-market, neoliberal principles.

Like the IMF, the World Bank is based in Washington DC, the American capital and is a special agency of the UN under the sub-jurisdiction of ECOSOC. It is technically comprised of two institutions; the **International Bank for Reconstruction and Development** (to lend to middle-income countries) and the **International Development Association** (to lend to developing countries).

The member-states of the World Bank elect the:

- Board of Executive Directors
- President of the World Bank

Each member-state has a number of votes in proportion to the financial contribution it makes. The USA therefore has the largest number of votes, although not a 'veto' majority as it has in the IMF. By convention, the World Bank President is an American (currently David Malpass). In 2011, the BRIC nations issued a statement calling for this tradition to be overturned.

Strengths of the World Bank	Weaknesses of the World Bank
Anti-poverty funds: The World Bank has provided significant funds in the fight against poverty and to create wealth across the globe. The World Bank can be partially credited for the halving of extreme poverty across the planet from its conception to 2015. In 2016, the World Bank provided $63bn in low-interest loans to 275 projects in developing; post-conflict; fragile; and middle-income states. The World Bank is crucial in providing these funds, since commercial banks would not loan to these states, or would charge predatory and extortionate interest rates. For example, the World Bank has:	Cash crops: A common conditionality for World Bank loans to developing countries is the rapid growth of an export-crop agricultural sector so that they can repay their loans effectively. These 'cash crops' are produced for high-profit exports rather than domestic consumption. Examples include cocoa beans in Cameroon, and coffee beans in Ethiopia. However, this can cause developing countries to become *dependent* on developed markets - what would happen to a developing economy if the demand for that crop fell in the West. It also makes them vulnerable TNCs that control processing and distribution, such as the declaration by the CEO of Nestle that water is not a 'human right' (in response to criticisms that local water supplies in various African countries had been diverted for crop

• Worked with the Arab League to reduce female unemployment and increase the economic participation of women • Expanded the electricity and power supply to rural areas in Tanzania and other East African countries • Built crucial infrastructure, like water supply, in the Palestinian territories • Provided funds for emergency coronavirus responses (lockdowns, furloughs, medical supplies) in Central American countries like Costa Rica • Built digital access and internet-capable infrastructure in Haiti, especially in the wake of natural disasters (earthquakes) • Funded programmes to extend emergency education in Yemen	growth)
	Corruption: Many World Bank loans are diverted from their intended purpose (infrastructure investment and poverty alleviation) to line the pockets of corrupt government officials in the states to which that money is sent. For example, in 2016, officials in the Afghan capital, Kabul, embezzled $700m of aid money from the World Bank. Another example is a $30m loan to Armenia to restore the crumbling Soviet-era piping system in the capital, Yerevan, which had dangerously contaminated the water supply. A significant amount of this money has gone mysteriously missing (the company tendered to carry out the repairs had financial links to the government); problems with the water supply persist
Adaptability and sustainability: The World Bank has been willing to adapt and has changed its practises to increase the efficacy of its loans and development projects. The principal problem with World Bank funding in the past is that it was often focused	Ecological damage: Pushing economic development at all costs as a conditionality of loan repayment has resulted in serious ecological damage in many parts of the developing world. Draining marshlands or cutting down forests

on grand infrastructure projects like hydroelectric dams. The issue with these 'high-tech' solutions to poverty were that:

- The local technical knowledge to sustain and repair such infrastructure was not present in developing countries
- They did not 'diffuse' their benefits throughout a whole community – the generation of power/wealth/food would usually be concentrated in the hands of a political, urban elite within the developing country

Now, there is much more of a focus on development involving local people and organisations, using local knowledge and giving greater consideration to the human and social impact of World Bank-funded projects.

An example of this is a current project to build low-cost schools in Eastern Afghanistan in collaboration with local educational officials, to raise opportunities for Afghan youth.

for farmland, for example, damages the local ecosystem and biodiversity – and can make areas more prone to poor drainage, floods or drought. Elsewhere, the World Bank invests in projects to generate rapid economic growth which may have negative environmental impacts, e.g.:

- Coal-fired power plants in South Africa (which contribute to carbon emissions)
- Oil rigs off the coast of Ghana (which contribute to carbon emissions)
- Gold mining in Peru; the purification processes means toxic 'heavy metals' like arsenic leach into the water table, poisoning animals and people

Insufficiency of funds: The scope of the World Bank is arguably too small. Its budget in 2016 was $63 billion, less than a tenth of the size of the US military budget in the same year. Since the World Bank only really benefits *developing* states, it is less likely that *developed* states will contribute since they see no immediate benefit

The World Trade Organisation (WTO)

The WTO was founded in 1995 (so, much more recently than the IMF and World Bank!) It superseded and replaced the **General Agreement on Trade and Tariffs (GATT)** which was a 1948 treaty between 23 states, which aimed to progressively reduce the level of tariffs between member-states through frequent negotiations. The average tariff levels for GATT participants went down from 22% in 1948 to 5% in 1999. The WTO:

- Organises negotiations to continue and extend the GATT reduction of tariffs
- Provides a forum for resolving trade disputes between member-states

WTO members are committed to trading with all other WTO members under what is known as **'most favoured nation'** status. What this means is that if they reduce tariffs on trade in a commodity with one country, they have to reduce tariffs on that commodity for *all* WTO member states. There are some exemptions to this rule for bilateral and multilateral trade agreements, regional trade agreements, and for providing favourable terms for developing countries which need help to build up their economies. WTO member-states may also deviate from these rules to protect the environment; public health; animal and plant health; or to prevent 'unfair' trade practices.

The highest decision-making body in the WTO is the **Ministerial Conference** in which the governments of all member states negotiate with one another directly to reach decisions. It meets every two years. Between meetings, the WTO is managed by a **Director General** and a **General Council** chosen by the Ministerial Conference. The WTO currently has 164 member-states, covering the vast majority of the world economy. It is *not* a UN agency, but works with the IMF/World Bank.

Strengths of the WTO	Weaknesses of the WTO
Relatively democratic: The WTO is considered to be much more democratic than its fellow institutions of global economic governance. Decisions are made by a	Negative externalities: The WTO prioritises free trade above issues like workers' rights, child labour and environmental damage. Consequently, many WTO meetings

simple majority, where each member-state has a single vote regardless of the size of their economy. Approximately 60% of WTO members are 'developing states', so it cannot be said that it is overly dominated by Western states. The rules of the WTO were collectively written by member-states, and member-states elect the leadership	have been targeted by violent protests (e.g. Cancun, 2003)
	Stalled negotiations: The 'Doha Round' of negotiations for reducing tariffs began in 2001 but have since stalled. This suggests that the WTO has hit something of a brick wall in terms of further free trade reform (*see next page*)
Tariff reduction: The WTO *has* successfully reduced tariff barriers, making it easier for states to trade and bringing down the affordable cost of manufactured goods and stimulating a growth in jobs and living standards. For example, in the 1990s, the 'Banana Wars' saw President Clinton (USA) bring a case to the WTO that the EU was unlawfully favouring banana producers in former African colonies by placing tariffs on US fruit corporations in Central America. The two sides reached an agreement in 2001, with the EU agreeing to gradually reduce tariffs on Central American bananas. This made bananas cheaper for EU citizens	Inability to compel powerful states: It is possible for powerful states to ignore WTO rulings. In 2012, the WTO ruled that Airbus (an EU aircraft manufacturer) had *not* received illegal subsidies from EU states; but that Boeing (a US aircraft manufacturer) *had* received illegal subsidies from the US. State subsidies are seen as a violation of fair competition and free trade. The US continued to provide government subsidies to Boeing anyway
	Threat to state sovereignty: Conversely, the WTO could be seen as forcing states to change laws/regulations against their sovereign will

The future of the WTO?

The **'Doha Development Round'** (DDA) is the trade-negotiation round of the WTO which commenced in 2001. Subsequent meetings have taken place in Cancun; Hong Kong; Paris; Potsdam; and Geneva. Progress in negotiations stalled after the breakdown of the July 2008 talks in Geneva. Despite attempts to resurrect the negotiations, they remain in limbo. The key issues preventing a consensus between member-states on trade negotiations are:

1. **Agriculture:** Around 75% of citizens in developing-world countries like India and Brazil live in rural areas and are dependent on agriculture for their livelihoods. Developing countries are therefore very reluctant to reduce tariffs on the importation of external agricultural goods, because this would expose domestic farmers to disastrous competition from goods produced in the mechanised, efficient, developed-world agricultural industry

2. **Subsidies:** It has also been alleged by developing-world countries that developed countries are unfairly boosting their domestic industries through subsidies (like the EU's Common Agricultural Policy; or significant US government support for the cotton industry). Developing-world countries have demanded that these subsidy policies, which are 'trade-distorting' by artificially reducing costs for Western corporations, be stripped back

It remains to be seen whether these issues could be resolved in future talks. They have been largely absent from the global agenda in the last four years in any case, under Donald Trump's presidency.

The Group of 7 (G7)

The G7 has no formal structure or staff. It is simply a convenient forum for the governments of advanced economies to have regular meetings with each other. The annual G7 summit is attended by the leaders of the G7 countries. Separately, the finance ministers of the G7 (e.g. Rishi Sunak for the UK) meet four times a year. Each G7 country holds the presidency for a year at a time; the presiding country is responsible for hosting the summit and setting the agenda for discussion. The G7 discusses coordination of domestic and international economic policy; debt reduction for developing countries; and coordinates Western responses to global economic crises.

Below is a brief history of the G7's development:

- **1975:** Founded as the 'G6' of the largest advanced economies in the world – the USA, Japan, Germany, the UK, France and Italy. It was formed in the aftermath of the 1973 'Oil Shock' (where in response to Western support for Israel in the Yom Kippur War, Arab countries quadrupled the price of oil, crippling Western economies), to coordinate economic policy

- **1976:** Became the 'G7' with the addition of Canada

- **1977:** The EEC/EU joined as a separate institution, but does not count towards the numbering

- **1997:** Became the 'G8' with the addition of Russia. Russia was not an advanced economy and was significantly less wealthy than all the other members, but was invited to join to encourage it to accelerate its post-Soviet, post-Communist free-market reforms

- **2014:** Russia was suspended from the G8 because of its invasion of Crimea

- **2017:** Russia left the G8, making it the 'G7' again

Strengths of the G7	Weaknesses of the G7
Effective discussion forum: The G7 provides a forum where states can discuss common concerns/interests openly. G7 meetings are very small – involving the leader and finance minister of each country; and sometimes the head of the IMF or another relevant global institution. Because all member-states share a	Internal divisions: There have been some serious divisions within the G7 in the past four years. President Trump argued that other states were 'exploiting' the US and responded by imposing steel tariffs on the EU, Canada and Japan). Trump also argued in 2018 and 2019 that Russia should be reinstated to the G7. In

belief in liberal-democratic capitalism, and because of the intimate size of meetings, it is easier to reach a policy consensus	2019, the G7 for the first time ever did not issue a 'joint communique' (a common agreement published at the end of the annual summit)
Internal legitimacy: The G7 utilises a rotating presidency system on an annual basis. The presidency brings with it the power to direct the agenda for the year's summit. This prevents any one state from dominating discussions and makes the group more internally democratic and legitimate, contributing to productive discussion	Global illegitimacy: The G7 has been accused of promoting neoliberal economic policy in the interests of developed countries, to the detriment of developing countries and other issues. In particular, the G7 has been unwilling or unable to seriously debate global poverty and climate change
Global economic power: Because of the overwhelming economic power of its member-states, the G7 is able to make important interventions in global economic governance. • 1999: Cancellation of $100bn multilateral and bilateral debt owed by developing countries to G8 countries • 2005: Doubling aid to Africa and cancelling debts owed by 19 developing countries at the Gleneagles Summit • 2008: Key role in coordinating responses to the financial crisis	Unrepresentative: The G7 is no longer representative of the dominant share of the global economy. In the late-1980s it accounted for nearly 70% of the global economy but today this is 46%, largely because of the rise of states like China, India and Brazil. The exclusion of China, the second-largest economy in the world, limits how influential it can be. Russia 'walking away' from the G8 after being sanctioned and suspended in 2014 shows that the G7 is no longer considered the main forum for economic policy discussions.

and increasing funding for the IMF • 2014: Punished Russia by expelling it from the G8 after it annexed Crimea	The rise of the G20 (discussed below) has arguably increased the irrelevance of the G7

The Group of 20 (G20)

The G20 was formed in 1999, of the USA, China, Japan, Germany, the UK, France, Italy, Canada, South Korea, Russia, India, Brazil, Indonesia, South Africa, Turkey, Mexico, Argentina, Australia and the EU. These are not the 20 richest countries in the world (otherwise the membership would be constantly changing), but they are in the top-30 and were selected in order to provide some representation to every 'important' geographical region. Collectively, the G20 accounts for 90% of global GDP; 80% of world trade; 2/3 of the global population; and half of the planet's land area.

Like the G7, the G20 has no formal structure or staff. There are regular (since 2011, annual) summits of the leaders of the G20 countries to discuss global economic issues. The G20 was founded in the wake of the debt crises that hit emerging/middle-income markets in the 1990s (these included the 1994 Mexican peso crisis; the 1997 Asian financial crisis; and the 1998 Russian financial crisis). The aim was to achieve a wider consensus on macro-economic policy than was possible within the narrower G7. In a more globalised world, it was seen as impossible to provide financial stability and responsible global economic governance whilst excluding major economies not in the G7. Since then, the G20 has also addressed issues like the ageing population in middle-income and developed states; IMF reform; World Bank reform; and the 2008 Financial Crisis. In 2009, the G20 announced that it would supersede the G8 (now G7) as the main economic council of wealthy nation-states.

Strengths of the G20	Weaknesses of the G20
Broad legitimacy: Because the membership of the G20 is wider than	Too exclusive: Although the G20 is more inclusive than the G7, it still

the G7, including critical middle-income and developing countries like China and India, it may be seen by these states as a more legitimate institution of global economic governance. The participation of more states also perhaps enables it to be more effective in tackling global problems like national debt crises that may spill over	excludes the vast bulk of the world's 195 countries. Many advanced economies (e.g. Poland, Norway and Singapore) and many developing economies (e.g. Nigeria) have criticised the G20 for excluding them from participation. The G20 often 'invites' these states as participant observers, but this isn't the same as membership
Forum for discussion: Like the G7, the G20 can provide a more intimate forum for economic policy discussion than a larger institution like the UN. This has led to some major successes – for example, the free trade deal struck between MERCOSUR (effectively the South American version of the EU) and the EU, announced at the 2019 Osaka Summit after decades of negotiation	Internal divisions: The G20's broader membership (compared to the G7) also increases the number of possible policy disputes, and therefore limits the efficacy of the institution. For example, the 2020 summit (hosted virtually by Saudi Arabia) was marred by arguments between the EU and Saudi Arabia for their numerous human rights abuses

GLOBAL ECONOMIC DEVELOPMENT

There are two main measurements of 'poverty' that we need to be aware of:

1. **The 'orthodox' measurement:** Poverty is being below the minimum income needed to ensure adequate access to safe drinking water, and adequate food,

clothing, shelter, health and education in the world's poorest countries. This is the definition adopted by the World Bank and is revised periodically upwards in line with inflation; currently this is $1.90 a day. In this view, poverty is purely a material affair – it is a lack of money and nothing more

2. **Alternative measurements:** Some would argue that poverty should also include racial, religious, class or caste-based discrimination; exploitative or abusive gender relationships; a lack of job or housing security; a lack of infrastructure; or corruption (these all come from the World Bank's 'Voices of the Poor' report that interviewed over 20,000 people in 23 countries). Others have argued that hours of work; environmental quality; and happiness should also be included as measurements of poverty

The North-South Divide

As things currently stand, the most widely accepted model of the distribution of global income is the **north-south divide** (also known as the **Brandt Line**). The **'global north'** consists of North America north of Mexico; Europe and Russia; Australia and New Zealand; and some developed parts of East Asia (Hong Kong, Singapore, South Korea and Taiwan). The **'global south'** is made up of Africa, Latin America, and 'developing' parts of Asia. It should be noted this is something of a crude oversimplification – there are states in the 'south' which are high-income, e.g. Saudi Arabia, and states in the 'north' which are middle-income, e.g. Russia.

The global north	The global south
1/4 of the world's population	3/4 of the world's population
4/5 of the world's income	1/5 of the world's income
90% of industry (located in the 'global north' or owned by companies based in the 'global north', with the factory physically located in the south')	10% of industry (located in the 'global south' and owned by a company or a state of the 'global south', rather than a 'northern' TNC)

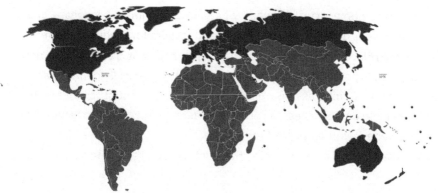

The north-south divide is not necessarily a static binary; it is obvious from history that states have the capacity to move from the 'south' to the 'north' of the Brandt Line. The classic case of this are the **Four Asian Tigers** (or Dragons) of South Korea, Taiwan, Singapore and Hong Kong. Between the 1960s and 1990s, they underwent rapid industrialisation and maintained exceptional growth rates of 7%+ annually. They are now high-income economies, specialising in areas of competitive and comparative advantage. For example, Hong Kong and Singapore became international financial

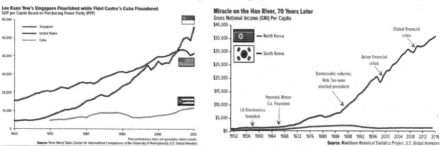

centres; whereas South Korea and Taiwan became world leaders in manufacturing electronic components and devices like microchips, phones, TVs, etc. In comparing (i) the relative growth rates in GDP per capita of Singapore, the United States and Cuba from 1960 to 2010; and (ii) the relative growth rates in GDP per capita of North and South Korea since the end of the Korean War; it is apparent how remarkable this growth has been.

The 'East Asian miracle' has been attributed variously to:

- Universal education policies pursued by national governments, involving English
- 'Confucian' values of hard work, discipline and respect for authority figures
- Initially dictatorial or semi-authoritarian governments that cracked down on internal instability and pushed forward modernisation policies, before gradually giving way to full democracy (as opposed to decolonised countries that were initially unstable democracies; or countries where authoritarian governments refused to cede power and opted for civil war)
- Targeted government investment in critical infrastructure, like ports, airports, etc.
- A willingness to embrace global free trade and orient their economies towards producing high-tech, specialised manufactured products for the export market

Indonesia, Malaysia, the Philippines, Thailand and Vietnam are sometimes referred to as **'Tiger Cub Economies'** because they are attempting to follow the same export-driven model of technological and economic development achieved by the Four Asian Tigers. The 'Tiger Cubs' and the 'Tigers' are sometimes referred to in conjunction as part of the **'bamboo network'** because of the disproportionate economic role played by ethnically Chinese business owners in all of these countries.

Theories of economics and global poverty
Given the obvious existence and continuation of global poverty in large parts of the world – whilst it does not exist in others – different theories have emerged to explain why this is the case. We will examine two of these theories. The questions you need to consider in conjunction with earlier information about institutions of global economic governance are:
- Which of the two theories is more convincing?
- Therefore, what is the 'solution' to global poverty?

Theory 1 – Dependency/structural theory (Frank)
To understand dependency or 'structural;' theory, we must first look at the 'world capitalist system' which emerged in the 16th century and lasted until the mid-1900s. Frank argued that colonialism in Latin America, Asia and Africa locked these regions

into an unequal and exploitative relationship with militarily, technologically powerful European empires. The relationship was structured as a:

- **Core/metropolis:** Wealthy European and Western nations
- **Satellite/periphery:** Impoverished Latin American/Asian/African colonies

The **core** generated enormous wealth by extracting natural resources (like sugar, cocoa, tropical fruits, precious metals, spices and slaves) from the **periphery**, the profits of which paid for their industrialisation and economic/social development, whilst the **periphery** was impoverished.

The periphery was treated as a bank of natural resources during the colonial period. In Frank's view, the process of colonisation was not merely one of 'robbery' which terminated with the end of empires and colonialism, but one with damaging long-term effects.

1. **Ethnic tensions:** In order to extract resources, organise local labour and maintain social order in colonies, European powers often established a native ruling class, rewarding them with wealth and status in exchange for maintaining the flow of resources. These policies enhanced divisions between ethnic groups and sowed the seeds of modern ethnic conflicts, e.g. the Rwandan Genocide in the 1990s perpetrated by the majority Hutu ethnicity against the minority Tutsi. The Tutsi had been made the 'ruling class' in Rwanda by Belgian colonists. Before this, there is little evidence of tension between the Tutsi and the Hutu

2. **Structural dependency:** Colonialism destroyed 'self-sufficient' national economies in the periphery, which were formerly able to grow or manufacture all the goods/resources needed in a particular area. Instead, colonies were converted into cash crop economies, where all labour was geared towards producing a crop (like sugar, tea or coffee) which would be exported back to the European 'core' in exchange for meagre wages. The wealth generated was used by European empires to industrialise; they would then sell manufactured goods back to the periphery. This locked the periphery into a cycle of *dependency*, since they did not have the capacity to produce manufactured goods at competitive prices; and had to continue with cash-crop production to generate minimal profits and purchase manufactured goods

Frank argued that after colonialism ended between the 1950s and 1970s, the global core (developed nations) had no interest in developing the global periphery (underdeveloped nations). Even though they no longer had formal political and military control of colonies, they wanted to keep poor countries in a state of economic underdevelopment so that they continue to benefit from this structural dependency; poor countries would be prepared to sell raw materials for cheap prices, and workers would work for less money than people in more economically powerful countries. Frank referred to this as **neo-imperialism**; a replication of the dependent core-periphery structure of colonialism, but upheld by economic force rather than military force.

Different mechanisms of this relationship are identified by Frank:

1. **Terms of trade:** Many ex-colonies are still dependent on primary (raw material) products for their export earnings. It is processing of those raw materials which adds value to them, and since this mostly takes place in the West, the 'core' still disproportionately benefits from trade. In addition to this, Western states often heavily subsidise agriculture in their own countries so that imported agricultural goods from the periphery are more expensive – this prevents the periphery from selling as much agricultural goods as it can actually produce

2. **Dominance of TNCs:** Because TNCs are mobile and can establish their presence in any country providing the raw material or labour they need, peripheral countries are forced into a 'race to the bottom' to make their country attractive to the TNC by lowering wages and workers' standards. They can also negotiate favourable tax deals – e.g. in Zambia, the mining TNC Glencore negotiated a long-term contract to mine copper in Zambia. They pay $50m in tax annually, but export $6bn of copper, and the Zambian government is contractually obliged to pay for the electrical costs of mining and processing the copper – about $150m annually. This restricts long-term social investment, education and development

3. **Aid money:** Western aid money can be seen as a means by which developed countries exploit poor countries and keep them underdeveloped/dependent by 'disincentivising' long-term development by providing short-term loans. Aid

could be viewed as bribery of a political/ economic elite in a developing country to maintain the existing relationship; or as a means by which to force favourable trade terms via attaching conditionalities to the loans

4. **Land grabs:** These are currently happening all over Africa, where a developed state or corporation buys up thousands of hectares of land in Africa with the intention of planting it with food or biofuel crops for export back to Western markets. In some case studies of land grabs, thousands of indigenous people are displaced. In the long-term, the land grab generates much more revenue for the developed state or corporation than it is initially sold for

A variation of dependency theory is **'world systems'** theory (Wallerstein). It is similar to classic dependency theory in that it argues that the global capitalist system requires some states, or regions within states, to be poor and underdeveloped in order for 'developed' states to reap the benefits of economically exploiting them. However, instead of considering a binary distinction between 'developed' and 'exploited' states, Wallerstein instead makes a distinction between three categories:

1. **Core:** Developed countries which control wages and monopolise high-tech manufacturing
2. **Semi-periphery:** States which resemble the core in urban areas but still have rural poverty
3. **Peripheral:** Countries which provide raw materials and cash crops to the core/semi-periphery

An example of a 'core' country might be the USA; the 'semi-periphery' would be a state like Brazil or China; the 'periphery' would mostly be located in sub-Saharan Africa. Crucially, Wallerstein argues that it is possible for states to be upwardly or downwardly mobile in the world system; their position is not fixed forever, as it is in classic dependency theory. This may explain how some countries, like the Asian Tigers, managed to move from the periphery to the core. However, Wallerstein acknowledges that this mobility is the *exception* and not the *norm*.

To summarise, the key tenets of dependency theory are:

1. 'Developed' countries became developed by exploiting colonies in the age of imperialism
2. They maintain this dominance in the present day through neo-imperial strategies
3. Poverty is a consequence of the dependent system established whereby core countries monopolise advanced manufacturing and peripheral countries rely on primary exports
4. It is impossible, or very difficult, for peripheral countries to break out of this system and 'escape' poverty, because the terms of global trade are established in such a way that they cannot be self-sufficient and must rely on primary good exports to sustain their economy
5. Poverty is a result of the *global capitalist structure* and the imbalances in global trade
6. The solution to poverty is for developing countries to become *self-sufficient*

Theory 2 – Classical/neo-liberal theory (aka. 'The Washington Consensus')

The second theory of global economics and poverty is inspired by the 18th and 19th century political and economic works of Adam Smith and David Ricardo. It is based on the idea that poverty is a lack of income or resources, which can be measured (typically this is done by considering GDP per capita). It argues that poverty is the *natural state of existence* for human beings – i.e. absent government, society, etc. we would all be impoverished – we would have insufficient food and water, would die of diseases or exposure or 'old age' at 40, etc. Therefore, the solution to poverty must be economic development, because economic development brings wealth and this solves poverty. The best way to generate wealth, in classical theory, is the 'invisible hand' of the free market. This is essentially similar to the neoliberal argument we looked at in the Ideologies unit, but writ large on a global scale. To tackle poverty, classical theorists argue that states should:

- Deregulate their markets
- Cut government/welfare spending
- Privatise state-owned industries
- Encourage private enterprise and businesses
- Focus their economies on products in which they have *comparative advantage*

- Trading freely with other states to generate profits

The set of solutions and policies inspired by classical/neo-liberal theory is known as the **Washington Consensus**. It became the dominant paradigm of global economic governance in the 1980s under the guidance of President Ronald Reagan and PM Margaret Thatcher, influencing the behaviour of the major institutions of governance like the IMF and World Bank.

CASE STUDIES: SAPs and the 2008 Financial Crisis
To compare dependency/structural and neoliberal/classical theory, and determine which is more convincing as an explanation of how the global economy works (and therefore how we should tackle the issue of poverty), it would be useful to first examine two case studies; **structural adjustment programmes (SAPs)** and the **2008 Financial Crisis.**

1. Structural Adjustment Programmes:
SAPs are imposed by the IMF and the World Bank when they loan money to a state. They follow the principles of the neoliberal theory/ the Washington Consensus and so usually involve:
- A balance of payments deficit reduction through currency devaluation
- Budget deficit reduction through higher taxes and lower government spending
- Eliminating subsidies for agriculture/food production
- Raising the price of public services to encourage the growth of private substitutes
- Cutting wages to 'competitive' levels
- Focusing economic output on exports and direct resource extraction

Below is a brief timeline of the implementation of SAPs. We should consider which parts of this support the conclusions drawn by dependency theorists and neoliberal theorists.

From the 1950s to the 1970s, developing countries tended to follow the dependency/ structuralist paradigm (i.e. trying to avoid participation on global trade, and building self-sufficiency by investing heavily in developing domestic industries). While the structuralist period led to rapid expansion of domestically manufactured goods and high rates of economic growth, there were also some major shortcomings such as stagnating exports, elevated fiscal deficit, very high rates of inflation and the crowding out of private investment.

However, the oil shocks (increase in oil prices) of the 1970s and early 1980s forced many developing countries to turn to the West for loans, since their structuralist economic policies meant they did not export enough to generate the hard currency needed to buy oil, and their economies were dependent on oil to function. The IMF and the World Bank used this as an opportunity to reshape their economies in line with the Washington Consensus, reforming their economic policies through structural adjustment programmes.

Interest rates in the West in the 1980s were very high, something which led the debt of developing countries to rise by an enormous amount (interest rates in the West mattered because that was where developing countries were borrowing from). In 2010 the total stock of external debt for all developing countries stood at approximately $4 trillion, according to the World Bank, an amount that represented 21 percent of the collective gross national income (GNI) of these countries. The heavy debt of developing countries left many of them dependent on the West for further loans, just so that they could service their debts.

SAPs are based on the condition that loans have to be repaid in hard currency. Developing countries were therefore forced to switch to exports to obtain such currency in the short-term (instead of focusing on developing 'self-sufficiency' in the long term). As dozens of countries did this simultaneously, and were often told to focus on similar primary goods (e.g. coffee), the situation resembled a large-scale price war: developing countries had to compete against each other, causing massive worldwide over-production and deteriorating world market prices.

While this was beneficial for Western consumers – where prices dropped massively – developing countries lost 52% of their revenues in exports between 1980 and 1992 (not because they were exporting less, but because prices were being driven down by competition).

The implementation of SAPs in Latin America/Africa/Asia had several effects:

1. Recipients of structural adjustment programmes in the 1980s were often encouraged to specialize in a single cash crop according to the neo-classical doctrine of comparative advantage, like cocoa in Ghana, tobacco in Zimbabwe and prawns in the Philippines, which made them highly vulnerable to fluctuations in the world market price of these crops

2. Structural adjustment programmes were typically introduced with no requirement to tackle corruption. This seems to have been an obstacle to their success since a significant amount of the money lent was stolen by corrupt officials at various levels of government

3. Since structural adjustment programmes require privatisations, they typically have a negative impact on health and education services in developing countries. Countries in receipt of structural adjustment programmes tend, for example, to suffer increasing rates of tuberculosis

4. Malnutrition seems often to have risen under developing countries in receipt of structural adjustment programmes (because of cuts to government spending); for example, in Zambia where average food consumption went down from two meals a day to one

5. Inflation fell dramatically in most South American countries in receipt of SAPs, something which helped balance their economies

Something that should be noted is that GDP tended to grow in developing countries in receipt of SAPs, although *not as fast as it grew in China, South Korea and Indonesia,* in which governments invested huge sums in infrastructure, something which was completely counter to the Washington Consensus (which instead argued for free market economics and privatisation). Many economists would argue the reason that China's economy is so successful today is because it built up a self-sufficient domestic economy through significant state intervention, nationalised programmes and industrial investment, and only opened up in terms of trade to the global market once its domestic economy was 'strong' enough to compete on a roughly level playing-field. SAPs were used in the 1990s to transform the countries of the Eastern Bloc to free market economies following the collapse of Communism, in some cases (such as the Czech Republic very successfully), in others less so (one million people are estimated to have died in the former USSR as a result of the transition to a free market economy). An NGO called Jubilee 2000 campaigned for the debt of developing countries to be cancelled, since it prevents them from dealing with poverty. In 2000 the G8 agreed to begin forgiving debt of the most impoverished countries. Since then 39 of the most heavily indebted developing countries have had part of the debt forgiven, typically that owed to the IMF and the World Bank. Debt owed to commercial banks tends not to have been forgiven. Debt forgiveness seems to have had a positive impact on poverty reduction, with Tanzania using the money saved to abolish school fees and Burkina Faso using it reduce healthcare charges.

Since 2002 the IMF and the World Bank have combined Structural Adjustment Programmes with Poverty Reduction Papers (PRPs). These are strategies to reduce poverty in the state receiving aid. They are based on the principle that they should be drawn up in partnership with civil society in the state receiving aid using local knowledge. Supporters of PRPs argue that they mitigate the weaknesses of the SAPs of the 1980s. Critics argue that many of the problems of SAPs still apply and that PRPs are still subject to influence by the donor countries.

2. The 2008 Financial Crisis:

The causes of the 2008 Financial Crisis are incredibly complex but are simplified below:
- In the early 2000s, the global economy was doing very well
- This meant that wages grew in the USA; house prices grew correspondingly
- Because of neo-liberal policy, banks were very deregulated and could do what they wanted

- Banks in the USA increasingly began to issue sub-prime mortgages; loans to people with poor credit histories who were in serious difficulty of not being able to repay money they borrowed
- Banks did this because if someone defaulted on their mortgage, the bank would have the right to repossess the house (and keep money already repaid!) and sell the house. Since house prices were rising, the bank would make a profit even if the mortgage was defaulted. This strategy is called 'predatory lending'
- In 2006, there was a slump in house prices in the USA. Now, if a mortgage was defaulted and a bank repossessed the house, the bank would still make a loss because when they sold the house it was not enough to cover the money they had initially loaned out as sub-prime mortgages to people they knew would likely not repay them
- This resulted in the collapse of Lehman Brothers, a major US bank; and AIG, an American insurance giant, in September 2008; as well as serious damage to other US banks
- Because many European banks had stakes in US banks; or had 'bought' debt from them (buying debt means that you pay an immediate sum to the institution to whom a debt is initially owed; you then have the right to collect the debt from the debtor), the instability spread to European banks (which European governments then had to bail out)

By examining the role played by different institutions of global economic governance in the 2008 Crisis, we can make judgements on how successful global economic governance have been collectively and relative to each other; and whether dependency or classical development theory seems to be the better explanation of the global economy's functioning.

The role of the IMF
Some have argued that the IMF is partially responsible for the global financial crisis because it encouraged the deregulation of global finance by promoting neo-liberalism through its SAPs and annual reports on the financial health of member states. The IMF (and other proponents of neo-liberalism) did not recognise the risk that in a deregulated environment, financial markets would engage in 'casino capitalism'- risky

practices, such as parcelling debt out to other financial institutions in the guise of high yielding securities. This was a major contributor to the 2008 Financial Crisis.

Before the financial crisis, the IMF was in danger of becoming irrelevant. Its currency exchange role had lapsed, its lending capacity was decreasing, its staff was shrinking, and few countries paid any attention to its surveillance reports. The IMF lacked the lending capacity to deal with the financial crisis and was accused of being slow to react.

The IMF used additional funding provided by the G20 in 2009 to take a prominent role in economic recovery, brokering rescue packages for Pakistan, Iceland, Hungary and Ukraine, providing $700 billion of crisis lending to member states, and $430 billion towards a rescue fund for countries in the Eurozone. The IMF has strengthened its surveillance reporting to give early warnings of trends which might cause financial difficulties. The IMF continues to believe in and argue for the neo-liberal Washington consensus. It has modified its position, however, in terms of arguing that banks be made to have large enough deposits to cope with mass-defaults on loans.

The role of the G8
The G8 had declined in terms of its share of world GDP since the organization was founded, and the G8 states were particularly hard hit by the financial crisis. It was therefore in no position to lead a response to the global financial crisis.

The role of the G20
The G20 held its first summit, the 2008 Washington Summit, in response to the financial crisis. Western leaders saw the G20 as a more appropriate forum than the G8 for dealing with the financial crisis, since the G20 economies had a much greater share of world GDP. The G20 reaffirmed their commitment to the free market, and agreed to tighten up regulation of financial institutions so as to prevent a recurrence of the financial crash.

The G20 also discussed how to prevent the financial crash becoming a full-scale depression at the 2008 Washington Summit. British PM Brown took a leading role at the conference, arguing for Western governments to adopt Keynesian stimulus packages whereby they cut interest rates, cut taxes, borrowed more and increased spending in order to ensure people carried on spending money so that the global economy did not grind to a halt. He was successful in convincing other governments to follow this approach. Thus, he is held in significantly higher esteem internationally than domestically.

The G20 held its second summit, the 2009 London Summit, to discuss additional measures to prevent the development of a full-scale depression. Gordon Brown again took a leading role, arguing for a global stimulus package against the objections of President Sarkozy of France and Angela Merkel. He got his own way and the G20 agreed to provide $1.1 trillion to various programmes designed to improve international finance and trade, and overall economic stability and recovery. The greater part of the money went to the IMF.

At the 2009 London Summit, the G20 also agreed to give developing countries more power in the IMF. China's influence at the G20 is widely believed to have grown at this meeting. These developments appear to have been concessions to persuade developing countries to agree to the wider stimulus agenda. At the 2009 Pittsburgh Summit, the G20 declared itself to be the new main forum of world economic cooperation instead of the G8. This represented a diminution of the global power of the West and the traditional 'developed world'.

At the 2010 Toronto Summit, the G20 decided that now financial recovery was underway, it was important to achieve financial consolidation. They agreed to cut government borrowing and return to a more neo-liberal approach in order to reduce debt-to-GDP ratios. Some have criticised the resulting austerity policies on the basis that they have resulted in a very slow recovery. Others have argued that they are essential for a stable global economy.

Comparing dependency and neoliberal theory

Dependency/structural theory	Classical/neoliberal theory
Poverty is a consequence of structural imbalances in the global	Poverty is the natural state of existence for human beings; the

economy which makes the 'periphery' dependent on the 'core' and prevents them from developing advanced manufacturing economies	question we should be asking is not 'why does poverty exist?' – this is like asking 'why does darkness exist?' – but rather, 'how do we create wealth?'
The solution to poverty is for 'developing' countries to stop participating in global free trade until they can develop self-sufficient economies capable of competing internationally. Structural adjustment programmes; aid; and conditional loans are hindrances to the development of self-sufficiency	The solution to poverty is for 'developing' countries to reorient their economies along the lines of the Washington Consensus and adopt neo-liberal policies; deregulation, privatisation, low taxes, low government spending, international trade; in order to incentivise the growth of private enterprise and wealth
Supporting evidence • Institutions of global economic governance (like the IMF, World Bank, G7) are dominated by 'developed' states who design policy in their interest • Some states which ignored IMF recommendations (like China and South Korea), instead investing heavily into infrastructure and manufacturing, have experienced a prolonged economic rise • Serial cancellation of debt shows an increasing awareness	Supporting evidence • Global GDP per capita has increased from $452 (1960) to $11456 (2019). Extreme poverty has fallen to 10% of the world population, from historical highs of 80%. Neoliberal theory, as applied by global institutions, does appear to be achieving its aims • The modification of SAPs to include PRPs; the increasing vote share of developing countries in the IMF, etc.; shows that the Washington Consensus is genuinely a force for progression

that past loans have been predatory and exploitative	
Criticisms • Dependency theory ignores other forms of 'oppression' – religious, racial, gender, etc. It is naïve to suggest that the structure of trade between nation-states is the sole reason for poverty • Countries that modelled their economic policy off dependency theory in the 1970s/80s found themselves unable to deal with price shocks; and were subject to high inflation and stagnating exports • Dependency theory does not seem to be able to explain how some 'peripheral' states which followed neoliberal policies have been so successful in shifting to the 'core' (e.g. Singapore) • Dependency theory ignores that countries which are the *most* self-sufficient are often those where incomes per capita are the lowest (e.g. North Korea, Bhutan, or Cuba)	Criticisms • Neoliberal theory, as applied by the IMF and major institutions of global economic governance, can be seen as partially responsible for the 2008 Crisis by encouraging risky practises • SAPs, frequently attached as neo-liberal conditionalities to IMF/World Bank loans, have had damaging impacts in many developing countries – such as violations of workers' rights; reduction in the provision of healthcare and education; environmental damage • Neoliberal theory can be viewed as posing an inherent threat to state sovereignty, because it involves the deregulation of economies; the reduction of trade barriers; and the increased power of corporations • Neoliberal theory has increased intra-state inequalities (rural/urban)

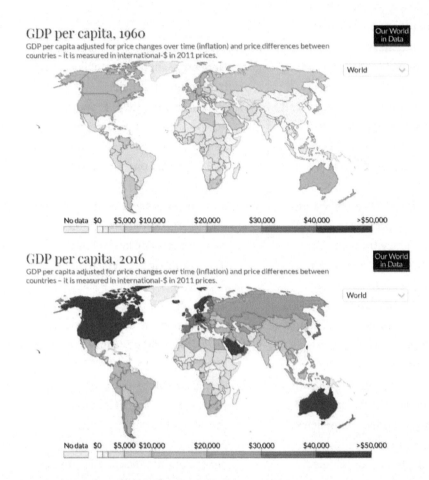

GDP per capita, 1960

GDP per capita adjusted for price changes over time (inflation) and price differences between countries - it is measured in international-$ in 2011 prices.

No data $0 $5,000 $10,000 $20,000 $30,000 $40,000   >$50,000

GDP per capita, 2016

GDP per capita adjusted for price changes over time (inflation) and price differences between countries - it is measured in international-$ in 2011 prices.

No data $0 $5,000 $10,000 $20,000 $30,000 $40,000   >$50,000

REALIST AND LIBERAL FRAMEWORKS (3.6)

Realism	Liberalism
The UN... • The UNSC reflects the harsh realities of global politics; those with power ultimately determine outcomes and policy (through the use of the P5 veto)	The UN... • The UNSC has a rotating membership which encourages participation from all areas of the globe, regardless of 'power'

• The General Assembly is toothless in that its resolutions are not binding – states retain sovereignty and are not compelled to follow collective decisions • The ICJ can only operate where states jointly agree to its jurisdiction; it does not have the authority to impose decisions on sovereign states	• The General Assembly gives all states a singular vote, regardless of their size or power – it is a truly cooperative institution where smaller states can outvote more 'powerful' ones • The ICJ has ruled on a number of inter-state disputes, and its rulings have been accepted and implemented; states respect it as an overarching arbiter
NATO... • During the Cold War, NATO functioned as an institution preserving a stable *balance of power* between the Western and the Soviet blocs • In the post-Cold War era, NATO's eastwards expansion has triggered a *security dilemma* vis-à-vis Russia, which has contributed to increased conflict in Eastern Europe • NATO is reliant on the military power of the USA – it would be non-functional without it. It is not a truly cooperative institution, but an extension of American power and influence	NATO... • In the post-Cold War era, NATO has adopted a key global role in upholding humanitarianism through interventions (which are not in 'self-interest') • NATO is evidence that rational states adopting liberal-democratic principles and cooperating to achieve a common good can be effective in spreading these values and securing mutual gains • The continued participation of states in NATO despite several disputes (France; the USA; Turkey) demonstrates that cooperation is not merely a

	temporary, short-term phenomenon
The IMF/World Bank... • The promotion of neo-liberal theory by the IMF and the World Bank is designed to entrench the power of the developed world and maintain a dependent, exploitative relationship in relation to the developing world. SAPs produce 'losers' so others can 'win' • The IMF and World Bank are dominated by the West (the USA and Europe) – it is not 'cooperative'	The IMF/World Bank... • The promotion of neo-liberal theory by the IMF and the World Bank (including specialisation in accordance with comparative advantage; and free trade) is a manifestation of rational, classical liberal thinking about the economy – it benefits all participants • IMF voting rules have been reworked recently to give more say to middle-income and developing states
G7/G20... • Both the G7 and G20 represent 'elite' clubs of powerful states which exclude an expansion of membership and try to maintain the status-quo in their favour • The G7 and the G20 undercut more democratic bodies like the UN Assembly; they represent raw power	G7/G20... • The shift from the G7 to the G20 demonstrates that decision-making is becoming less exclusive • The G7 (and G20) have made many policies which are clearly not purely the result of amoral self-interest, like debt cancellation to developing countries
WTO... • The WTO does not properly enforce its rulings against	WTO... • The WTO has progressively slashed tariffs on trade, which

powerful states, which allows them to maintain subsidies and undercut developing countries by artificially depressing prices • Negotiations for the expansion of WTO rules have stalled; states want to preserve their sovereign capabilities	benefits consumers worldwide (this suggests gains are mutual, not zero-sum) • WTO decision-making gives every state an equal say; it is a cooperative project, not one which gives uneven say to more powerful states
Development theory... • The global economy is a zero-sum game • For some countries to 'win', others must be 'losing' (structural theory) • States must be sovereign and self-sufficient in order to tackle poverty • Institutions of global economic governance are designed in order to benefit the interests of some states (the 'core') over others (the 'periphery') → this is demonstrated by SAPs, conditionalities, and global debt	Development theory... • The best way to tackle poverty is through economic growth; the best way to achieve economic growth is through cooperative international trade • This is not a 'zero-sum' game; by making use of comparative advantage, all countries can maximise their benefits • Institutions of global economic governance are designed so that *all states* benefit (to different degrees) – this is the crux of rational liberalism

Global Politics – Unit 3.3
Global Governance (Human Rights and Environmental)

GLOBAL GOVERNANCE

Governance is all of the processes of governing (making and enforcing laws/policy/conventions), whether this is undertaken by:

- A government(s)
- A market or network
- A social/religious group

: over any social system – a family, tribe, formal or informal organisation, a territory or multiple territories; and whether this is done through:

- Laws
- Norms
- Language

In this way, **governance** differs from **government.** 'The government' as the classically-conceived sovereign political entity is one way of executing 'governance', but 'governance' is a broader concept which may be carried out by actors other than 'governments'. Consequently, **global governance** is different from the idea of a **world government.** A 'world government' requires a single political sovereign for the planet, whereas it is possible for 'governance' to be carried out on a global scale between a coalition of nation-states and non-state actors, even if there is no single world sovereign.

In this unit, we will explore institutions/mechanisms of 'human rights' and 'environmental' global governance – those elements of global governance that primarily concern human rights and environmental issues. However, it is not possible to completely disentangle the two from each other (or indeed from issues of political or economic governance); they are separated for reasons of analytical ease, rather than because they are qualitatively distinct categories.

HUMAN RIGHTS GLOBAL GOVERNANCE
The creation of international law

After the Second World War, the Allies collected evidence of extensive human rights abuses by:

- **Nazi Germany:** The Nazis were responsible for the mass-murder of around 17 million people, including 6 million Jewish people in the Holocaust, and large numbers of Gypsies/Roma; LGBT people; Communists; socialists; Slavs (Eastern Europeans, who were seen as racially inferior) and Jehovah's Witnesses (a pacifist Christian denomination)
- **Imperial Japan:** Japan was responsible for the mass-murder of 14 million civilians and prisoners-of-war in China, Korea and South-East Asia through deliberate massacre, starvation, forced labour, human medical experimentation; as well as a programme of systematic rape as a 'weapon of war' against occupied populations

After the Second World War, the Allies put the leading German and Japanese politicians and military officers on trial for war crimes at the **Nuremburg Trials** (Germany) and the **Tokyo Trials** (Japan). The majority of defendants were convicted and sentenced to death or long prison sentences, but a small minority were acquitted. A number of Nazis who had escaped to South America at the end of the war were later captured by Mossad (the Israeli secret service) and tried/sentenced in Israel. Although the guilt of the sentenced parties is generally considered beyond doubt (other than by conspiracy theorists and genocide-deniers), the procedure and legitimacy of the trials themselves were heavily criticised on several grounds:

1. *Ex post facto* **charges:** 'Ex post facto' is a Latin phrase referring to a law which retroactively changes the legal consequences of actions that were committed before the enactment of the law. In the case of the Nuremburg/Tokyo trials, the actions carried out by political and military leaders were not technically illegal – because they happened within the jurisdiction of Nazi Germany and Imperial Japan, and such actions were both legal and encouraged. How could defendants be convicted for actions which were not crimes when they committed them?

2. **Allied hypocrisy:** Most of the Allied nations overseeing the trials had undertaken questionable actions themselves. In the case of the Soviet Union, they began the war on the side of Nazi Germany, agreeing to invade and partition Poland between them (the USSR also then conquered the Baltic states); they only

turned against Germany when Hitler betrayed Stalin and invaded the Soviet Union in 1941. The Soviet Union was guilty of many atrocities in the recapture of Eastern Europe and the invasion of Germany, including the extrajudicial massacre of purported Nazi 'collaborators' and the rape of over half a million German women. Prior to WWII, the Soviet regime had executed over 680,000 people in 1937-38 alone as part of Stalin's 'Great Purge' of suspected enemies of the state. Although the Americans had not participated in this level of barbarity, they had conducted bombing campaigns deliberately targeting civilians, most infamously the atomic destruction of Hiroshima and Nagasaki in Japan, killing over 200,000 civilians. The trials were therefore seen as an expression of imbalanced 'victor's justice'

3. **Legitimacy:** There were also some questions about the legitimacy of the procedural evidence. In several cases, the chief Soviet prosecutor attempted to submit falsified documentation to convict Nazis for massacres which the *Soviets* had committed; and the USA withheld evidence that would have exonerated some of the Nazi generals of specific charges

The Allies responded that even though the actions committed were not crimes when they were committed, they were so obviously in violation of the 'universal' moral rules of human behaviour and conduct that they should be prosecuted. The Nuremburg and Tokyo trials led to the development of a new kind of international law; one that was not merely concerned with non-intervention between sovereign states, but also with the behaviour of sovereign state governments towards citizens. The Nuremburg and Tokyo trials established new principles of international law, most importantly:

- **Principle II:** *"The fact that internal law does not impose a penalty for an act which constitutes a crime under international law does not relieve the person who committed the act from responsibility under international law."* – i.e. 'it is legal' (domestically) is not a defence against the committing of a war crime

- **Principle IV:** *"The fact that a person acted pursuant to the order of his Government or of a superior does not relieve him from responsibility under international law, provided a moral choice was in fact possible to him."* – i.e. 'I was just following orders' is not a defence against the committing of a war crime unless your life is directly at risk if you don't do it

- **Principle VI:** The punishable crimes under international law are (i) <u>crimes against peace</u> (planning, preparing or initiating a war of aggression); (ii) <u>war crimes</u> (murder, ill-treatment, enslavement of an enemy civilian population or prisoners of war, unnecessary destruction of cities); (iii) <u>crimes against humanity</u> (murder, extermination, persecution and/or enslavement of *any* civilian population)

The Universal Declaration of Human Rights (UDHR)

In an attempt to further codify the principles of contemporary international law that had emerged at Nuremburg and Tokyo, the newly-created UN began to consider the creation of an international 'Bill of Rights' that should apply between and within all states, regardless of their domestic laws. The process of drafting the document began in 1946 under the auspices of ECOSOC and was a very difficult process. 18 philosophers, politicians, theologians, etc. from a variety of national, religious and political backgrounds were involved in the drafting in order to facilitate a 'representative' document. Prominent members included the Canadian scholar Humphrey; French jurist Cassin; the Lebanese academic Malik; and Chinese philosopher P.C. Chang.

Major sticking points in the construction of the text involved:

- The extent to which the draft was just a reflection of 'Western ideas' (P.C. Chang, in response to arguments based on the works of Thomas Aquinas suggested the committee should spend several months studying the fundamentals of Confucianism)

- The role which religion should play in the construction of the text – especially ideas of 'Christian democracy' which were advocated by Malik, a Lebanese Arab Christian

- Whether 'socio-economic' rights (in effect, positive liberties) should be included in the document along with the classic 'political' rights (negative liberties) – Hernan Santa Cruz, the Chilean representative, was particularly in favour of their inclusion

The UN General Assembly passed the **Universal Declaration of Human Rights** in 1948 to set out the principles that all states should abide by in peace or war, as universal moral obligations that states should fulfil with regards to their citizens. Of the 58 members of the UN at the time, 48 voted in favour, 8 abstained and 2 did not vote. The finalised text can be found here:

https://www.un.org/en/universal-declaration-human-rights/

Debates over the UDHR

The UDHR is a complex and contested legal work. It has obviously been massively influential in international and domestic law, and is the most translated document in human history (a total of 524 languages as of January 2021 - https://www.ohchr.org/en/udhr/pages/searchbylang.aspx). The UDHR has influenced at least 90 national constitutions drafted since 1948. At least 20 African constitutions which gained independence in the decades following the UDHR's creation explicitly reference the UDHR in their national constitutions. Several specific provisions of the UDHR, e.g. the obligation of the government to provide health services, can be found verbatim in national constitutions e.g. those of Armenia, Finland, South Korea, Paraguay and Thailand. Judicial figures in many countries have invoked the UDHR in domestic cases, including India and the USA.

It must be noted, however, that the UDHR is not a **treaty** – as such, it does not impose legal obligations on signatories. In addition, there have been many debates about whether the document is truly a 'universal' work or whether it reflects 'relativist' Western positions on ethics and morality which should not be applied as the foundation of global governance in human rights.

Some would argue that the UDHR is a valuable document because it reflects genuinely, objective universal moral principles that everyone in the world should abide by. The drafters of the document intended it to draw upon the common threads that united most of the world's major philosophical, religious and secular belief systems about what a 'good' life and 'moral' actions are. Conversely, it might be said that this is an unconvincing view as several prominent belief systems have mutually irreconcilable precepts, e.g. whether blasphemy should be tolerated. However, it is still possible to make the case that even if these rights are not *inherently* true, they are valuable in the *constructivist* sense. That is to say, they do not reflect a fundamental truth of nature, but they are extremely worthwhile beliefs for building a peaceful and prosperous world (much like the concept of coins/notes having 'monetary value', which is a collectively agreed-upon fiction).

Nevertheless, there is opposition to the UDHR on a number of fronts:

1. Islamic relativism:

Saudi Arabia abstained on the initial vote, and many Muslim states since (e.g. Pakistan and Iran) have critiqued the UDHR as a set of 'Western' principles rather than a truly 'universal' set of rights. They instead argue for moral *relativism*, and that the UDHR should not apply where it contradicts 'Islamic' principles that they wish to apply. There has been particular opposition to:

- **Article 16:** Freedom to marry (where this involves same-sex marriage)
- **Article 18:** Freedom of religion, including the right to change religion/ to be an atheist
- **Article 19:** Freedom of opinion and expression (where this contradicts with blasphemy laws)

In 1990, the Organisation of Islamic Cooperation (OIC) adopted the **Cairo Declaration on Human Rights**, which reaffirmed many of the principles of the UDHR but explicitly allows for sharia-compliant corporal punishment; forbids blasphemy or conversion to atheism/another religion as features of free expression; and does not regard LGBT identity or expression as a feature that should be protected under the umbrella of equal rights.

2. Asian relativism:

East Asian states have also objected to the UDHR on the basis that it is a 'Western' rather than a 'universal' document. In 1993, several Asian states signed the **Bangkok Declaration**; this reaffirmed a general commitment to human rights, but also:

- Emphasised the principles of sovereignty and non-interference between states
- Emphasised economic, social and cultural 'developmental' rights

- Argued that the UDHR is too individualistic in nature, and emphasised **'Confucian values'** of societal cohesion, the nuclear family, collectivism and loyalty to the state

In general, the 'Asian values' argument against the UDHR presumes that the right to economic development is more important than the political rights of democracy, free speech, etc. and that the preservation of a cohesive society and culture is ultimately more important than the extension of these negative liberties. In particular, the ex-Singaporean PM Lee Kuan Yew was an advocate of this view.

3. Inclusion of socio-economic rights:

The inclusion of 'socio-economic' rights, e.g. those to healthcare; certain standards of living; education; etc. were controversial amongst Western and developed states. The concept of a 'right' implies there is an obligation to provide it – in the case of negative liberty rights, this is fairly straightforward, as 'providing' the right consists of abstaining from an action (e.g. providing the right to freedom of speech merely requires a state to not restrict speech). However, in the case of positive liberty rights, (e.g. the right to healthcare), someone needs to *actively provide* it. If a developing state does not have the capacity to do so, who has the obligation to do so? The worry that developed states would be burdened with an unlimited liability of fulfilling these rights is one reason why politicians from developed states have critiqued the UDHR.

Another related critique is that some states have referred to 'socio-economic rights' as a rationale for suppressing 'political' rights, suggesting they cannot both be developed simultaneously – for example, President Duterte (Philippines) has made extensive use of extrajudicial death squads to combat the drug trade (literally executing suspected drug dealers and drug users without trial in the streets), arguing that even though he is violating the right to a fair trial, he is doing it in order to provide rights to security and standards of living for others.

Institutions of global governance of human rights

Now that we have established the general foundation of international law and human rights, and the theoretical controversies of its application, we can examine in greater depth the actual institutions which allow for global governance of international law and human rights.

International Court of Justice (ICJ)
We have previously looked at the ICJ as the principal judicial organ of the UN. Its primary role is to settle legal disputes between member states and give advisory legal opinions to UN agencies who request them. It will usually only hear contentious cases if they are *between* states and if the participant states involved agree to abide by its ruling. The UNSC is permitted to enforce these rulings, although it has not always done so. The ICJ is somewhat of an anomaly amongst the other institutions we are looking at in that it is focused on *inter-state* disputes and does not typically have jurisdiction over *intra-state* disputes, which is what the majority of human rights issues are. Generally speaking, therefore, the ICJ does *not* deal with human rights issues.

A recent case that might indicate a break away from this existing convention is **The Gambia v Myanmar (2019-present)**, in which the Gambia (a small, predominantly Muslim, West African state) filed an application with the ICJ against Myanmar as a result of the **Tatmadaw** (the Myanmar military) conducting genocidal actions including mass murder, rape, and destruction of villages against the minority Rohingya ethnicity in the Rakhine state of western Myanmar. The Gambia argued that even though the issue concerned actions happening solely within Myanmar's borders, it qualified as an inter-state dispute because Myanmar was a signatory of the 1951 Genocide Convention which involved *'erga omnes'* – owed towards all – obligations enshrined in the constitution (as opposed to contract obligations which are only owed towards a specific party).

The ICJ issued a temporary order in January 2020 to fulfil the Gambia's suggested 'provisional measures', to compel Myanmar to prevent genocidal acts against the Rohingya and to report on its implementation of this pending a final decision. Optimistically, one may view this temporary decision as the precursor to a more extensive use of the ICJ as a mechanism to uphold human rights obligations by utilising the principle of 'erga omnes' obligations. Conversely, a final judgement is still pending; it is unclear whether the UNSC would enforce the ICJ's ruling; and it is unclear whether a case involving a more powerful state (for example, China) could even make it to this stage.

International Criminal Court (ICC)

Discussions in the UN regarding the need for an international criminal court to deal with such crimes began in the late 1940s, but stalled for much of the Cold War as both the Soviets and Americans disliked the idea of a judicial institution that could prosecute them for the numerous coups, invasions, death squads, terrorist paramilitaries etc. that they were responsible for. It would have been impossible for such an institution to function as votes would have been conducted purely along partisan lines – if a Soviet-aligned country committed a war crime, the Soviet-aligned judges would have voted to acquit and the US-aligned judges would have voted to convict (and vice versa).

After the Cold War ended in the 1990s and the US was left as the sole global 'superpower', discussions restarted and accelerated. The **Rome Statute** was agreed in 1998 via the UN General Assembly and ratified in 2004, bringing the ICC into being. Although it was founded through the UN, it is not a UN institution. The ICC is physically based in The Hague, in the Netherlands. There are 18 judges elected for nine-year terms from the member states.

The International Criminal Court (ICC) was established to try individuals for:

- **Genocide:** Intentionally attempting to destroy a 'people' (ethnic, national, religious or racial group) in whole or in part, including through - killing; serious harm; imposing conditions that make its survival impossible; preventing births; or forcibly transferring children

- **Crimes against humanity:** *Systematic or widespread attacks* on civilian populations including murder; massacres; dehumanisation; ethnic cleansing; deportations; human experimentation; extrajudicial punishments; use of weapons of mass destruction; terrorism or sponsoring of terrorism; death squads; kidnappings and forced disappearances; use of child soldiers;

enslavement; torture; rape; and other human rights abuses

- **War crimes:** Essentially identical to crimes against humanity, except (i) they must take place in the context of an armed conflict; (ii) they can be perpetrated against soldiers/combatants as well as civilians and (iii) they do not have to be 'widespread' or 'systematic'

- **Crimes of aggression:** Planning or executing an unprovoked attack on another state

Strengths of the ICC	Weaknesses of the ICC
International justice: The ICC has established the principle that in states under its jurisdiction, everyone is subject to prosecution for the crimes outlined in the Rome Statute, regardless of their political or military role in the country. As well as this, the ICC grants procedural rights to victims of genocide; crimes against humanity; war crimes; and crimes of aggression. They have the possibility under the ICC's trial procedures to present their views and observations, and shape the outcomes of truth, justice and reparations in the Court. This is important, because as well as providing 'retributive' justice by convicting and punishing criminals, the Court provides 'restorative' justice by making clear what atrocities had been committed and	'Anti-African' bias: A number of African leaders have accused the ICC of being a tool of Western imperialism, only punishing leaders from small, weak African states while ignoring crimes committed by richer and more powerful states. Statistically, there is some basis for this – 10 of the 11 'situations' being investigated by the ICC are in Africa (the exception is Georgia). Of the 44 individuals indicted (formally accused or charged of a crime), all have been African. As a result of this, Burundi withdrew from the ICC in 2017. Kenya is considering withdrawal. There have also been some controversial convictions, such as that of Dominic Ongwen. Ongwen was a leader in the Lord's Resistance Army, a Christian terrorist rebel group in Uganda. He was charged

not allowing them to be swept under the carpet and forgotten.

Some prominent convictions include:

- Thomas Lubanga: Lubanga was the leader of a militia group, the Union of Congolese Patriots (UPC). The UPC was dominated by the Hema ethnic group and committed atrocities against the Lendu ethnic group in the gold-rich Ituri region of north-eastern Congo. These atrocities included massacres, murder, torture, rape and mutilation and the recruitment and use of child soldiers. He was the first person to be arrested as a result of an ICC warrant, and was convicted in 2012 alongside another rebel leader, Germain Katanga

- Jean-Pierre Bemba: Bemba was a rebel leader (of the MLC) in Congo, and later a vice-president of the country. The ICC issued an arrest warrant for rape, pillaging and murder (individual crimes) and also other war crimes committed with war crimes, including murder; mutilation of civilians; pillaging; use of child soldiers; enslavement; and rape. However, he himself was kidnapped as a child and forced to participate in violent LRA initiation ceremonies including the killing of captives, and physical/ psychological torture. The conviction was therefore morally and legally controversial, because Ongwen could be seen as a victim (as well as a perpetrator) of war crimes who was unfairly punished

Limited jurisdiction: The ICC's jurisdiction is limited to states which have signed and ratified the Rome Statute. Currently, this is a majority (123 of 195) of states, but most of those who have not signed and ratified are amongst those with the worst records of human rights, domestically and internationally, e.g.:

- China: Uighur concentration camps
- Israel: The occupation of Palestine
- Russia: Airstrikes on civilian targets, e.g. hospitals and schools, in Syria

by his rebel forces. He was arrested near Brussels, Belgium in 2009 (the first person to be arrested in another country based on an ICC warrant) and convicted in 2016 (the first conviction based on sexual violence) • Ahmad al-Mahdi: Al-Mahdi was a member of Ansar Dine, an Islamist terrorist militia operating in Mali, North Africa. He was convicted after pleading guilty in 2016 for the war crime of attacking religious and historical buildings in the ancient city of Timbuktu (believing the tombs to be idolatrous/ shirk). This was the first international conviction for this crime	• Saudi Arabia: Airstrikes on civilian targets in Yemen; execution of atheist, Shia and pro-democracy activists • USA: War crimes committed in the course of the 'War on Terror' Some legal theorists have suggested that the ICC could prosecute individuals from a third-party country which has *not* ratified the Rome Statute if they commit a crime in a country which *has* ratified the Rome Statute. To head this off, the US Congress passed the American Service-Members' Protection Act (ASPA) which authorises the US President to use military force to prevent any US soldier being detained by the ICC for trial – this theoretically means the USA could invade the Netherlands if the ICC were ever to put an American soldier on trial for war crimes
Deterrent effect: The drafters of the Rome Statute argued that the ICC would have a 'deterrent' effect – i.e. that those who were committing war crimes; genocides; crimes against humanity (or preparing to do so) would not do so because of fear of	'Cobra effect': Arguably, the fear of facing trial and conviction in the ICC has created a 'cobra effect' or perverse incentive for dictators who have committed crimes against humanity, genocide or war crimes to try to hang on to power because if

ICC prosecution and conviction. Whilst this clearly has not worked in all cases, there are some instances where it can be shown the threat of ICC prosecution contributed to a reduction in violence and an increased chance of peace (especially when those crimes are committed by rebel groups as opposed to the government):

- Uganda: The issuing of ICC arrest warrants against the leaders of the Lord's Resistance Army (LRA) Christian terrorist rebel group in 2005 may have contributed in bringing the LRA to the negotiating table with the Ugandan government

- Colombia: Since the ICC announced its interest in opening a Colombian investigation in 2006, several paramilitary rebel groups, e.g. Vincente Castrano, the leader of the AUC militia, decided to demobilise and stop fighting

they were removed, this would make their appearance at the ICC more likely.

An example of this is Omar al-Bashir, the former dictator of Arab-dominated Sudan (ruling since 1989). In 2003, he oversaw the ethnic cleansing of non-Arab minorities in the western province of Darfur. This was carried out by the pro-government Janjaweed militia group. Over 300,000 were killed and 3 million were displaced as refugees. In 2009, the ICC issued an arrest warrant for al-Bashir, but he refused to comply and continued as dictator until 2019. In 2019, when popular protests broke out against his rule, he attempted to hold onto power by force, deploying the Janjaweed militias to slaughter and rape protesters in Khartoum. He was eventually overthrown by the military.

This 'cobra effect' or fear of ICC conviction is also one of many reasons that Bashar al-Assad is fighting so hard to hold onto power in Syria.

- Democratic Republic of Congo: Since the conviction of Thomas Lubanga for his role in the Ituri conflict, local rebel commanders (whilst still operating) have generally not been engaging in indiscriminate violence against civilians, partially driven by a fear of potential ICC prosecution

- Kenya: Uhuru Kenyatta, the Kenyan President, was indicted by the ICC in connection with post-election ethnic violence in 2007-8 in which 1,200 people died and 600,000 were displaced. Whilst the ICC was forced to drop charges because Kenyatta (the President) refused to cooperate and share evidence, the following 2013 and 2018 elections were relatively peaceful

It is not tenable to argue that the ICC has completely eliminated war crimes, genocide and crimes against humanity through the 'deterrent effect', but the empirical evidence does suggest it has had a dampening

Questionable efficacy: The ICC does not have its own enforcement mechanisms and therefore requires states or other international agencies to cooperate to arrest the individuals it has indicted. This is often difficult for a number of reasons, which is why out of the 22 individuals whom the Court has current proceedings against, 15 are still at large as fugitives. The ICC has only secured 4 convictions.

- Unless a conflict is already 'over' and a leader has been overthrown, it is virtually impossible to bring the leader of a state to trial at the ICC

- Even if the conflict is over, if it took place in an unstable region like the Democratic Republic of Congo, then it is very easy for war criminals to disappear into ungoverned wilderness

- Even if the conflict is over, state leaders may choose not to cooperate with the ICC if they fear that it will damage their political position (e.g. Alassane Ouattara, the Ivorian

effect on the extent or scale of violence. It should be noted that this argument is partially counterfactual, since it depends on a comparison to a situation that did not happen (i.e. a situation where the ICC did not intervene, indict or open investigations)	President, cooperated with the ICC to hand over the former President and his political rival, Laurent Gbagbo; but refused to cooperate when the ICC began investigating his political allies)

Special UN Tribunals

In the mid-1990s (prior to Rome Statute and the creation of the ICC), special tribunals were established to investigate particular sets of crimes:

- **The International Criminal Tribunal for Yugoslavia (ICTY)** from 1993-2017, in order to try cases related to the Yugoslav Wars between Serbia, Bosnia and Croatia as the former Yugoslav state collapsed into brutal inter-ethnic conflict

- **The International Criminal Tribunal for Rwanda (ICTR)** from 1994-2015, in order to try cases related to the Rwandan genocide perpetrated by the Hutu majority against the Tutsi minority (and also against Hutus who were seen as 'collaborators' with the Tutsi)

Even after the ICC was established, the UN has continued to set up special tribunals on an ad hoc basis, where there is a need to try cases relating to human rights according to *domestic* rather than *international* law; and (i) the state concerned does not have the financial or judicial resources to try a large number of dependents; and/or (ii) there is still popular support for the defendants which would make a 'fair trial' conducted only on a domestic basis impossible. These tribunals are called **hybrid tribunals** because they combine judges/lawyers from the state concerned as well as those from the international community, and because they are international courts applying domestic law. There have been three post-ICC special UN tribunals:

- **The Special Court for Sierra Leone** from 2002-2013, in order to try cases related to the Sierra Leonean Civil War and intervention from neighbouring states, particularly Liberia

- **The Extraordinary Chambers in the Courts of Cambodia** from 2006-present, in order to try cases related to the genocidal Communist Khmer Rouge dictatorship in Cambodia (the Khmer Rouge killed anyone who was seen as an 'enemy' of the regime – in practise this meant all professionals, intellectuals and religious figures. ¼ of the Cambodian population was killed by the Khmer Rouge regime

- **The Special Tribunal for Lebanon** from 2009 onwards, in order to investigate the assassination of former Lebanese PM Rafic Hariri in an explosion which killed 21 others and injured 226 bystanders – this investigation would be difficult for Lebanon to achieve on its own because it is likely its powerful neighbour, Syria, played a role in the assassination and this would make a fair and objective investigation impossible

Strengths of Special UN Tribunals	Weaknesses of Special UN Tribunals
Holds leaders accountable: Special UN Tribunals mean that anyone can be punished for crimes and egregious violations of human rights, even major political or military leaders – it shows that no-one is above human rights law. This in turn creates a genuine deterrent effect because of the threat of conviction and life imprisonment by a UN tribunal. Leaders who have been indicted by UN Tribunals include: - ICTY: Mladic and Karadzic, the Serb generals who orchestrated the Srebrenica massacre of 8,000 Bosnian	Only 'symbolic' justice: Special UN Tribunals can be seen as only providing 'symbolic' justice by convicting only the leaders or figureheads overseeing war crimes and genocide. In the case of the ICTR (Rwanda), for example, 500-600,000 Tutsi were murdered in around 100 days of genocidal violence; and 250-500,000 women were raped (often with the intention of purposefully infecting them with HIV for a slow death. Most victims were killed in their own towns or villages, often by their neighbours or fellow villages (incited by the government and Hutu militias).

Muslims in 1995; and Milosevic, the Serb president, were all captured and put on trial by the ICTY. Mladic and Karadzic are serving life sentences in Holland, whilst Milosevic died on trial

- ICTR: Jean Kambanda, the former President of Rwanda, was charged and convicted of genocide. To date, he is the only head of state to plead guilty to genocide. He is currently serving a life-sentence in prison in Mali

- ECCC: Kang Kek lew (nicknamed 'Duch'), was a senior Khmer Rouge official who ran the S-21 Tuol Sleng prison during the Cambodian genocide. Over 18,000 'enemies of the regime' were killed here, most after brutal torture. Duch was convicted of crimes against humanity and sentenced to life in prison in 2010 along with several of his Khmer Rouge comrades

The application of the 'Yamashita' or 'Medina' standard in the case of

The ICTR indicted (brought to trial) a total of 96 individuals, of whom 61 were convicted and imprisoned. Although this did include the main instigators of the genocide and its local orchestrators, it obviously omits several thousand perpetrators of violence 'on the ground' for whom it would be impossible to gather sufficient evidence given the chaotic nature of the genocide. One may argue that if the ICTR is unable to bring these individuals to justice, it cannot be seen as an effective body.

The ICTR was also controversial in its provision of 'symbolic' justice because it focused exclusively on Hutu perpetrators of genocide and crimes against humanity. Paul Kagame was the Tutsi leader of the Rwandan Patriotic Front (RPF), the rebel group which eventually brought down the Hutu government and ended the genocide. After the genocide ended, approximately 2 million Hutu fled to refugee camps in neighbouring countries, fearing reprisals from Kagame's Tutsi-dominated RPF. Kagame's attacks on the refugee camps to stop the remnants of Hutu militias from

tribunals means that commanders are culpable for actions committed by their men; if they directly ordered them or were aware of them but did not stop them	attacking Rwanda led to around 200,000 civilian deaths. Kagame was *not* indicted by the ICTR – this has led to accusations of 'victor's justice' and a flawed judicial structure of the tribunal
Pathway to long-term stability: UN-backed tribunals can be seen as way for a country to come to terms with violence, punish those responsible, and establish the foundations for future peace. The Special Court for Sierra Leone is widely considered to have been successful at doing this. The tribunal convicted: • 3 ARFC leaders (anti-government) • 2 CDF leaders (pro-government) • 3 RUF leaders (anti-government) • Charles Taylor (the President of a neighbouring state, Liberia. He had supported the RUF rebels in exchange for payment in 'blood diamonds'. He is now, surprisingly, imprisoned in HM Prison Frankland in Durham, UK) : for a range of crimes, including murder; torture; mutilation; sexual	Requires state cooperation: Special tribunals are not 'purely' international courts and therefore require the participation and cooperation of the government of the state in which human rights abuses have occurred. For a range of reasons (local support for the criminal; political deals), it is sometimes not possible to secure this cooperation which may lead to some crimes going unpunished by the tribunal. In the case of Ratko Mladic, the Serb general who oversaw the siege of Sarajevo and the Srebrenica genocide of Bosnian Muslims in 1995, the indictment was immediate but he was not arrested until 2011. When the US put a $5 million bounty on his head, he went into hiding and was sheltered by Serbian citizens who sympathised with his actions (polling suggested approximately 53% of the population was strongly against his arrest)

violence; and widespread use of child soldiers. The conviction of all major culprits from both sides of the conflict, as well as a head of state, meant that the Tribunal was viewed as providing something of a sense of closure for Sierra Leone. Sierra Leone is today a functioning multiparty democracy that has not seen serious violence since the end of the civil war	More recently, the Special Tribunal for Lebanon convicted Salim Ayyash, a Hezbollah militant, for the killing of former Lebanese PM Rafic Hariri. However, he is not actually serving his life sentence because Hassan Nasrallah, the leader of Hezbollah (which is very prominent in Lebanese politics) has refused to give him up to the authorities to serve the sentence

European Court of Human Rights (ECtHR)

Traditionally, the European Court of Human Rights is abbreviated as the ECtHR to distinguish it from the 1950 European *Convention* on Human Rights, the document which forms the operational basis of the Court. It was established by the Council of Europe (an organisation of European democracies which is separate to the EU) in 1959. Initially, this corresponded roughly with Western Europe but after the end of the Cold War, the number of member-states under the jurisdiction of the ECtHR increased dramatically as post-Soviet and formerly Communist states joined. There are currently 47 signatories, including Russia.

The ECtHR hears cases where member-states are accused of violating the ECHR. Cases can be brought by other states, but are most commonly brought by individuals or groups. Only seven cases have ever been brought by a state against another state (the most recent being Armenia v Azerbaijan 2020, relating to the Nagorno-Karabakh conflict) whereas tens of thousands of cases are brought every year by citizens. The court is physically based in Strasbourg, France. Each signatory of the ECHR has the right to nominate three candidates for judgeship – the Council of Europe elects one judge per country from the three candidates they put forward. Judges serve nine-year terms, and each case is heard by 17 randomly selected judges (which cannot include a judge from the state concerned).

N.B. The ECtHR is <u>not</u> the same as the ECJ (European Court of Justice), which is the judicial body of the European Union. All EU countries are party to the ECtHR, but* *there are also many European countries outside the EU which are party to the ECtHR*

Strengths of the ECtHR	Weaknesses of the ECtHR
Common European standards: The Court establishes a common set of European standards based upon core values of liberal democracy and rights. This was especially important in maintaining a cohesiveness of political culture in Western Europe after WWII, and of strengthening general European identity since the end of the Cold War. Although the ECtHR is not a body of the EU, the two institutions are closely interlinked. EU member states are all members of the Council of Europe and signatories to the ECtHR; the EU works on the general principle that its member states should adhere to the ECHR. Chapter 3 of the EU-UK Trade Agreement (2021) states that the UK must continue to be part of the ECtHR, or the EU will withdraw cooperation in law enforcement and security in response	Threat to state sovereignty: A number of European jurists see the ECtHR as a threat to state sovereignty. Lord Hoffmann (UK) argued in 2009 that the ECtHR is "unable to resist the temptation to aggrandise its jurisdiction and to impose uniform rules on Member States." Marc Bossuyt (President of the Belgian Constitutional Court) criticised the court in 2010 for being too 'activist' and re-interpreting the rights laid out in the ECHR as part of a 'living instrument', but in a way that was clearly not intended by the writers of the document. For example, Article 8 of the ECHR refers to a right to 'family life'; the ECtHR interpreted this in Oliari v Italy (2015) to include same-sex marriage and imposed an obligation on member-states to provide legal recognition for same-sex marriage. Several European countries (predominantly in Eastern Europe) have been very opposed to this
Empowerment of individuals: The ECtHR, unlike other institutions of global judicial procedure, allows	Lack of enforcement powers: The ECtHR lacks formal enforcement powers. Many states have ignored

individuals to bring cases against states (either those where they currently reside; or other states who are members of the Council of Europe). This empowers individuals to challenge abuses of state power and gives them the tools to defend their human rights. E.g.

Some landmark cases include:

- Article 3 (Prohibition of torture): In Selmouni v France (1999), the applicant successfully argued that his treatment in police custody amounted to torture and led to formal compensation awarded
- Article 6 (Right to a fair trial): In Salduz v Turkey (2008), the applicant successfully argued that his conviction for participating in a demonstration in support of the PKK, an illegal Kurdish political party, should be quashed since he was forced to admit guilt in custody without a lawyer present

ECtHR verdicts and continued practises which the Court has judged to be a violation of the human rights stipulated in the ECHR. The number of non-implemented judgements has risen significantly over time, from 2,624 in 2001 to 9,944 at the end of 2016. The worst offenders for non-implementation are Italy, Russia, Turkey and Ukraine. Of these non-implemented judgements, around 3,200 concern human rights violations by security forces and poor conditions of imprisonment. Some other specific examples of note include:

- Hirst v UK (2005): The ECtHR ruled that prisoners should have the right to vote. The UK has not implemented this
- Fedotova v Russia (2011): The ECtHR ruled that Russian laws banning children from being exposed to information about homosexuality violated freedom of speech. Russia has retained these discriminatory laws

Evolution of case law: The ECtHR operates as a 'living instrument' –

Excessive caseload: The caseload of the court expanded rapidly after the that is, the rights laid out in the ECHR are interpreted by judges according to the contemporary context. This has allowed the ECtHR to defend human rights effectively against new and unforeseen threats.

S. and Marper v United Kingdom (2008) is a good example of this; the case concerned the retention by the authorities of DNA samples taken during criminal proceedings, which did *not* result in conviction. The applicants successfully argued that this was a violation of Article 8 (right to respect for private and family life) and the police were ordered to pay compensation of 42,000 euros per applicant and to begin destroying 'innocent' DNA samples

Taking DNA samples as part of police procedure was technologically inconceivable at the time of the ECHR's drafting (1940s), demonstrating the Court's flexibility in dealing with new challenges

fall of the Soviet Union and the incorporation of Eastern European states into the Court's jurisdiction. This is because there is generally less trust in court systems in former Communist states; and a greater prevalence of state violence against citizens. In 1999, only 8,400 cases were filed; by 2009, this number had risen to 57,000. Because the ECtHR's capacity has not grown correspondingly, it faced an increasing backlog of pending cases (peaking at 151,600 in 2011).

This has since been reduced as a result of the 2010 Interlaken Declaration, which allows single judges to reject applications as inadmissible or bypassed, especially if they dealt with 'repetitive' issues (i.e. issues the Court had previously ruled on). Although this has reduced the backlog of pending cases, it has also meant that cases which were perfectly sound and *could* have been heard have been rejected because of a lack of capacity

Humanitarian intervention

Humanitarian intervention has no universally accepted legal definition, but can be approximately described as a state's use of military force against another state, with the aim of ending human rights violations in that state (some would also include the threat of force). This is the case even if that state has only committed human rights violations against its *own* citizens and has not committed any human rights violations or acts of aggression against another state. Of course, it is not possible for any military action to be *purely* humanitarian – some strategic benefit to the intervening state always exists, however distant or abstract. However, if the primary aim of the military action is humanitarian, then the intervention is said to be humanitarian.

The concept of humanitarian intervention arguably goes back to the 1800s, with British-French-Russian intervention against the Ottoman Empire to secure Greek independence in the 1827 naval Battle of Navarino. JS Mill also discussed in depth the theoretical liberal basis for interventions, where a state was violating the negative liberties of its citizens (although he did also justify intervention against 'uncivilised' states more generally as an argument for imperialism).

The formation of the UN in 1945, and its adoption of the UDHR in 1948, laid the framework for modern humanitarian UN **peacekeeping missions**. The UN was endowed with peacekeeping forces 'donated' by member-states to serve under the UN flag, and the UDHR provided the basis by which the UN could identify rights, when they were being violated, and deploy these peacekeeping forces appropriately for humanitarian purposes.

During the Cold War (1945-1990), there were only 18 such interventions undertaken under the aegis of the UN. Some examples include:

- **Republic of the Congo:** To preserve the territory of the Republic of Congo. In 1960, Congo gained its independence from Belgium. Belgium had then supported the secession of the resource-rich provinces of South Kasai and Katanga and the country collapsed into a violent civil war with multiple rebellions which lasted until 1964

- **Cyprus:** To prevent conflict between Greek and Turkish Cypriots after the invasion of the island by Turkey and its partition between the internationally-recognised Republic of Cyprus (Greek) and the Turkish Republic of Northern Cyprus. The UN peacekeeping mission patrols the neutral, demilitarised buffer zone between the two territories

- **Iraq-Iran:** To supervise the ceasefire and the disengagement of Iraqi and Iranian forces from their shared border after the Iran-Iraq War ended after eight years in 1988 (with over 1 million military deaths and over 100,000 civilian casualties)

Since the end of the Cold War, the UN has staged far more interventions (53 in total, with 37 happening in the 1990s alone). The primary reason for this is that during the Cold War, the rivalry between the USA and the Soviet Union meant that situations where human rights were being violated and interventions *should* have been called were vetoed or blocked by the USA or the Soviets where they felt this would damage their strategic interests. The USSR would have vetoed any interventions against a Communist state; the USA would have vetoed any interventions against a capitalist state (as they did several times to resolutions condemning South Africa for its system of apartheid, and its continued occupation of Namibia which was effectively ruled as a black colony by a white minority). However, after the conclusion of the Cold War, the USA's dominance as a global hyperpower and the absence of opposition allowed it to direct Security Council debates and push through resolutions enabling interventions with much greater frequency. As China and Russia have become more assertive in the last decade or so, the frequency of UN-sanctioned interventions has again diminished.

Who gets to carry out interventions?
Another aspect of humanitarian interventions which is worth considering (and has no concrete legal answer, since international law in this area is more a series of evolving norms and conventions than 'enforceable' strictures) is who has the authority to sanction and carry out interventions.

One view is that only the UN should have the authority to do so. As a body which represents all of the world's nation-states, it is the only global institution which has the broad legitimacy necessary to propose the violation of state sovereignty – the most 'sacred' element of the global political system. If other regional organisations (e.g. NATO), organisations with narrower membership (e.g. the G20) or individual states were to decide for themselves when humanitarian intervention was necessary, then it would be more likely that they would abuse the concept of humanitarian intervention to carry out military interventions for their own strategic interests, cloaked in the language of humanitarianism.

Another view is that, contrary to the above, the UN is often ineffective as a forum for deciding on resolutions given the veto power of the P5 in the Security Council. Often, interventions are not sanctioned by the UNSC – not because there is not a clear humanitarian issue, but because an intervention would go against the interests of one of the P5. For the US, this generally refers to proposed interventions against US allies, but China more broadly utilises its veto to prevent any perceived interference in 'state sovereignty', because the fierce defence of this principle helps to insulate it from criticism over issues in Xinjiang, Tibet and Hong Kong. Therefore, it is necessary for other organisations and states to step forward and fulfil universal humanitarian obligations if the UN is unwilling or unable to do so.

The theory of humanitarian interventions

The argument for humanitarian interventions is that international law and human rights are a set of obligations, moral and legal, which exist above and beyond state law. If a state violates human rights and international law, then it should be asked to stop doing so; sanctioned if it refuses; and as a last resort, military force must be applied to prevent the state violating the human rights of its citizens. Proponents of humanitarian intervention view this as an ethical obligation of the global community.

The principal theoretical arguments against humanitarian intervention are:

1. **'Purity' of humanitarian motives:** Some would argue that interventions are never truly 'humanitarian' but rely on ulterior motives – strategic, economic or political gain. Where other gains can be made, intervention will take place whereas if they are absent, it will not. For example, there was clear strategic benefit to (i) NATO in the interventions in Bosnia and Kosovo in the 1990s, because it prevented a total collapse of order in the Balkans and a massive refugee crisis which would have spilled over into Western Europe, and (ii) NATO in the Libyan intervention of 2011, for similar reasons (potential refugee flows across the Mediterranean from Libya to Italy/Greece). However, there was little benefit to intervention in Rwanda, Myanmar or Sudan, where significant interethnic violence was taking place but they were far distant from NATO's

borders and had little chance of imminent consequence. If humanitarian intervention does not take place in all humanitarian crises, does this selectivity undermine its rationale - should it not take place at all?

2. **Imposition of Western values:** Humanitarianism is based on the principle of universal 'human rights', which as we have seen previously are not accepted everywhere as neutral values. Particularly in the Middle East and East Asia, state leaders often invoke the idea that there are particular sets of 'Islamic rights' or 'Confucian/Asian rights' which exclude certain 'Western rights' like democracy, freedom of speech, freedom of religion, etc. Some therefore argue that humanitarian interventions are not about protecting the rights of individuals, but about imposing Western values on non-Western states who do not want or need them. For example, China would likely veto any intervention in Myanmar (it has already vetoed resolutions condemning the military coup) on the basis that Myanmar's degree of democracy or state repression is an entirely internal affair and should not be held to 'Western standards'

3. **The acceptable threshold:** Humanitarian intervention inherently undermines state sovereignty, which is the bedrock of the international political system. The UN Charter explicitly notes that this should not be violated except in the most extreme circumstances. Humanitarian interventions must therefore be triggered only at an 'exceptional' threshold of human rights violations. Clearly, it would be unworkable and ridiculous for a state to face military intervention every time it committed a 'minor' human rights violation. The more general theoretical question is then – when has a sufficient threshold of human rights violation been reached so as to make intervention justifiable? How persistent does the violation have to be; how many people have to be under threat; what rights should intervention be used as a mechanism to protect?

4. **The question of legitimate authority:** As discussed above, it is unclear which international bodies have the legitimacy to give permission for any carry out interventions. Does only the UN have the authority to make these decisions, or can other major organisations like NATO permit and execute interventions?

Sometimes, this is not so contentious if the UNSC doesn't explicitly disagree with an organisation's use of military force for humanitarian purposes, e.g. ECOWAS' (Economic Community of West African States)' intervention in the Gambia, a member-state of ECOWAS, when President Yahya Jammeh refused to step down after losing the 2017 election. However, if the UNSC disagrees with an organisation's use of military force, this becomes much more of an issue – e.g. opposition to NATO's intervention in Kosovo from Russia and China on the UNSC

Given the criticisms outlined above, the Canadian government developed the principle of **'Responsibility to Protect' (R2P)** which has since been adopted more widely in international circles. The report argues that a state's sovereignty gives a state the right to control its affairs, but also the 'responsibility' for protecting people within its borders. When a state fails to do so – either passively (by allowing famine, violent rebel activity, etc.) or actively (by undertaking the persecution of individuals or groups itself) then the responsibility for protecting civilians shifts to the broader international community.

R2P therefore (i) sets the bar for intervention at the potential for large-scale loss of life or ethnic cleansing; (ii) proposes that rather than a 'right', intervention should be considered a 'responsibility'; and (iii) emphasise the responsibility to rebuild and stabilise as well as that to militarily intervene. R2P has been endorsed by some Western and African states, but is widely dismissed as a continuation of previous justifications to infringe on state sovereignty by major Asian states and Russia.

CASE STUDIES – Humanitarian crises (interventions and non-interventions)

The following is a selected list of humanitarian emergencies over the past few decades, some of which have seen humanitarian interventions triggered in response, whereas others have not. Some of the cases of humanitarian intervention have been successful, whereas others have not.

Red = no intervention, Green = intervention, Yellow = partial intervention

<u>**Israel-Palestine (1948-present):**</u> Since the creation of an independent Israeli state in 1948, it has progressively encroached on Palestinian territory (in 1948, this was not an independent state – the West Bank was under Jordanian jurisdiction and the Gaza Strip

was Egyptian). Israel has built settlements and 'imported' Israeli settlers into what was formerly Palestinian territory in the West Bank – the replacement of a civilian population is considered a war crime under international law. There has been no intervention because the US would veto any resolution of this nature in the Security Council, because Israel is seen as a key regional ally.

The Iran/Iraq War (1980-1988): In 1980 Iraq (under the leadership of Saddam Hussein) invaded Iran, sparking the Iran-Iraq War which lasted until 1988 and was one of the bloodiest conflicts of the late 20th century. The USA, which was bitterly opposed to the new Iranian government, supplied Iraq with military hardware, although not actual weapons. The USSR, also bitterly opposed to the new Iranian government, also supplied Iraq with weapons. Iraq used chemical weapons, including mustard gas and sarin, against the Iranian armed forces and also its own Kurdish population. It is now clear that the USA helped it to gas the Iranian army by providing it with the locations of troops it wanted to hit (although it played no part in the attacks on the Kurds). The UN passed numerous resolutions calling for a ceasefire in the Iran-Iraq war and condemning the use of chemical weapons. All its resolutions condemned 'both sides' even though Iraq had invaded and was the only country to use chemical weapons. None of the resolutions imposed sanctions

The Yugoslav Wars (1991-1995): The Yugoslav Wars were a series of civil wars from 1991 which resulted in the break-up of Yugoslavia into a number of smaller states based on ethnic divisions. The UN Security Council deployed peacekeepers there in 1992 initially in order to ensure peace talks could proceed between Serbia and Croatia. The fighting then spread to Bosnia-Herzegovina where Serbian forces launched a campaign of ethnic cleansing against the Bosniak (Bosnian Muslim) population. The UN Security Council gave its forces in the area the additional mission of keeping the Bosniak population alive. They succeeded in keeping Sarajevo airport open and connected to the city of Sarajevo, then besieged by Serbian forces, which enabled 2,476 aircraft to be brought in carrying 27,460 tons of food, medicines and other relief goods. If they had not done so thousands of people would certainly have died of starvation in Sarajevo, and Serbian forces might well have taken the city, which would probably have led to a massacre. UN forces also declared a number of places as safe areas under their protection, including the town of Srebrenica. In 1995 a Serbian force captured Srebrenica, massacred 8,000 Bosniak men and forcibly deported 25,000-30,000 Bosniak women, children and elderly people, many of whom were raped. 375 Dutch peacekeepers from the UN force were present in the town, but they did not prevent the massacre – the reasons for this are still controversial. NATO played a part in carrying out the UN mandate to protect the population of Bosnia-Herzegovina by establishing no-fly zones where the Serbian air force could not operate bombing missions, and then by carrying out air strikes against Serbian positions

The Sierra Leone Civil War (1991-2002): The Sierra Leone Civil War began in 1991 when the Revolutionary United Front (RUF), intervened in Sierra Leone in an attempt to overthrow the Joseph Momoh government. The resulting civil war lasted 11 years, enveloped the country, and left over 50,000 dead. During the first year of the war, the RUF took control of large swathes of territory in eastern and southern Sierra Leone, which were rich in alluvial diamonds. In 1995, the government hired Executive Outcomes (EO), a South African private military company with a dubious reputation, to repel the RUF, which they did very effectively. The retreating RUF signed the Abidjan Peace Accord. Under UN pressure, however, the government terminated its contract with EO before the accord could be implemented. Because the EO was no longer present to deter the RUF, the RUF resumed hostilities, and in 1997, it captured the capital, Freetown, with little resistance. In 1999, the UN helped the RUF and the government negotiate the Lome Peace Accord. Lome gave Foday Sankoh, the commander of the RUF, the vice presidency and control of Sierra Leone's diamond mines in return for a cessation of the fighting and the deployment of a UN peacekeeping force to monitor the disarmament process. RUF compliance with the disarmament process was inconsistent and sluggish, and by 2000, the rebels were advancing again upon Freetown. As the UN mission began to fail, Tony Blair declared the UK's intention to intervene in the former British colony in an attempt to support the government. With a renewed UN mandate and Guinean air support, the British Operation Palliser finally defeated the RUF, taking control of Freetown. On 18 January 2002, President Kabbah declared the Sierra Leone Civil War over

The Rwandan Genocide (1994): The population of Rwanda is primarily comprised of two ethnic groups, the Hutus and the Tutsis. Rwanda had once been a colony of Germany and then Belgium, both of which had intensified divisions between the groups in order to help them rule. These intensified divisions remained after they left. The Rwandan Civil War began in 1990 as a conflict between the Hutu dominated government and the Tutsi dominated Rwandan Patriotic Front (RPF). In 1993 the two sides agreed the Arusha Accords to create a power-sharing government, and the UN Security Council voted to deploy a small peace-keeping force of about 2,500 soldiers to act as a neutral party to help them achieve that. In 1994 a plane carrying the President of Rwanda was shot down. Anti-Tutsi elements in the government reacted by launching a concerted attempt to kill all of the Tutsis in Rwanda. An estimated 500,000 to 1 million Rwandans were killed over the next hundred days, including 70% of the Tutsi population. The UN peacekeepers had not been given a mandate by the Security Council to use force, so they did not prevent this. One of the first victims of the genocide was Agathe Uwilingiyimana, the Prime Minister of Rwanda. She was being guarded by ten Belgian peacekeepers, but she and they were killed after they were advised by their commander to surrender their weapons to Rwandan government forces. Another group of Belgian peacekeepers, who had been sheltering 2,000 Rwandans in a technical school, were ordered by their government to evacuate, and all the people they had been protecting were killed. New Zealand, which held the rotating presidency of the UN Security Council, wanted to reinforce the peacekeeping mission and give it a mandate to use force, but Bill Clinton, then President of the USA, was opposed to doing so, even though he was aware that a genocide was taking place, because American interests were not threatened. He got his own way and the UN did nothing. In the end the RPF brought the genocide to an end by resuming hostilities and overthrowing the government

The Kosovo War (1998-1999): The KLA (Kosovo Liberation Army) was a rebel group formed by Albanians who formed the ethnic majority in Kosovo, then a region of the Federal Republic of Yugoslavia (by this point really only Serbia and Montenegro, since all the other parts had become independent). It was formed in response to Serbian persecution of Kosovo Albanians and began launching attacks on Serbian law enforcement from 1995, sparking a general insurgency. Serbia responded by sending paramilitaries and soldiers into Kosovo in a retributive campaign that killed around 2,000 civilians and KLA combatants. The UN later found that there had been "a systematic campaign of terror, including murders, rapes, arsons and severe maltreatments". Around 230,000 Kosovans were displaced by the violence. Consensus in the Security Council was impossible because of Russian opposition; subsequent negotiations between NATO and Yugoslavia/Serbia broke down, leading to a NATO bombing campaign against Serbia. Around 520 civilians were killed in these airstrikes, including 87 Albanian refugees who were hit in a mistaken-identity incident. Serbian forces eventually withdrew and the country was occupied by NATO forces, securing its transition to independence. Russia protested this intervention as an act of Western aggression

East Timor (1999-2002): East Timor, or Timor-Leste, was a Portuguese island colony surrounded by Indonesia. When it became independent in 1975, Indonesia immediately invaded leading to the development of one of the longest and bloodiest guerrilla wars in history, in which about a third of East Timor's inhabitants were killed by the Indonesian government. In 1999, Indonesia agreed to a referendum on independence, in which 75% of East Timorese voted for independence. The government did not accept the result and stepped up its campaign of military intimidation and suppression. A multinational UN force, (INTERFET) was established by the Security Council with Australia as the leading member to bring peace and support Timor-Leste's self-determination. A UN administration was set up; in 2001, democratic elections were held; and in 2002, East Timor formally became independent. East Timor has seen outbreaks of sporadic violence between rival military factions, the police and various militia since independence

The Libyan Civil War (2011): The First Libyan Civil War began in 2011 as part of the wider 'Arab Spring'. Pro-democratic protests in Libya led to clashes with the security forces of the dictator, Muammar Gaddafi, who fired into peacefully protesting crowds. Protests then escalated into violent revolution and the establishment of an interim rebel government – the National Transitional Council (NTC). When Gaddafi threatened to destroy Benghazi, the city that had become the centre of the rebellion, via airstrikes, a UN resolution authorised the establishment of a no-fly zone over Libya and "all necessary measures" to prevent attacks on civilians. Under this UN mandate, NATO enforced the no-fly zone and conducted a bombing campaign against military installations. The NATO bombing campaign then escalated to air support for advancing rebel forces, leading to the rebel capture of the capital Tripoli and the capture and execution of Gaddafi in Sirte, his desert hometown. A low-level insurgency persisted after the end of the Civil War from pro-Gaddafi loyalists. Arguments between the various rebel factions, the army, and ISIS then led to a second civil war in Libya (2014-present)

The Syrian Civil War (2011-present): The Syrian Civil War is an ongoing and incredibly complex multi-sided conflict fought between the Baath Party government led by President Bashar al-Assad and various domestic and foreign forces opposing the Syrian government and each other in varying configurations. Like the Libyan Civil War, the conflict was rooted in a violent government response to pro-democratic protests inspired by the broader Arab Spring movement. Currently, the Syrian government is being militarily supported by Iran and Russia; the main opposition group is being supported by Turkey; and Kurdish forces in NE Syria were until recently supported by the USA; ISIS also operated widely in the country. All factions of the Syrian Civil War have engaged in some level of war crimes and ethnic cleansing, although those perpetrated by the Syrian government and Russia are the most egregious, including the use of chemical weapons and the widespread bombing of civilian targets in rebel-held cities like Idlib and Aleppo such as hospitals. Russia commonly makes use of 'double-tap' strikes, with one airstrike to hit a target, and a second a few minutes later to kill medics looking to save survivors. An estimated 387,000 to 593,000 Syrians have been killed; there are nearly 8 million Syrians internally displaced and over 5 million refugees who have left the country. Humanitarian intervention was stalled in the Security Council by Russia and China's opposition (which still continues); unilateral Western intervention against Bashar al-Assad is impossible, because Russia has already deployed soldiers and aircraft through Syria and there is a high risk of accidentally engaging a Russian target and sparking a world war. However, there *has* been broad international intervention to eradicate the ISIS Caliphate which all state parties view as an illegitimate terrorist group and not subject to the protections of 'state sovereignty'

The Yemeni Civil War (2015-present): This has been going on since 2015. Saudi Arabia (a close ally of the USA and UK) and the UAE have intervened on the side of the internationally recognised (but unelected) government, which was resisting an armed uprising led by the Houthi militia and the former dictator, Saleh. There have been human rights abuses on both sides, including widespread and indiscriminate bombing campaigns by the Saudis, targeting hospitals and other civilian infrastructure. Saudi naval and air forces are also blockading the coastline, claiming that this is to stop the flow of weapons to the Houthis, but also cutting off food, water and medical supplies. A UN resolution has been passed condemning the rebels, but not the pro-government forces. UN agencies predict that if the fighting continues 13 million Yemenis face starvation in what is likely to be the worst famine anywhere in the world in the last century. There has been no intervention by the UNSC because the USA has threatened to veto any resolutions that endorse humanitarian intervention

The persecution of the Uighurs (2017-present): Somewhere between one and three million Muslim Uighurs are believed to have imprisoned in concentration camps in the Xinjiang region of western China. Reports suggest that they are forced to learn Mandarin Chinese, memorise large tracts of Chinese Communist Party doctrine and renounce their Islamic faith. The evidence also points towards widespread beatings, torture, systematic rape, and the sale of organs from deceased prisoners; although there is not yet evidence of intentional mass killing (the aim seems to be to 'convert' Uighurs into 'loyal Chinese citizens' by forcibly eradicating their culture, rather than killing them). There is also a more widespread campaign of cultural genocide, with the razing of Muslim graveyards in Xinjiang and the destruction or modification of major mosques and shrines. The UNSC has not acted, because China has threatened to veto any resolutions that endorse any interference or even sending UN missions to Xinjiang with the ability to freely travel and observe conditions

Analysis of the case studies
There are three main questions to answer with regards to the case studies above:
1. **Is humanitarian intervention just Western neo-imperialism/hypocrisy?**

One perspective is that humanitarian intervention is inherently a product of Western neo-imperialism:

- Humanitarian intervention is based on the concept of 'universal' liberal rights, which are not really universal – they are the product of a particular Western culture. The 'West' has taken on a role as 'global policemen' which they have no exclusive entitlement to (this includes in states such as Yugoslavia)
- Humanitarian interventions by Western institutions and states seem to have been conducted very selectively and only where there is some wider strategic benefit to the West. For example, NATO was quick to intervene in Bosnia/Kosovo (1990s) where there was a risk of spill-over refugee crises; and in oil-rich Libya, where there was also a potential for a massive refugee crisis across the Mediterranean (2011). However, intervention has been lacking in instances where there is no direct threat to Western interests or regional stability (Darfur, Sudan; Rakhine, Myanmar; Rwanda)
- The 'West' (although this is a generalisation) does not always live to the humanitarian standards which it uses to justify interventions in other states. For example, the USA has operated a prison camp at Guantanamo Bay, Cuba since 2002. Nearly 800 men have been held in the camp on the basis that they were involved in Islamic terrorism – most were eventually released without charge. Torture and the sexual humiliation of prisoners have been widely used in the camp; prisoners are frequently chained up for 18 hours or more so that they soil themselves. It would be fair to describe Guantanamo as a concentration camp, with the exception that 'only' 8 prisoners have died there (a historically low figure for a concentration camp). Obama stood on an election pledge in 2008 to close Guantanamo, but did not do so; the camp still exists with fewer than 100 prisoners. Other examples of Western hypocrisy include the use of torture in the Abu Ghraib prison during the Iraq War; and Trump's pardoning of several US soldiers accused of war crimes (e.g. Edward Gallagher, who shot random Iraqi civilians for sport and was reported by his fellow soldiers)

Another perspective is that humanitarian intervention is not *inherently* a product of Western neo-imperialism, but that certain interventions (Afghanistan and Iraq are most commonly referred to) *are* examples of Western neo-imperialism. However, there are some *genuinely* humanitarian interventions, which should be viewed as positive developments for global governance of human rights (Bosnia, Kosovo and Sierra Leone are most commonly referred to).

A central difficulty remains; it is difficult to judge whether a humanitarian intervention is 'good' until it has been conducted and the aftermath can be analysed – this is almost always tied up with judgements about whether it is 'humanitarian'. It is possible that interventions carried out for the 'right' reasons can have disastrous consequences, and that those carried out for the 'wrong' reasons can have beneficial consequences. In the sense of the contemporary lack of humanitarian intervention, in many cases it could also be argued that the lack of interventions is not because of Western 'hypocrisy' or unwillingness to intervene where there is no strategic benefit; but because intervention is precluded by the possibility of sparking a larger war with a major global power, e.g. Russia (Syria) or China (Xinjiang). It is also worth noting that the argument that 'the West only intervenes for strategic benefit' is also raised by those who argue against intervention in Syria and Xinjiang to imply that the West intervening in these regions/states is only because the West wants to weaken its geopolitical enemies and that they are manufacturing evidence to justify this.

2. Why has the rate of humanitarian intervention declined since the 1990s?
In the 1990s, humanitarian interventions became much more common for a number of reasons:

- **Media coverage and exposure:** In a world of 24/7 news and current affairs, global television coverage and digital communications, governments often came under considerable public pressure to act in the event of humanitarian emergencies. This was particularly demonstrated by the impact of 'non-interventions', such as the failure to prevent the Rwandan genocide and the Srebrenica massacre. The 'CNN Effect' put more pressure on Western governments and international bodies to fulfil moral responsibilities and obligations

- **The end of the Cold War:** The end of the Cold War, the collapse of the Soviet Union and the emergence of the USA as the world's sole superpower meant that it was easier to build consensus in the Security Council for intervention. Russia, in a condition of political and economic turmoil; and China, still in the early phase of its emergence as an economic powerhouse, were not in a position to oppose US-backed resolutions

- **The role of individual leaders:** Certain policy-makers were very willing in the 1990s to embrace the doctrine of universal human rights and its interventionist implications. Kofi Annan, the UN-Secretary General (1997-2007); President Clinton of the USA (1993-2001); Prime Minister Blair of the UK (1997-2007) were particularly prominent is establishing a 'right' or 'responsibility' to intervene. For Blair, this logic of benevolent liberal humanitarianism can be tracked through his interventions in Kosovo, Sierra Leone and Iraq
-

All of this contributed to what has been described as a 'human rights regime' or a 'new world order' in the 1990s, in which ideas of liberal universalism informed widespread humanitarian interventions. However, the frequency of interventions has declined somewhat since the turn of the millennium. There are two main reasons for this:

I: The impact of the 'War on Terror':
In 2001, the Islamist terrorist group Al-Qaeda conducted the 9/11 attacks in the USA, killing nearly 3,000 American civilians. In response, the USA invoked Article 5 of NATO to invade Afghanistan, where bin Laden, the Al-Qaeda leader was correctly suspected to be hiding with the support of the Taliban regime. Two years later, the USA also led a coalition to invade Iraq, arguing principally that they were in possession of WMDs (weapons of mass destruction) of a nuclear or chemical nature. In both instances, 'humanitarian' logic was invoked to justify the invasions. In Afghanistan, the Taliban regime was a theocratic dictatorship which persecuted Shia Muslims and other religious minorities, and was vehemently against any womens' rights. In Iraq, Saddam Hussein had attempted genocides in the past against the Arab al-Ahwar (Marsh Arab) and Kurdish ethnic minorities and ran a brutal dictatorial regime with many political opponents routinely arrested, imprisoned, tortured and executed. It is estimated that Saddam's regime was responsible for around 250,000 civilian deaths over the course of his presidency. Nevertheless, in both cases, there was no imminent threat of large-

scale loss of life or ethnic cleansing, so the humanitarian grounds for intervention were shaky at best

The execution of both interventions was also heavily criticised. For example, neither the UNSC nor NATO sanctioned the Iraq invasion, which was carried out independently by the US, UK, Australia and Poland. Kofi Annan, the UN Secretary General described the invasion as illegal The post-invasion situation has been characterised by an unstable democracy; a serious pro-Hussein insurgency against the US occupation; considerable sectarian violence between Sunni and Shia Iraqi; and the emergence of ISIS from the chaos in 2014. The total death toll in 2006 was estimated at 655,000 – it has clearly grown since, but there are few reliable estimates. Many US soldiers and mercenaries operating on behalf of the US government were accused of war crimes, but very few were convicted and most received very light prison sentences. In Afghanistan, intervention was carried out on a broader basis by NATO, but the Taliban regime still controls large parts of the country

The conduct of Western forces and the inability to secure long-lasting, stable political gains led many Western citizens to criticise the (i) motivations; (ii) cost and (iii) effectiveness of humanitarian intervention. Consequently, it has become much harder for democratically-elected Western leaders to convince an averse electorate of the need for humanitarian intervention. For example, when Bashar al-Assad began to shoot Syrian protestors in 2011, Barack Obama considered US intervention but decided against it because he was already in a difficult domestic position and didn't want to raise another tricky argument in Congress. In 2013, after Assad's use of chemical weapons on civilians, David Cameron proposed airstrikes on Assad's military facilities but was defeated 285-272 in a fractious Parliamentary vote in which the precedent of the Iraq War was frequently invoked both by Labour and Conservative MPs who argued that intervention would be an act of neo-imperialist aggression or that Britain should not bear the costs for conflicts happening elsewhere in the world

II: The rise of Russia and China on the UNSC:

A second reason for the decreased frequency of humanitarian interventions today compared to the 1990s is the resurgence of Russia (which under Putin has re-established itself as a major military power, if not an economic one) and the emergence of China (which has become increasingly willing to flex its geopolitical muscles as its economic boom has continued). This means it has become harder to pass UNSC resolutions justifying interventions; or that unilateral Western/NATO intervention is impossible in some cases against a Russian or Chinese client state (e.g. Syria).

3. Is humanitarian intervention effective in achieving its goals?
A central question in assessing the success of global governance in human rights is assessing the success of humanitarian intervention. On what criteria should we make these judgements? It seems reasonable that this includes the immediate prevention of mass human rights abuses, but also the 'legacy' of human rights that the intervention leaves behind, i.e. a stable political system in which human rights are safe and respected. One might also consider the 'cost' of intervention in lives relative to the outcome. A complication in this analysis is the counterfactual nature of judgements – we can tell how 'good' or 'bad' a situation currently is, but the world in which the intervention didn't happen does not exist, so we are making comparisons to a non-existent hypothetical reality.

Of the case studies and examples mentioned above, interventions took place in:
- **Bosnia:** Generally successful in preventing a total genocide of Bosnian Muslims, but specific failure in the case of the Srebrenica Massacre; and criticised by some for deaths of Serbs civilians in the bombing of Belgrade during the conflict
- **Sierra Leone:** Initial UN mission somewhat unsuccessful, because the Abidjan Peace Accords quickly broke down. The UK mission (Operation Palliser) was much more effective in defeating the rebel forces and re-establishing a parliamentary democracy
- **Rwanda:** UN peacekeeping mission sent to stop the civil war failed to prevent the genocide, because it was not given a mandate to use force against Rwandan troops/government militia

- **Kosovo:** Generally successful in preventing a genocide/ethnic cleansing of Kosovan Muslims; but criticised by some for deaths of Serb civilians and Kosovan refugees in the NATO bombing campaign
- **East Timor:** Generally successful in re-establishing stability in East Timor after Indonesia's brutal campaign of suppression, and allowing the conditions for elections and independence. However, East Timor's stability and prosperity since has been questionable
- **Iraq:** Successful in the short-term objective of removing Saddam Hussein; generally deemed a long-term failure in terms of establishing a stable post-invasion state. Iraq quickly buckled under the weight of insurgencies, sectarian violence and the rise of ISIS
- **Libya:** Successful in the prevention of Benghazi's destruction; arguably a long-term failure in terms of establishing a stable post-invasion state. Libya devolved into a quagmire of warring factions including various militia, the transitional government, the army and ISIS

From these case studies, we can identify some 'ingredients' for successful intervention:
1. Limited, specific military objectives (a lack of 'mission drift')
2. A mandate for the use of force to protect human rights
3. A willingness to invest resources and troops to keep order after the intervention
4. A specific plan for the post-invasion reconstruction/rebuilding of the political system (rather than assuming that liberal democracy will magically take root)

3-4 perhaps correlate with the proximity of the main states contributing forces to the intervention to the humanitarian crisis. If the crisis is more likely to spill-over in the form of violence or refugee movements, then a state is more willing to invest long-term resources to rebuild. E.g. Australia/East Timor, or NATO/Bosnia & Kosovo. The 'responsibility to rebuild' is, in terms of achieving effective interventions, as important as the 'responsibility to protect'.

Of course, another school of thought is that there is no such thing as a successful humanitarian intervention and they are all just examples of the West extending its neo-imperial network and that the 'best' interventions are the ones that never take place. It can reasonably be inferred from the Syrian case that 'non-intervention' does not generate a utopian peace and that the price of non-intervention can be just as high, or higher, than intervention itself.

ENVIRONMENTAL GLOBAL GOVERNANCE

The environment is broadly defined as the 'natural world' – that is non-human and non-manufactured aspects of Earth, like plants and animals; ecosystems; the atmosphere; terrain; the oceans; etc. There is a philosophical argument about whether the distinction between 'humans' and 'Nature' is valid, but this is outside the remit of the Politics course (but is somewhat relevant in terms of arguments over the effectiveness of environmental global governance).

Climate change
The greenhouse effect

There are many environmental problems facing the world today, but the most pressing and encompassing is that of climate change. To understand climate change, we must first understand the **'greenhouse effect'** which means that life on Earth is viable, as opposed to every other rocky planet we have discovered, which are either far too cold or far too hot to sustain life.

The source of nearly all energy, and therefore life, on Earth is the Sun. Solar radiation travels through space from the Sun to the Earth, providing heat and light. If there were no **atmosphere** (a thin layer of gases surrounding the Earth's surface), nearly half of this solar radiation would reflect off the planet's surface back into space and be lost. However, the fact that Earth *does* have an atmosphere means that:

- 23% of incoming solar radiation is immediately absorbed by the atmosphere
- 48% of incoming solar radiation is absorbed by the Earth's surface
- 29% of incoming solar radiation is reflected back into space

In total, that means around 71% of solar radiation is retained by the Earth (about 23% more than would be the case in the absence of an atmosphere). That 23% is critical – it means that instead of being a cold, dead ball of rock like Mars, the Earth has sufficient heat to sustain a liveable temperature. The gases in the atmosphere which contribute to the insulation/absorption effect are commonly referred to as 'greenhouse gases' –

carbon dioxide, methane, and water vapour.

Changes to the atmosphere

It logically follows, then, that changes to the composition of the atmosphere will lead to changes in the scale of the 'greenhouse effect'. Less greenhouse gases means less insulation/absorption and lower global temperatures, whereas more greenhouse gases means more insulation/absorption and higher global temperatures. The Earth's level of greenhouse gases and therefore temperature has varied significantly in the geological past due to natural factors like volcanic activity and increased solar radiation. However, the current increase in greenhouse gases and global temperatures is **anthropogenic** (caused by humans), a fact over which there has been long-established and near-unanimous scientific (if not political) consensus.

Human activity since the advent of the Industrial Revolution has led an increase in the level of greenhouse gases in the atmosphere in a number of ways:

- **Combustion** – the burning of fossil fuels like coal, oil and gas – is the main way by which we have generated electricity and power over the last century and half, but also produces CO2. This is not just the case for 'power plants' but also any mechanical engine – cars, planes, etc.
- **Deforestation** – the cutting down of forests, contributes to greenhouse gases through (i) burning of the wood and (ii) the removal of trees, which naturally absorb CO2
- **Agriculture** – livestock are reckoned to be responsible for around 14% of all greenhouse gas emissions, because animals produce CO2; NO2 (nitrous oxide) is a common by-product of fertilisers and wastes; and CH4 (methane) is a product of cattle flatulence and belching. As global demand for meat has risen, so has the climatic impact of agriculture

Increased greenhouse gas emissions and reduced capacity for its absorption has led to changes in atmospheric composition and global climate.

https://climate.nasa.gov/vital-signs/global-temperature/

Weather is short-term atmospheric conditions in a given location (precipitation, temperature, winds, humidity, etc.) whereas **climate** is a long-term pattern of atmospheric conditions – i.e. 'weather observed as an average over a period of time'. A global rise in temperature of the following degrees from the pre-industrial global temperature is predicted to have the following effects:

+1°C	This is the situation now:
	• Extreme weather events (such as floods, hurricanes, wildfires and droughts) are increasing and weather forecasts are becoming less reliable
	• Agriculture is becoming less productive because changes in heat, precipitation and humidity affect crops. There is some evidence that drought-induced food shortages were responsible for the conditions leading to the Arab Spring in 2011
	• The extinction rate is at the highest level in global history (although that is definitely not just down to global warming) – because organisms with very specific environmental niches suffer from small climatic changes. E.g. polar bears, which require sea-ice; or corals, which require neutral water pH (the absorption of CO_2 into the oceans makes them more acidic)
	• Africa's last glaciers are melting
+2°C	As before, and:
	• The Greenland ice sheet is likely to collapse, causing a gradual seven metre rise in sea level. This will eventually result in the flooding of coastal cities like Dhaka, Miami and London and the total disappearance of island nations like the Maldives
	• The last of the coral reefs will die off, as will significant numbers of the 'higher' (larger + further up the food chain) fish and whales in the oceans
	• Agricultural production will fall even further and famines will become frequent
+3°C	As before, and:
	• Australia, southern Africa and northern Africa will become entirely desert – the Sahara Desert will swallow up everything south of the Mediterranean coastline. Desertification will also

	occur in north-west India/Pakistan, Central Asia, and the southwest of North America, leading to critical water shortages • The last glaciers in India and Pakistan will melt, leading to serious droughts and famines across the subcontinent • Northern Europe will still be climatically viable, so there will likely be an exodus of refugees moving there from Northern Africa • The Amazon Rainforest will die off – since this helps keep global temperatures down, stopping at this level of global warming is not possible; if this point is reached, global temperatures will rise by at least another degree
+4°C	As before, and: • The Arctic ice sheet, the Arctic permafrost in Siberia and possibly the West Antarctic glacier will collapse, causing sea levels to rise by another five metres (by this point, twelve metres in total taking into account previous effects) • The boundary Sahara Desert will cross the Mediterranean and absorb southern Europe – Italy, Greece, Turkey and Spain • Summer temperatures in southern England will routinely reach highs of 45°C • Northern Europe, the north of North America and Siberia will be the only truly liveable places on the globe; there will be mass refugee exoduses there
5°C+	It is difficult to predict with any accuracy what would happen at this point. The last time temperatures on Earth rose suddenly by 6°C was 299m-252m years ago – the result was the Permian Extinction, a mass-extinction event in which 95% of life on Earth was wiped out

The urgency of tackling climate change

Part of the reason that climate change is so difficult to deal with is because its self-sustaining characteristics. Climate change involves **positive feedback loops** – that is, climate change causes things which *in turn* contribute to additional climate change. The main feedback loops are:

1. **Permafrost melting:** Most of northern Eurasia (Siberia, part of Russia) and northern North America (Canada and Alaska) is covered with permafrost, semi-frozen ground. This permafrost contains significant deposits of methane. As it melts, the methane is released into the atmosphere, which causes further warming

2. **Ice melting:** Ice has a high albedo (reflectivity) which means that solar radiation hitting it is more likely to reflect back into space and 'escape' the Earth's system. When ice melts, the bare rock underneath is exposed. This is darker and has a lower albedo; it is therefore more likely to absorb solar radiation and contribute to Earth's warming

3. **Water vapour:** Higher temperature means that more water exists as gas/vapour rather than in its liquid form. Water vapour is a greenhouse gas, and means more solar radiation is absorbed, contributing further to the Earth's warming

These feedback loops mean that even if all industrial activity and agriculture on Earth were to cease instantaneously and our greenhouse gas emissions dropped to zero, climate change would slowly grind to a halt rather than stopping instantaneously (like applying brakes to a landing airplane). It means that at this point (bar the development of new and miraculous technologies), it would be impossible to keep global temperatures from exceeding +1°C from the pre-industrial average. It also means that if we pass +3°C, we will not be able to stop a runaway greenhouse effect because the positive feedback loops will continue to accelerate the process.

1.5°C seems to be the 'ideal' target, as it avoids any further irreversible processes (like the collapse of the Greenland ice sheet predicted to happen with around 2°C of warming). This target increasingly seems like it will not be reached. If global emissions had peaked in 2000 and declined thereafter, we could have reached the 1.5 target with a 3% reduction in global emissions per year. By contrast, limiting warming to below 1.5 starting in 2019 would require a 15% cut in global emissions each year through to 2040. If emissions continue rising (as they have done, with only a minimal blip during the coronavirus pandemic), then by 2030 the 1.5 target could only be reached by cutting emissions to zero instantly. Beyond 2030, the 1.5 target could only be reached if we developed **negative emissions** technology (some way to remove, capture and store greenhouse gases on an industrial scale).

Global emissions have continued to rise every year for decades, and they do not appear to be slowing down by any appreciable amount. If climate change is such an existential threat to the human race, why are there not more concerted efforts to deal with the crisis?

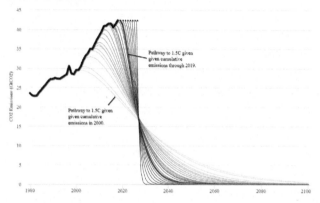

Each line on the graph shows the rate at which emissions would have to fall in order to reach no more than +1.5°C from the pre-industrial average

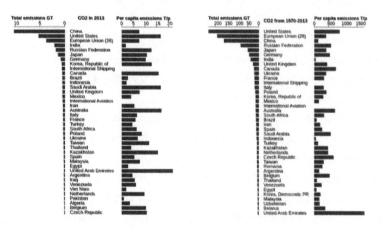

(Left) Emissions in 2013 per country and per capita (Right) Emissions between 1970-2013 per country and per capita

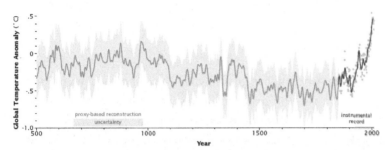

It is worth noting that there are natural fluctuations in temperature over time (and that in the past, the Earth's climate has certainly been warmer than it is today). The issue is that today, humans exist and will suffer from climate change (whereas they didn't in the past!); and that the rate of change is far too quick for Nature and ecosystems to adapt and evolve in response. Every similar jump or collapse in global temperatures in the past has led to widespread extinction

Political obstacles to tackling climate change

A number of political obstacles to tackling climate change can also be identified:

1. **Living standards:** High living standards in the West are based on industrial technology, which contributes to climate change since most of our energy generation still relies on the combustion of fossil fuels. It may well be possible to retain an advanced standard of living on the basis of renewable energy, but some aspects of 'developed' life like private cars, current levels of central heating use, meat consumption and commercial air travel will almost certainly have to go. It is difficult for democracies (either ones whose populations already have these things, or those whose populations would like to have them) to make such commitments. It is also difficult for autocracies which rely on delivering a steady growth in living standards to stave off calls for democracy to make these commitments

2. **Sovereignty:** Greenhouse gas emissions and pollution cannot be solved by unilateral action, since continued emissions elsewhere in the world make unilateral reductions ineffective. Effective action requires implementation by most (probably all) states; and definitely the most powerful. This in turn requires collective decision-making and the creation of international

organizations. Inevitably this leads to loss of sovereignty since decisions will be made by majorities rather than unanimity. No state wants to lose out on its economic interests

3. **Historical responsibility:** Greenhouse gas emissions have mostly been produced by the burning of fossil fuels - this began in earnest with the Industrial Revolution in 18th/19th century Europe and North America. It follows that developed states which industrialised earliest are historically more responsible for anthropogenic climate change than developing states and have benefited far more from it. There is therefore an argument that they should cut their emissions at a greater rate than developing states. However, it has also been argued that developing countries cannot be held responsible for historical levels of emissions which occurred at a time when nobody scientifically understood they would lead to climate change, and that reductions should be calculated on the basis of current levels of emissions only

4. **Current responsibility:** Developed states still have higher emissions levels than developing states, but the gap has narrowed considerably. A 2016 study found that developed states contribute approximately 53%–61% of emissions, and developing states contribute approximately 39%–47%. Some developed states such as the USA therefore argue that the cuts made by developed and developing states should be made at a rate that reflects this spread. There is a counter-argument that approximately one third of carbon dioxide emissions from the developing world come from the manufacture of goods which are consumed in the developed world, and that these emissions should be counted as coming from the developed world. Many leaders of developing states, such as Narendra Modi of India and Jiang Zemin of China in the 1990s, have also argued that any requirement for developing states to cut emissions will jeopardise their much-needed economic growth, and that the majority of cuts should be made in the developed world (since they can 'afford it')

5. **Calculating entitlement to emissions:** There is disagreement between some states as to how to calculate a country's share of emissions (and therefore their

share of responsibility). China argues that it should be done by calculating a country's per capita share of emissions (i.e. emissions per person). According to this measure the USA produces four times more emissions than China. The USA argues that it should be calculated by country's total emissions - according to this measure the USA is responsible for 16% of world emissions and China is responsible for 29%. China's government have argued that the American measure means states with small populations will have no incentive to cut emissions. The American government has argued that most can be achieved by targeting the highest polluters

6. **Unevenly distributed effects:** Climate change will not affect all parts of the world evenly. This means some states will treat it as a more serious and pressing problem than others:

   - *Desertification/drought:* This will affect areas on the periphery of existing deserts, like North Africa; southern Africa; Central Asia; the Indian subcontinent, and areas closer to the Equator (where temperatures are higher than the global average). Areas far to the north of the globe (Northern Europe, Canada, Alaska, Russia) will not face drought or desertification as impacts of climate change

   - *Sea level rises and flooding:* This will affect coastal states – like Bangladesh – and island states – like the Maldives, Tuvalu, and Nauru – more than inland areas. 1.5°C of warming would mean survival for these regions; 2°C would mean widespread obliteration. A significant proportion of the global population lives along coastlines; a significant proportion of this coastal population lives in developing countries, which cannot afford mitigation technologies like flood barriers

   - *Extreme weather events:* Extreme weather events like storms (hurricanes and cyclones) and wildfires will take place respectively more commonly in coastal/oceanic areas; and areas with a combination of high temperatures and forests

7. **Climate change denialism:** Climate change denialism takes two forms – firstly denialism of climate change *itself*, and secondly denial that climate change is *anthropogenic*. This was particularly common in the US as the result of lobbying efforts from oil companies like ExxonMobil. Under President GW Bush (2000-2008), the USA withdrew from the Kyoto Agreement. Under President Trump (2016-2020), the USA withdrew from the Paris Agreement. It is difficult to see how climate change could be tackled without the USA's full support, given its share of total emissions and position of global leadership

A comparative case study

Another serious ecological problem faced by the world was that of **ozone depletion** (this is a separate issue to climate change). In the late 1970s, it was observed that the ozone layer in the earth's atmosphere was becoming depleted by about 4% and there was a hole in the ozone layer in the Antarctic region. Since ozone is an effective absorber of UV radiation, the depletion of the ozone layer meant that there was a scientifically verifiable link to increased levels of skin cancer. The depletion of the ozone layer was found to have been caused by manufactured chemicals used in fridges and deodorants called **CFCs** (cholorofluorocarbons). In 1987, the **Montreal Protocol** was signed in which virtually every state agreed to ban the production of CFCs and related chemicals. By 1990, ozone levels had stabilised and began to rise back towards their natural levels in the 2000s.

One could see ozone depletion/the Montreal Protocol as an optimistic precedent that climate change could be similarly dealt with. However, one could also point out that the CFC issue:

1. Could be more easily dealt with, since CFCs are not the bedrock of modern civilisation and there were readily available technological alternatives
2. Was less complex, because all states had begun to emit CFCs at approximately the same time and no one had really disproportionately benefited from their emissions in a 'permanent' way
3. Had more 'immediate' consequences on all people across the world, which sparked immediate cooperative counteraction; as opposed to climate change,

where the effects in some parts of the world are marginal whereas in others they are already very serious

Frameworks of global governance of the environment
The Intergovernmental Panel on Climate Change (IPCC)
The IPCC was founded in 1988 by the World Meteorological Organisation (WMO) and the United Nations Environment Programme (UNEP), and was later endorsed by the UN General Assembly. It currently has 195 members.

The purpose of the IPCC is to provide impartial information and advice about climate change. The panel consists of leading climate change scientists who volunteer to review the latest scientific research on climate change. The IPCC does not conduct its own 'original' research. It makes regular reports, the most important being its Assessment Reports, which assess the risk of climate change, its current and project impact, and comment on the options for **adaptation** (coping with climate change) and **mitigation** (how to reduce emissions). The 2007 AR predicted that if nothing more was done to curb greenhouse gas emissions, the world's temperature would rise by between 2.4-6.4°C by 2099. A full list of IPCC assessment reports can be found here: https://www.ipcc.ch/reports/

The decision to found the IPCC was taken by President Reagan of the USA who was concerned that official UN climate change predictions would otherwise be made by independent scientists working with no political oversight – he wanted to predict 'excessive' predictions that would compel strong action against fossil fuel industries. The IPCC is unusual amongst global institutions as a **hybrid institution**, neither fully 'scientific' nor fully 'political':

- **Scientific:** Scientists of the IPCC are renowned climatologists and experts in their field

- **Political:** Scientists of the IPCC are selected by and act as official representatives of their governments; IPCC reports have to gain consensus from participating governments

Strengths of the IPCC	Weaknesses of the IPCC
Establishment of a consensus: Although the IPCC does tend to 'err	Too conservative: IPCC reports tend to be conservative and consistently

on the side of caution', it has been remarkably successful at establishing a consensus around the science of climate change. It is now undeniable that climate change is happening, and nearly every major government also agrees that it is anthropogenic. This is a first and necessary step to tackling the problem.

The IPCC releases Assessment Reports on a regular basis (AR1 1990; AR2 1996; AR3 2001; AR4 2007; AR5 2014; AR6 scheduled for 2022) which help to inform policy discussions on a domestic and an interstate level.

AR5 stated that "warming of the climate system is unequivocal", that greenhouse gas levels are "unprecedented in at least the last 800,000 years" and that "It is extremely likely (95-100% probability) that human influence was the dominant cause of global warming between 1951 and 2010." This consensus to a large degree spurred the 2015 Paris Agreement.

Most major states and scientific bodies globally have endorsed the IPCC's reporting

underestimate the pace and impacts of climate change (which are then updated in later reports). There are two main reasons for this phenomenon:

1. Politicisation: The IPCC, because of political pressure from state governments on their scientists, tends to report conservatively on the 'lowest common denominator' scenario of the range of possible outcomes. The leaking of a memo from ExxonMobil (an oil company) to the Bush administration showed heavy corporate lobbying attempts behind the scenes to remove some scientists from their IPCC posts

2. Reliance on prior research: Because the IPCC does not conduct research of its own, but instead relies on a review of previously published research, its reports are often outdated by the time they are published because of new understandings of climate science. For example, the 4th IPCC Assessment Report (2007) was already out of date when it was published and omitted the thawing permafrost → methane feedback loop from its explanations

Scientific basis for predictions: The IPCC bases its predictions on rigorous science and cross-referencing between many different academic articles and reports. The reliance on work which is already peer-reviewed means that is conclusions are likely to be solid, and this means that they are more likely to be accepted. They cannot be reasonably disputed because they draw on such a broad base of knowledge	Disputed assumptions: Some specific IPCC predictions have been questioned because they rely on assumptions which are not concretely proven, e.g. the capacity of the oceans to absorb carbon dioxide, or the fragility of the Himalayan glaciers. It is worth noting that these assumptions are minor parts of the overall climate change picture, but they may still reduce trust in the institution if they do not 'come true'

Projected change in temperatures by 2090
If CO$_2$ emissions drop to zero by 2080 (RCP2.6)

If CO$_2$ emissions triple by 2080 (RCP8.5)

Max 12°C
6°C
5
4
3
2
1
0°C

Visualisation from Working Group I of AR5 (published 2014). In the map at the top, the scenario is global emissions falling to zero by 2080 – this would result in global warming of somewhere around 2°C by 2090 and the worst of climate change's effects would be avoided although we would still see more droughts, flooding, extreme weather events, etc. In the map at the top, the scenario is global emissions tripling by 2080 – this would result in global warming of 4-6°C by 2090 and catastrophic consequences for human civilisation. It is worth noting that recorded global emissions have continued to rise every year since the publication of this report, although there is an expected 7% dip for 2020 as a result of the coronavirus pandemic, lockdowns and reduced economic activity

The United Nations Framework Convention on Climate Change (UNFCCC)

The UNFCCC is an international environmental treaty established at the Earth Summit in Rio de Janeiro in 1992. It entered into force in 1994 after a sufficient number of countries had ratified it – it currently has 197 signatories. The objective of the UNFCCC is to 'stabilise greenhouse gas concentrations in the atmosphere at a level that would prevent dangerous anthropogenic interference with the climate system'. Parties to the treaty have to make national inventories of their sources of carbon dioxide emissions and possible **sinks** (ways carbon dioxide could be absorbed).

The UNFCCC says that requirements on states will be determined in accordance with the principle of 'common but differentiated responsibilities' – i.e. states that have contributed most to global warming, had industrialised earlier, or were more developed were expected to accept greater reduction in their emissions, while developing states were not expected to reduce theirs at the same rate. The parties to the convention have met annually from 1995 in 'Conferences of the Parties' to assess progress in dealing with climate change. The principal agreements made at UNFCCC Conferences were the Kyoto Protocol (1997), the Copenhagen Accord (2009) and the Paris Agreement (2015), discussed in more depth below:

- **Rio Summit (1992):**

    o Led to the creation of the UNFCCC; the Convention on Biological Diversity; and the United Nations Convention to Combat Desertification

    o Began promoting the idea of **'sustainable development'** (economic growth without environmental damage that would prevent long-term human existence)

- **The Kyoto Protocol (1997):**

    o Committed signatories to reducing greenhouse gas emissions to a level that would prevent "dangerous anthropogenic interference with the climate system"

- Parties to Kyoto are classified as 'Annex I' and/or 'Annex II' countries; **Annex I** countries (40) are industrialised countries and countries in economic transition, whereas **Annex II** (23) countries are developed countries which should pay for the costs of developing countries. Annex II is a subset of Annex I. All Annex I countries are committed to reduce their emission levels of greenhouse gases to targets generally set below their 1990 emission levels

- Under the Kyoto Protocol, developing countries are *not* required to reduce their emissions unless developed countries (Annex II) supply funding and technology – this is to (i) avoid restrictions on their economic development; (ii) allow for the sale of emissions credits; (iii) allow for the transfer of money and technology for low-carbon investments from the developed world. The idea that different countries have different capabilities is called **'common but differentiated responsibilities'**

- Kyoto included three **flexibility mechanisms** – emissions trading; the Clean Development Mechanism (CDM) and Joint Implementation (JI). In general, these mean that if a country has emitted less than its permitted emissions, it can 'sell' the unused capacity to a country which has emitted *more* than its permitted emissions. It also allows for developed countries to record a 'reduction' in emissions if they help provide technology or funds to reduce emissions in a developing country

- The USA signed the Protocol in 1998 under President Bill Clinton, but the Senate blocked the ratification of the Protocol on a 95-0 vote on the basis that it "would seriously harm the economy of the United States". Bush repeated this critique when he became President (2000) and added that it "exempted 80% of the world, including China and India, from compliance" (the coal and oil lobbies played a major role in this). Canada, Japan and Russia withdrew from the Protocol in 2012

- Total GHG emissions for Annex I parties decreased from 19 gigatonnes per year (1990) to 17.8 gigatonnes (2012), a reduction of 6%. On paper, this suggests that the Protocol was a success. However, (i) 10 countries only achieved their targets by buying carbon/emissions credits, so these were not 'true' cuts (ii) the collapse of the Soviet Union meant that industrial activity contracted sharply in Eastern Europe and Russia, but are now starting to rise; (iii) without the impact of the 2008 Financial Crisis, it is possible that the targets would have been missed

- **Copenhagen (2009):**

  - Recognised the existential threat of climate change and agreed that actions should be taken to prevent any temperature increases above 2°C from the pre-industrial average

  - A commitment to limit temperature rises to 1.5°C and cut emissions by 80% by 2050 were dropped as consensus could not be reached in the UNFCCC

  - Commitment from the developed world to provide $30bn to the developing world from 2009-2012, rising to $100bn by 2020 to help them adapt to climate change

  - Was "taken note of" but not "adopted" by the UNFCCC – the distinction meaning that it is not legally binding and is rather a general statement of intent

- **The Paris Agreement (2015):**

  - Agreed a legally binding commitment to "well below 2°C" and "pursue efforts to limit the increase to 1.5°C" to reduce the risks and impacts of warming

- Each country is to set its own NDC (nationally determined contributions) which are required to be "ambitious", "represent a progression over time" (Article 3) with a view to securing the overall legally binding commitment. NDCs themselves are non-binding and there is no hard enforcement mechanism. States are, however, required to declare their NDCs and progress towards them, so there is a 'name and shame' or 'name and encourage' system for enforcing NDCs

- Unlike Kyoto, there is no distinction between developed and developing countries in Paris – all countries are required to submit NDCs. However, the flexibility and 'nationally determined' character of NDCs means that developing states will likely submit less comprehensive targets than developed states, taking into account their need for economic development

- The maintenance of a 'Green Climate Fund' was reaffirmed, with £100bn per year until 2025 being committed by developed countries to developing ones for actions on climate change adaptation and mitigation

- The Paris Agreement was signed and ratified by nearly all states with the notable exceptions of Iran and Turkey and a handful of other very low emitters. The US temporarily left under Donald Trump but re-joined under President Biden

- All countries have submitted NDCs which involve a reduction in GHG emissions over an extended period; e.g. China is aiming for zero-emissions by 2060. However, scientific estimates suggest that if the current NDC commitments are adhered to, global temperatures will have risen by around 3°C by the end of the century. To hit a 1.5°C target, global emissions must be below 25 gigatonnes annually – given current NDC projections, they will be around 56 gigatonnes (i.e. double the required amount)

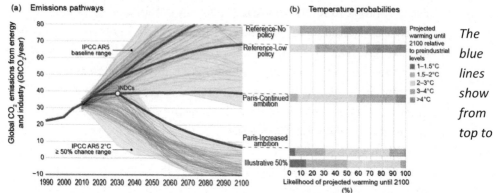

(a) Emissions pathways

(b) Temperature probabilities

The blue lines show from top to

bottom; (i) emission growth over time based on AR5 projections, (ii) emission growth over time based on AR5 projections and minimal policy intervention, (iii) emission growth over time based on current Paris NDCs, (iv) emission growth over time based on Paris NDCs becoming more ambitious over time. To have more than a 50% chance of keeping warming below 2°C, the reduction in emissions would have to be within the light-blue shaded area. The emissions pathways connect to 'temperature probabilities' on the right – i.e. given current NDCs, the most likely outcome is a temperature rise of between 2-4°C.

Strengths of the UNFCCC	Weaknesses of the UNFCCC
Legally binding commitments: UNFCCC-derived agreements are designed such that they do not come into force unless at least 55 states, representing 55% of global emissions, ratify them. However, the commitments are then legally binding – for example, Kyoto (1997) committed Annex I participants to reductions in their greenhouse gas emissions; Paris (2015) commits states to keep warming "well below 2°C" and aim to "limit the increase to 1.5°C." States are committed to	Fundamentally unenforceable: Treaties created under the UNFCCC framework are fundamentally unenforceable – although states may be legally bound to general *commitments*, their specific *actions* are open to a great degree of interpretation. It could be reasonably argued that even though Paris' NDC system has encouraged more states to sign and ratify the Agreement, this has come at the expense of effective and enforceable action. NDCs are largely self-regulating, or rely on a

regular reporting of their efforts to reduce emissions, which adds a layer of accountability to the system	sense of intangible reward/guilt from the wider international community to generate results
Increasing participation: Over time, it is clear that the UNFCCC has been able to secure participation from a greater number of states. In the Kyoto Protocol, many major developing countries did not sign on to either Annex I or II, meaning that they made no commitment to reducing emissions (notably India and China), and the USA did not ratify the Protocol under President GW Bush. This is in stark contrast to the Paris Agreement, in which nearly every state signed and ratified the agreement (the US briefly left under Trump but has re-joined under Biden; the only notable emitters that are not part of the Agreement are Iran and Turkey, collectively accounting for only about 2% of global emissions together	Uneven participation: In the Kyoto Protocol, developing states did not participate in any commitments to cutting carbon emissions. Thus, whilst Annex I emissions fell slightly from 19 to 17.8 Gt, total global emissions rose significantly from 38 Gt to 50 Gt. Between 1990 and 2010 alone, China nearly doubled its emissions. In the Paris Agreement, even though virtually all states are participating through NDCs, the ambition of targets varies significantly. Some countries have targets, which if replicated globally, would be sufficient to reach the 1.5°C target, e.g. Morocco and the Gambia. Most countries' NDCs would be insufficient to even reach the 2°C target (tinyurl.com/45jtxw4a)
Positive steps forward: Many countries, on the back of the Paris Agreement, have put forward statements of intent or pledges to reduce emissions and achieve carbon-neutrality (net zero emissions):	Rate of change is too slow: Although the UNFCCC has provided a framework for the agreement of global targets and actions, the rate of change that has been agreed is far too slow to prevent catastrophic climate change. Current trends of

	emissions, based on current NDCs from Paris, would make it near impossible to reach the 1.5°C target and would only provide around an 8% chance of keeping warming below 2°C. Current changes are cosmetic and are not ambitious enough to meet the scale of the environmental challenge
• China: 2060 • UK: 2050 • USA: 2050 These have been accompanied by promises for additional 'green' funding and technologies	

Shallow and deep green ecology
The tragedy of the commons

The 'tragedy of the commons' describes a situation in which multiple individuals, all of whom have unfettered access to a common resource which is not governed by any rules or laws, exploit the resource for their individual benefit whilst the negative consequences are externalised. Eventually, this uncoordinated exploitation leads to a depletion/destruction of the resource.

It was initially used as a literal description of a **commons** (an area of unenclosed public pasture/ grassland in medieval and early modern Europe which anyone could access and use). The 'tragedy of the commons' here was that farmers would bring their cattle to graze on the commons, which would fatten the cattle but deplete the grass. The benefit would be individual (a farmer getting bigger cattle) whereas the negative consequence (reduction of grass) was externalised and not specific to the individual, since the commons was owned by everyone. In the long run, the individually selfish nature of each farmer would lead to the overgrazing of the commons – in the short run, since the action was individually beneficial, no-one would want to unilaterally stop (because to do so might entail others carrying on and benefiting whilst the individual forgoes the benefits!)

In the sense of global environmental governance, this might apply to:
- Overfishing of the oceans
- Over-pollution of the atmosphere
- Mass deforestation

In all cases, individuals (or corporations, or states) extract resources from the commons for their own personal profit, whilst diminishing the overall commons. Given that all actors are simultaneously doing this, in the absence of a sovereign to enforce rules and order, the commons will be destroyed.

There are two main schools of thought as to how the tragedy of the commons can be solved:

1. **Governmental solutions:** Governmental solutions to the tragedy involve some kind of sovereign regulating authority, which may (i) privatise the commons, to convert common negative externalities into specific negative externalities; or (ii) regulate the amount of a common good that is available for any individual, e.g. via a permit system

2. **Non-governmental solutions:** Non-governmental solutions deny that the tragedy of the commons is an inherent problem and argue that it is possible to build cooperative systems that rational individuals do not over-exploit because they wish to prevent its overall collapse

Deep v shallow green ecology

Deep and shallow green ecology are two schools of thought to do with environmental issues. The salient differences are summarised below:

Shallow green ecology	Deep green ecology
People should love and protect the biodiversity of the natural world and ecosystems so that they can continue to sustain human life in the future (enlightened anthropocentrism)	People are not more important than the natural world – we are all valuable components of an overall ecosystem. Nature should be protected because it is of intrinsic value (ecocentrism)
Different environmental issues (e.g. climate change, oceanic pollution, deforestation, fracking, animal rights, etc.) are all separate issues which can be tackled with individual campaigns	Different environmental issues (e.g. climate change, oceanic pollution, deforestation, fracking, animal rights, etc.) are all interlinked issues and fundamentally rooted in humanity's

161

and solutions	problematic relationship with the environment
The answer to consumerism (increasing consumption = increasing happiness) and materialism (physical goods bring us happiness) is to 'do more than less' – we don't have to stop consuming material goods, but we need to be satisfied with less consumption	The answer to consumerism and materialism is to 'do less with less' – we need to break the false psychological link between happiness and consumption, and build a society which is poorer in the conventional economic sense but which is richer in respect for Nature

Sustainability is the capacity of the ecological system (the Earth) to maintain its 'health' over time

Shallow greens favour weak sustainability or sustainable development – the idea of continuing industrialisation and getting richer, but at a slower pace. Earth's 'natural capital' (resources) can be used up, as long as we replace it with 'manufactured capital' (infrastructure) of equal value. Specific 'weak sustainability' solutions might be: 1. Green capitalism: Using private companies and the free market to deliver 'green' technology like renewable energies (wind, solar, nuclear) as consumers become more ecologically aware and demand changes.	Deep greens favour strong sustainability – they believe that 'weak sustainability' and 'sustainable development' are merely symbolic concessions which will not solve fundamental environmental crises. In this view, economic growth; industrialisation; materialism; and consumerism are fundamentally incompatible with preserving the environment. It is not enough to develop 'green, clean' technologies or to manage capitalism; there will always be greed and rising consumption, and to truly achieve sustainability and protect the health of the Earth, we need to redefine the relationship between humans and nature.

The rising price of fossil fuels will naturally shift corporations to pursuing cheaper renewable substitutes

2. Mangerialism: Using government regulations to impose targets and some limits on corporations to prevent excessive environmental damage. This could be achieved by individual states (e.g. the UK Climate Change Act 2008) or by global bodies like the UNFCCC and international treaties (Kyoto, Paris). Governments can impose taxes to make harmful activities more expensive and incentivise a shift to alternatives

3. Technological solutions: We can innovate new solutions to reduce environmental crises, e.g. 'carbon-capture'; more efficient farming methods using less water; better battery technology so renewable energy can be stored and becomes used more widely (solar energy is cheaper than coal/ oil/ gas – it is just hard to

'Sustainable development' does not make changes quickly enough to tackle the scale of the environmental crisis we are facing. States will not want to deliver meaningful change, because this would mean accepting lower standards of living (which as a policy would be electoral suicide in a democracy). Corporations will attempt to look more environmentally friendly and spend huge sums on PR so as to assuage public worries, but will not really make fundamental changes to their damaging practises behind the scenes (greenwashing).

The only real solutions to achieve strong sustainability in the deep green view are:

1. Living economies: Rooting economies in sustainable local production, instead of global trade networks; and moving away from materialistic consumption

2. Living democracy: Politics should be based on 'bio-regions' and local democracy, instead of existing national and

store electricity)	state boundaries
Shallow greens would argue the solutions to the tragedy of the commons are governmental solutions – the problem can be solved with greater intergovernmental regulation; some kind of 'permit system' for carbon emissions; or privatisation of aspects of the global commons	Deep greens would argue the solutions to the tragedy of the commons are non-governmental. As long as our harmful, exploitative attitude towards Nature persists, no level of regulation and law will fix things. We need to radically reformulate our way of life and perspectives

The structures and institutions of global environmental governance are clearly based on **shallow green** rather than **deep green** ideas. The reason for this is that the latter would involve a radical reformulation of how we understand and carry out politics on a global, national and local level – none of the state actors and governments dealing with climate change have the appetite to make these changes (which would effectively amount to disestablishing themselves).

It is worth considering whether **sustainable development** (the shallow green idea that both economic growth and protection of the environment) can be achieved simultaneously.

- If we believe this is the case, then current models of global governance of the environment based on shallow green theories could solve the climate crisis and other ecological issues

- If we believe this is not the case, and that deep green ecology correctly identifies our exploitative attitude towards Nature as the root of the problem, then current models of global governance of the environment are doomed to fail

There are, I think, grounds for optimism. Currently the greatest problem facing renewable energy is battery technology; it is hard to have energy 'on demand' from renewables (which are already cheaper than fossil fuel derived energy) because you cannot turn wind, sunlight etc. on and off in the same way as you can turn a power plant on and off. Lithium-ion batteries are not good enough to store massive amounts of energy, so we rely on fossil fuel derived energy for our electric grid. However, it is also worth noting that we are now in a 'race against time' to unlock this holy grail of technology *and* roll it out worldwide by 2030 if we wish to keep emissions below 1.5°C. It may seem unlikely that governments and corporations will cooperate to achieve this, especially given the rapid growth of the developing world and a desire of its citizens to access cheap and low-tech sources of energy (which in practise means the combustion of fossil fuels).

REALIST AND LIBERAL FRAMEWORKS (3.6)

Realism	Liberalism
Realists would view human rights as an unenforceable fiction – the world is inherently amoral and there are no universal codes of ethics. Realists would argue that the deployment of 'human rights' doctrine is a Western-specific development, utilised in order to increase the hegemony of Western states over other states (N.B. they are not making a comment on whether this is 'good' or 'bad', merely that human rights are used as a rationale by some states to extend their power over others). Human rights can be ignored by powerful states when this clashes with their national self-interest, illustrating the realist belief that states act in a fundamentally amoral and power-seeking way	Liberals would view human rights as genuine (whether natural or constructivist) ethical principles which should underpin and regulate the behaviour of governments towards their citizens, and states towards each other. Human rights are the product of states cooperating and working together to design liberal principles, and the adherence of all states to these ideas will promote greater interstate trust, peace and a reduction of conflict both within and between nation-states. Human rights *can* be ignored by powerful states, but increasingly states are 'buying into' the concept of human rights and view them as important mechanisms for governance and political legitimacy

International courts and tribunals, in the view of realists, are not particularly effective. They are not sovereign institutions, have limited jurisdiction and cannot compel states to act • The ICJ can only rule on inter-state disputes with state consent • Tribunals can only really be set up after the resolution of a conflict • The ICC has limited jurisdiction (only parties to the Rome Statute) • The ECHR has no enforcement mechanism for its rulings	International courts and tribunals, in the view of liberals, are nascent institutions but they are becoming more effective over time at embedding a human rights doctrine • The ICJ has made rulings based on the Genocide Convention (Myanmar) • Tribunals hold national leaders to account and apply universal standards • The ICC's jurisdiction is expanding and has reduced violence and war crimes • The ECHR's rulings are largely followed, and it has expanded over time
Humanitarian intervention is generally ineffective and rarely happens because all powerful states block it when it goes against their amoral national self-interests. Where it does occur, it is not to uphold a universal morality or individual rights, but to extend the strategic power of the intervening states and – it is just Western neo-imperialism. State sovereignty remains the key axis of IR	Humanitarian intervention is generally effective where it occurs and represents the international community working together to secure universal rights (above the narrower concerns of state sovereignty and self-interest). Sometimes interventions do not happen, but this is largely correlated with the obstructionism of non-democratic states; as the world becomes more democratic, intervention will work better

The IPCC and UNFCCC are ineffective because they have no way of imposing binding targets on sovereign states. Both bodies show that sovereign states act in their own selfish interest, to the detriment of the global community, and will not cooperate because they see the calculation as a zero-sum game	The IPCC and UNFCCC are effective examples of inter-state cooperation, with a growing consensus on anthropogenic climate change and increasingly ambitious agreements and targets over time which include more and more of the world's states (Kyoto; Copenhagen; Paris). Cooperation leads to mutual gains

POWER

Power is typically defined as the ability to exert influence or coerce others to do something that they would not otherwise do without that intervention. It is important to note that power is strictly **amoral**; it is not about **legitimacy**, but **ability** – having the resources, might, persuasiveness or integrity to bend others to your will. A general distinction between two types of power can be made:

1. **Hard power (i.e. 'twisting arms'):** Command or coercive power – to compel other actors to follow your orders via threats ('sticks') or incentivise them to do via material rewards ('carrots'), *even when they don't want to do so*

2. **Soft power (i.e. 'twisting minds'):** Power via attraction and identification, by sharing common values and ideas with other actors – in other words, co-opting them to 'want what you want' and thereby indirectly achieve your aims by changing *their* aims

A way to think about this theoretical distinction might be in the hypothetical example of wanting someone else's wallet. The use of hard power to acquire the wallet would involve threats or the use of violence, or offering them something in return. The use of soft power to acquire the wallet would involve convincing them that it would be in their interest to hand over the wallet; that the money could be used for a beneficial purpose; and/or that it would serve a 'common good'.

Below, we will examine different types of power that are deployed in international relations by states, and consider their effectiveness and how/why patterns of their use have changed over time.

Hard power
Military
Military power is the capacity of a state to:
1. *Commit* aggression against another state or non-state actor **(actively deployed)**

2. *Threaten* aggression against another state or non-state actor **(deterrent or threat)**

This may commonly involve assassinations and limited drone strikes, bombing campaigns, militarisation of territory, and the possession of nuclear weapons; all the way to 'full' conflict.

Advantages of using military power	Disadvantages of using military power
Deterrent effect: Displaying significant military power allows a state to safely deter acts of aggression that might otherwise take place against it, even if they never actually have to 'use' their weapons. The ultimate expression of military power is the possession of nuclear weapons and the ability to deliver them to targets – by ICBMs (intercontinental ballistic missiles) or bomber jets. This explains why some states have been so keen in the development of nuclear weapons Israel developed nuclear weapons in the 1960s after several wars with neighbouring Arab states (Egypt, Syria, Jordan, Iraq) with a view that they would prevent a future con invasion of Israeli territory. Israel maintains a position of "nuclear opacity" which means it does not admit it has nuclear weapons, but very heavily hints that it has them and would use them if existentially	Potential retaliation: A state building up its military power, whether or not it actually utilises it, could trigger a security dilemma – i.e. other states perceive it as a threat and either (i) retaliate against its use of military power or (ii) act pre-emptively to contain it before it becomes a more serious threat to international peace For example, Saddam Hussein instigated the Iran-Iraq War in 1980 shortly after becoming the dictator of Iraq. In 1981, the Israeli air force destroyed the Osirak nuclear reactor in Iraq, fearing that Hussein might produce nuclear weapons. In 1990, Hussein invaded the small neighbouring oil-rich country of Kuwait; a global coalition involving the USA, UK and most Arab countries counter-attacked and expelled Iraqi forces from Kuwait. Arguably, this pattern of military violence against other states (as well as genocides against Kurdish, Marsh Arab and Shia

threatened. Israel has not been attacked by any of its neighbours since 1973 North Korea developed nuclear weapons in the late 2000s under the dictator Kim Jong Il (since continued under his son Kim Jong Un). The risk that North Korea could launch nuclear strikes on Tokyo and Seoul, the Japanese and South Korean capitals respectively, as well as potentially hit targets on the West Coast of the USA has prevented any serious military action against the existing dictatorship	minorities in Iraq) were significant contributing factors in the Anglo-American decision to invade Iraq in 2003 Another example could be Russia' response to NATO's increasing global role; NATO's actions in Yugoslavia, Libya and Afghanistan as well as rising military spending are arguably why Russia has adopted a more aggressive stance with regards to Ukraine, the Baltic states, the Caucasus and Syria to counter the expansion of NATO's military influence
Secures objectives: In many cases (moral and ethical concerns aside), it is clear that military hard power 'works' in terms of securing a state's objectives, if it applies it intelligently. For example, Russia's increasingly belligerent foreign policy since 2008 has achieved key objectives. The 2008 invasion of Georgia and the 2014 intervention in Ukraine secured the *de facto* independence of South Ossetia and Abkhazia, and the Russian annexation of Crimea respectively. Russia's intervention in the Syrian civil war and destruction	Ineffective vs non-state actors: 'Classical' international relations is seen as an affair that takes place mostly between state actors (governments). In these cases, targets for military action are fairly well defined and it is easy to distinguish between 'enemies' and 'civilians'. The use of military power becomes much trickier when faced with insurgencies (rebellions against an occupying force) or terrorist groups which do not have strictly delineated territories. This is perhaps one of the reasons that the USA and UK found it so difficult to restore

of rebel cities ensured the survival of Assad's government, a key regional ally in the Middle East Another example in Chinese militarisation since 2009, with a particular focus on building up naval power. China now has two aircraft carriers (Liaoning and Shandong) and is constructing a third – this allows China to launch air attacks far away from land bases. In turn, this has enabled China to successfully press its claim to a series of oil-adjacent islands in the South China Sea which are disputed by Vietnam, Brunei, Indonesia, Malaysia, and the Philippines	stability in Iraq after the 2003 invasion, because the Baathist (pro-Saddam) uprising against the US-UK occupation did not have a 'command base' or fortresses that could be taken out, uniformed armies that could be distinguished from civilians, a clear battlefield where Western armed forces could manoeuvre easily (most of the fighting took place in cities) etc. Consequently, the UK and USA became embroiled in a long-term, costly and violent occupation. Arguably, the threat posed by non-state actors, primarily terrorist groups, negates the military power of major states because it cannot be deployed effectively in full force
Sometimes necessary: Arguably, the exercise of military power is sometimes necessary as a last resort and there sometimes no other alternatives for a state to achieve its goals In the 'moral' sense, this can be seen in the case of humanitarian interventions; in the face of imminent or ongoing genocide, war crimes and crimes against humanity, the use of force is the only thing that will prevent a catastrophic loss of life.	'Moral' concerns: For most states, there are moral and ethical concerns associated with the use of military power (whether or not these are genuine or for the sake of 'appearances'). Military conflicts are inherently violent and unpredictable, and whilst it is possible to minimise civilian collateral damage it can never be completely eliminated. Civilian casualties from war, whether intentional or not, reflect badly upon a state actor; they may face condemnation from the international

We might refer here to NATO interventions in Bosnia, Kosovo and Libya, as well as UN-backed interventions in East Timor, Sierra Leone and Haiti, amongst others The use of military power is also sometimes necessary for a state to secure its survival if it is attacked by other states. Here, we might refer to the fighting of 'defensive wars' such as by Iran, in response to an Iraqi invasion led by Saddam Hussein (1980-1989). Hussein wanted to cripple Iran and prevent the exportation of the Shia-led Islamic Revolution movement to Iraq, where it might threaten the Sunni-dominated Baath Party government, led by Hussein. Without its own independent military forces (the USA, UK, Soviets and France all backed Iraq), Iran would have lost most of its territory to Iraq	community that damages their ability to achieve other aims For example, the 'War on Terror' which has involved Western military interventions in Afghanistan, Iraq, Syria and Libya (as well as indirect support for Saudi Arabia's war in Yemen) has been perceived by many other states as an example of careless, callous Western neo-imperialism because of the rate of civilian casualties. There is credible evidence that nearly 30,000 civilians have been killed by the coalition airstrikes against ISIS in Syria. In turn, this has damaged the relationship of the USA and UK with Muslim-majority countries and made it harder for them to garner support for humanitarian interventions generally

Economic

Economic power is the capacity of a state to induce another actor to do something by:

1. *Threatening* to apply economic penalties (trade barriers, tariffs, suspending loans)
2. *Offering* favourable terms (new trade agreements, loans, investments)

This may commonly involve trade deals, trade wars and embargoes, sanctions (both on individuals and on a state more generally), infrastructure loans and deals, and wider investments.

Advantages of using economic power	Disadvantages of using economic power
Compels peaceful change: Sanctions allow states to achieve their aims bloodlessly against other states without having to resort to violence, instead relying on economic pressure. For example, joint American-Japanese-European sanctions on the apartheid regime in South Africa during the 1980s and early 1990s were instrumental in leading to the collapse of apartheid. The sanctions targeted agriculture, uranium and precious metals, which were the key sectors of South Africa's export profile. The ensuing 15% inflation rate contributed to President de Klerk's willingness to negotiate with Nelson Mandela (then a political prisoner) and agree to multiracial democratic elections Another example were sanctions imposed by the UN on Iran in 2006 as a result of Iran's pursuit of nuclear enrichment (building a nuclear bomb), in violation of the Non-Proliferation Treaty. Sanctions targeted oil, gas, and financial	Indiscriminate impacts: The operating principle of sanctions is that they make the economy of a state worse, citizens suffer, and consequently protest against the government, which modifies its policies so that the sanctions are lifted. There are questions about the efficacy of sanctions and the ethics of imposing a sanctions regime which disproportionately affects the poorer and more vulnerable in society (whereas those who are richer or more connected to the regime are able to access resources, albeit they are scarcer and dearer) For example, sanctions on apartheid-era South Africa in the 1980s disproportionately affected poor black Africans and raised the price of everyday food, supplies and resources (as well as causing the collapse of many white-owned South African businesses) Another example would be the current US sanctions on Venezuela and Cuba's regimes; these have had demonstrable impacts on food and

business dealings of the government. The annual $60 billion hit to the economy partially explains the loss of President Ahmadinejad's party (hardline conservative) in the next election to the more moderate President Rouhani. Rouhani negotiated an end to sanctions in 2015 in exchange for (i) ending enrichment to weapons-grade level and (ii) allowing the IAEA (International Atomic Energy Agency) to send inspectors to confirm this was taking place

medical supplies in those countries (although the US has only sanctioned companies which are directly connected to the regime via funding or shareholding). Some would argue that Venezuela and Cuba are only in such a dire economic situation at the moment because of the pressure caused by US sanctions. Whilst this is not true, sanctions definitely have contributed to current shortages for everyday people

Structural dependencies: The exercise of economic hard power allows a state to build up a durable, long-term network of structural dependency that ties other states to it via an incentive/ threat approach

For example, the BRI (Belt and Road Initiative) of China, spearheaded by Xi Jinping, has entrenched Chinese power across Asia and Africa. The development strategy involves the building of ports, railways, roads and airports – in total, it is expected to cost more than $1 trillion and nearly $300 billion has already been spent. Most of these building projects are carried out by Chinese companies

Mutually destructive effects: The utilisation of economic hard power, especially in terms of restricting trade with another country to 'punish' them, has inevitably mutually destructive effects in the globalised and economically interdependent world. This can most clearly be seen in Trump's trade war against China

In 2018, Trump began imposing American tariffs and other trade barriers on China with the goal of forcing it to make changes to what were quite legitimately described as 'unfair trade practises' and theft of intellectual property. The trade war

using Chinese materials. China's massive spending has driven other countries into debt in such a way that China is able to leverage concessions to write off the debt; e.g. having control of Chinese-built ports ceded to China in Malaysia, Sri Lanka and Pakistan; or pressuring countries to drop criticism of China's policies in Xinjiang by threatening withdrawal of investment Arguably, the USA's dominance in the IMF and WTO is also an example of building long-term structures of power through economics	negatively impacted China's economy – it contributed to a slowdown in the rate of economic and industrial output, and some companies have shifted their supply chains elsewhere in Asia. However, it was also heavily damaging to the US economy – prices rose for consumers, and China's retaliatory tariffs on agriculture meant that the US government had to bail out the farming industry with over $21 billion of public funds In January 2020, the USA and China signed a 'Phase One' trade deal with a view to gradually reduce tariffs and restore favourable trade terms

Soft power

Soft power is often discussed as coming in cultural or diplomatic forms. Cultural soft power is about the projection of a country's moral, cultural and political values in a way that makes them seem attractive to imitate; diplomatic soft power is concerned with the art of negotiation, deal-making and engineering treaties and compromises. This is in opposition to the coercive nature of hard power.

Examples of soft power include:

- **The UK:** The UK often tops rankings of 'soft power' states. One reason is that English is the most common second-language in the world, spoken by an estimated 1 billion people (both as a result of British imperialism and the influence of the USA). Across the world, there is some level of admiration for British culture and a desire to imitate it, where it seen as 'upper class' or 'refined'. many international organisations, such as the Council of Europe, the European Court of Human Rights and the Security Council. Through these institutions, it is able to influence and persuade other states diplomatically. British media is broadcast internationally, notably the BBC World Service (broadcasting in 28 languages and offering online services in Arabic and Farsi). British film and literature have international appeal. Schools and universities in Britain are popular destinations for students of other states. The UK also exhibits its cultural power in sporting events, with London (as of 2012) being the only city to have hosted the Olympics three times, and finishing 2nd at the 2016 Olympics. Following the poisoning of Sergei Skripal in 2018, the UK responded with diplomatic efforts that led to nations around the world expelling one hundred and fifty Russian diplomats, described by CNN as a "remarkable diplomatic coup for Britain"

- **China:** China's traditional culture has been a source of attraction, building on which it has created several hundred Confucius Institutes around the world to teach its language and culture. In 2005, the first Confucius Institute was established in Africa. The institute is funded by the Chinese government and it provides Chinese language and cultural education to the public, promoting 'Confucian' ideals of prizing stability and order over liberty and freedom. There are 19 institutes today in Africa and China has planned to spend 20 million renminbi for education projects in South Africa, including the teaching of Mandarin in 50 local high schools. The enrolment of foreign students in China has increased from 36,000 a decade before to at least 240,000 in 2010. China's increasing soft power can be explained by looking at China's economic growth and regarding economic engagement with many African countries. China has made a systematic effort to expand and give greater profile to its soft-power policies in Africa ever since the first Forum on China-Africa Cooperation in 2000. The commitments of China's soft power ranges from health and humanitarian assistance to academic, professional and cultural exchange. China has consequently been able to secure lucrative mining, resource and construction deals across the African continent

Soft power can clearly be very effective in terms of allowing a state to co-opt other states and align their interests. Nevertheless, two major limitations to soft power should be noted. Firstly, it takes time to build up the cultural and diplomatic capital that allows soft power to be wielded effectively. A relatively 'young' country or one which does not have an established history does not have soft power and cannot acquire it in the near future (this is why most soft power states are Western states, with the exception of Japan, China and South Korea). Secondly, soft power is arguably less 'tangible' than hard power – soft power strategies may be unable to effectively counteract hard power strategies if a state is faced with aggression (however one may also argue that adopting soft power strategies makes a state less likely to face conflict – e.g. Canada, Sweden, the Netherlands, etc.)

Smart power?

'Smart' power is a concept established by the IR theorist Nye, which describes the need for a state to simultaneously deploy hard and soft power to effectively achieve their objectives. He argues that the deployment of either type in isolation is ineffective, and both 'minds' and 'arms' need to be twisted. The utilisation of only hard power leads to resistance and backlash (e.g. the American-led War on Terror); the utilisation of only soft power means progress is slow and limited (e.g. international criticisms of Myanmar's genocide against ethnic minorities like the Kachin, Shan and Rohingya, as well as the recent military coup). States must 'speak softly, and carry a big stick'.

A historical example of this would be the Roman Empire, which combined legions and armies of unprecedented strength and technological advantage **(hard power)** to conquer new territories, with the spread of Roman culture, religion and laws and the extension of citizenship to the elites of non-Roman ethnic groups **(soft power)**. A more modern example would be the eastwards expansion of the European Union, combining membership of the single market and customs union, and the financial benefits this entailed **(hard power)** with membership of an organisation requiring a commitment to values like liberalism, democratisation and the 'rule of law' **(soft power)**, shifting the political culture in the former Communist sphere of influence. In the Balkans, many EU states were involved in the NATO intervention in the Yugoslav Wars. The current consideration of Serbia's membership of the EU and extension of economic loans/investments in Serbia was then predicated on the government arresting Yugoslav war criminals like Mladic and handing them over to the ICTY to stand trial. In this way, the EU's expansion can be considered as an example of 'smart power', combining both materially coercive/ persuasive and 'values-based' elements.

Sharp power?

Nye also discusses the potential emergence of new manifestations of power utilising modern technology, which he describes as 'sharp power'. Sharp power is defined as the use of manipulative diplomatic policies by one state to influence and undermine the political system of a target state. Two recent examples of this concept include:

- **Russia:** Although it is unclear how far these changed the overall result, it is now known that Russia has participated in mass disinformation and propaganda campaigns via social media, Russia Today news (RT) and armies of 'bots' in both the US Presidential Election (2016) and the Brexit Referendum (2017). The main aim is to sow socio-political division within Western states by funding right-wing movements – there is significant evidence to suggest Russian funding of Arron Banks (a leading Brexiteer), the National Front in France, and the National Rifle Association (NRA) in America and 'divisive' stories about race, gender, etc.

- **China:** China's government has intervened worldwide against portrayals of China which are seen to be against Chinese interests. China has also used the 'Confucius Educational Institute' to spread a specific view of Chinese society abroad (whilst ignoring more unsavoury elements like mass detention and persecution of minorities); and pressuring foreign governments, technology companies (Google, Facebook) and media institutions (Marvel – Ancient One in *Doctor Strange* changed from a Tibetan to Celtic character) to limit criticism of the Chinese government. Chinese IW (information warfare) also includes the spreading of disinformation about Xinjiang, Hong Kong and Tibet and attempts to discredit critics of the CCP

Sharp power is arguably distinguished from soft power because it is not conventionally 'attractive' and from hard power because it is not conventionally 'coercive' – it instead relies on distorting the political and civil system in other states. Some theorists (Walker 2018) argue that sharp power is inherently **asymmetric** in that it is carried out by authoritarian regimes against democratic ones, but not vice versa, because authoritarian regimes can damage democratic political environments abroad, whilst shielding their own domestic spaces from criticism by limiting free expression.

The changing face of power in global politics

Some would argue that the use of hard power by states has declined over the past few decades relative to the historical 'norm', and that the use of soft power has become more common. That is to say, major states are now more likely to utilise diplomacy, negotiation and encouraging the spread of their political cultures to achieve their goals instead of military or economic coercion. It is empirically verifiable that the occurrence of significant conflicts or trade wars between major states has decreased massively since the 1950s (with the notable exception of India/Pakistan). To explain this, we should consider the 'advantages' that soft power has over hard power.

1. Soft power does not cause casualties; there is less concern of moral backlash to its use

2. Soft power has more 'predictable' outcomes (unlike messy and protracted wars)

3. Achievements derived from soft power are more likely to be durable and longer-lasting than those derived from hard power, since they involve the target state *changing the way they think and act of their own free will* rather than being 'coerced' to do and ceasing to do so once that coercive framework is removed. This is perhaps why American influence in global politics has been so pervasive; it relies on institutions, values and ideas that other states 'buy into'

Nevertheless, states do sometimes deploy hard power (military and economic) to achieve their aims in contemporary global politics. It is therefore also worth considering the 'advantages' that hard power has over soft power in certain circumstances.

1. Hard power can be acquired relatively quickly compared to soft power, which requires a slow build-up of cultural and diplomatic capital over decades or even centuries

2. Hard power can achieve limited, specific aims more rapidly than soft power – especially where these involve territorial acquisition or removing a potential threat

3. In the realist view, hard power is the only 'real' power. Soft power is ineffective unless a country has hard power (military and economic) to back it up; a state cannot become globally dominant on the back of soft power alone

CLASSIFICATIONS OF STATE POWER
Factors influencing state power
A state can derive power through:

- **Capabilities:** Resources such as population, wealth, military strength or geography (e.g. China's 1.4 billion-strong population, mineral wealth, sprawling territory and modernised military forces). A poor country with a small population and few resources cannot become a military power and will always lack hard power (e.g. Lesotho – a tiny state landlocked within South Africa and a population of slightly over 2 million)

- **Partnerships:** Also known as 'relational power'. Making the right strategic alliances or joining international institutions can confer power on a state far beyond the extent of its inbuilt capabilities (e.g. the UK's 'special relationship' with the USA, or membership of a small European state like Croatia in the European Union)

- **Structures:** A state's establishment or control of knowledge, financial networks, security networks and production networks across the globe (e.g. the USA's leading role in major international institutions like the IMF, World Bank, UNSC, etc.)

'Levels' of state power

We can identify three broad categories or 'levels' of state power based on a combination of capabilities, partnerships and structures outlined above.

1. Great Powers:

The term 'great power' originates from the early 19th century, when it was used to describe the main combatants of the Napoleonic Wars – Austria, France, Great Britain, Prussia and Russia. After the defeat of France in the Napoleonic Wars, it was these states that came together to redraw the map of Europe and attempt to impose a lasting peace on the continent. There is no single academic definition of 'great power' but considerations usually include:

- A substantial population and territory (including colonies and empires)
- Resources and a high degree of economic development
- Political stability (lack of revolutions, insurgencies, etc.)
- Military strength and modern technology
- Ability to **project power** beyond the state's immediate geographic region (through alliances, empire, institutions, trade networks, cultural influence, etc.)

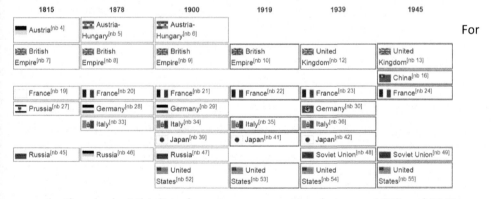

1815	1878	1900	1919	1939	1945
Austria[nb 4]	Austria-Hungary[nb 5]	Austria-Hungary[nb 6]			
British Empire[nb 7]	British Empire[nb 8]	British Empire[nb 9]	British Empire[nb 10]	United Kingdom[nb 12]	United Kingdom[nb 13]
					China[nb 16]
France[nb 19]	France[nb 20]	France[nb 21]	France[nb 22]	France[nb 23]	France[nb 24]
Prussia[nb 27]	Germany[nb 28]	Germany[nb 29]		Germany[nb 30]	
	Italy[nb 33]	Italy[nb 34]	Italy[nb 35]	Italy[nb 36]	
		Japan[nb 39]	Japan[nb 41]	Japan[nb 42]	
Russia[nb 45]	Russia[nb 46]	Russia[nb 47]		Soviet Union[nb 48]	Soviet Union[nb 49]
		United States[nb 52]	United States[nb 53]	United States[nb 54]	United States[nb 55]

For example, if we look at this list of great power over time between 1815 and 1945, we can see that a state's classification as a great power depends on its specific circumstances.

- The United States was not defined as a great power until 1900, even though it was already an industrial and economic powerhouse prior to this, because it was largely focused on consolidating territory in North Africa (fighting genocidal wars against Native Americans) rather than projecting its power more broadly around the world

- Likewise, Japan was not considered a great power until 1900, because for most of the 1800s it had not been particularly well developed in economic terms and adopted a very isolationist approach to global politics. The Meiji Restoration, the rapid industrialisation of Japan, and Japanese colonialism in Korea/China, meant that by 1900 it was a great power

- Germany and Austria-Hungary were not considered great powers in 1919 having lost WWI and being subjected to a harsh peace settlements which stripped away much of their territory and forced it to pay substantial reparations to the Allies. The same was true of Germany, Japan and Italy after WWII in 1945 (being on the 'losing side' and suffering as a result)
- Russia/the Soviet Union was not considered a great power in 1919 because it was in the midst of a bloody and destructive civil war and could not project its power. The same was true for China throughout the 1800s and early 1900s (an incredible degree of internal instability), preventing it from projecting its power globally even though it had substantial capabilities

Modern great powers are commonly classified as the G7, Russia and India, although this is by no means an objectively 'true' categorisation, merely the general consensus of political theorists.

2. Superpowers:

The term 'superpower' emerged in the aftermath of the Second World War to describe the two main protagonists of the Cold War; the USA and the Soviet Union.

After WWII, the traditional European powers had been heavily damaged. Germany, being on the losing side of the war, was occupied by Britain, France, the USA and the USSR. However, Britain and France, even though they were 'victors' were significantly weakened and lost their global empires in the decades that followed. It was in this power vacuum that the USA and the Soviet Union emerged as leading states of the new global system. The USA and the Soviet Union were immediately distinguished as more powerful than all other states by their possession of nuclear weapons (the USA in 1945, the Soviets in 1949), which had the capacity to wipe entire cities from the map. Although other countries also later gained nuclear weapons, the US and Soviet arsenals were orders of magnitude higher. Although the growth rates of the Soviet economy lagged far behind most Western European economies (Britain and France for example), Soviet military expenditure was orders of magnitude higher, which meant that a Soviet invasion of Western Europe was always an imminent threat. The Soviet and American economies were the largest in the world by some margin throughout the Cold War. In 1989, Soviet GDP was $2.5 trillion and US GDP was $4.8 trillion.

Both sides were not averse to supporting brutal regimes or violent rebellions, if they aligned with their ideological aims. The USA was particularly active in supporting anti-Communist dictatorships in Central America (Guatemala, Nicaragua) whilst the Soviets were active across South America and Africa, especially in post-colonial countries. Nearly every major state acted as an arena for some form of US-Soviet rivalry. Most wars fought in the Cold War era were backed by the USA, the Soviets, or both (Korea, Vietnam, Chile, Afghanistan, Arab-Israeli conflicts). Even where no actual wars took place, both sides attempted to gain an advantage over the other – e.g. the USA's stationing of Jupiter missiles in Turkey, and the Soviets' retaliatory stationing of missiles in Cuba.

Both countries established military bases across the globe – achieving a reach of military power that only the British Empire had come close to in the early 20th century. Rival alliance systems were created, under which all other major states were subsumed. For the USA, this was NATO; for the Soviets, this was the Warsaw Pact. Even with Britain and France's acquisition of nuclear weapons, they remained under the NATO umbrella and reliant on American support. The USA and the Soviets also dominated international institutions such as the United Nations and took leading roles as part of the P5. The two established rival global economic paradigms, with the US championing the free market and the Soviets extensively propping up Communist states such as Cuba and North Korea.

More generally, therefore, we can distinguish between 'great powers' and 'superpowers':

Great power	Superpower
Significant capabilities that match several other 'great powers' in scope and potential	Overwhelming capabilities that only one or two other powers can match in scope and potential
Ability to project power (hard or soft) in some areas of the globe beyond their 'home' region	Ability to project power (hard and soft) in all areas of the globe beyond their 'home' region
Has independent interests, objectives and aims to other 'great powers' in the global system	Is able to coerce/convince other 'great powers' to align with its interests, objectives and aims
Some control of global institutions and networks – one voice amongst other great powers	Dominant role in global institutions and networks – directs other 'great powers'

Some would argue that after the end of the Cold War that the USA was a 'hyperpower' – we shall later assess if this appellation is warranted.

3. Emerging powers:

The term 'emerging power' has been utilised since the early 21st century to describe states which have newly acquired levels of power which could be projected beyond a regional scale, but have not previously held such power in the last few generations. Russia is somewhat an exception to this, given that it existed in a markedly different political and territorial form (the Soviet Union) for the majority of the 20th century. It is generally agreed that an emerging power must have a growing economy giving the state the potential to be an important global actor. An 'emerging power' may *be* or eventually *become* a great power or a superpower. 'Emerging' is therefore more a description of the direction in which a state's power is travelling rather than a description of where it currently is.

The main states classified as emerging powers today are the BRIC nations (Brazil, Russia, India and China). The group sometimes also includes South Africa as 'BRICS'. All of these have begun to expand their economic, cultural, military and political influence beyond their borders due to two significant recent global developments:

- **Globalisation:** As we have discussed in the previous sub-unit, globalisation has created an interconnected international economy with trade now accounting for 70% of global GDP. Countries with considerable natural resources and manufacturing sectors (such as Brazil and China) or tech/services sectors that can be easily outsourced to (India), can take advantage of this and immensely boost their economies as a whole (although internal inequality may persist). This increased economic clout allows a country to invest more in the military, and to exert influences on other states through new international organisations

- **Post-2001 changes:** Post 9/11, the 'War on Terror' and the 2008 financial crash, Western economies have suffered greatly, as has the willingness of Western states to intervene meaningfully on a global stage. This has allowed other 'emerging powers' to fill the vacuum in places that the USA seems to have 'abandoned' as its sphere of influence – particularly Russia and China in the Middle East and Asia. It has also meant that the role of the BRIC nations has increased in institutions like the IMF, World Bank and G20

The BRIC nations have the *potential* to become superpowers given their populations, access to significant natural resources, and technological quality. Other emerging powers may be identified that do not have the potential to become superpowers, but could definitely extend influence beyond their immediate region. These include many members of the G20 (Mexico, Nigeria, Indonesia, Saudi Arabia, South Korea, Turkey), which is beginning to be seen as more important than the G7 in many circles of international politics. In particular, Turkey under Erdogan has shown a desire to expand its influence further afield from home, with military action in the Afrin region of Syria to expel Kurdish forces, and intervention in the Nagorno-Karabakh conflict on the side of Azerbaijan; as well as significant investments Somalian infrastructure and an increasingly vocal claim to global leadership of the Islamic world. Saudi Arabia has used its 'petro-dollars' to expand its influence across the Middle East, funding madrassas to spread its ideology as far away as Pakistan and Afghanistan, and investing considerable sums in global 'PR' to improve the diplomatic connections of Saudi Arabia with Western states.

POLARITY
Polarity, or world order, is a description of the distribution of power and authority amongst state actors in the international system. When describing systems of polarity, a 'pole' is a major state which has the power to define and achieve its objectives independently and on a global scale. There are three main systems of polarity:

1. **Unipolarity:** A system with one single pre-eminent state (a **hegemon**) in global politics, which is relatively unconstrained and has no serious rivals (either as individual states or alliance blocs). All other states 'tend towards' the pole, either willingly or reluctantly

2. **Bipolarity:** A system revolving around two major states, with other states clustering around one of the two dominant states to form 'blocs'. Between the two blocs, a near-equal balance of power exists and neither is able to challenge the other decisively

3. **Multipolarity:** A system with three or more states with significant global power, which have independent interests and goals. They constrain each other and none are able to decisively affect the actions of the others alone (although they may cooperate to do so)

We can now illustrate these systems of polarity with historical examples, and consider what realists and liberals might say about each of them – especially in terms of how stable they are.

1. **The C19th British Empire (unipolarity):** After the end of the Napoleonic Wars against France in the early 1800s, there was a period of relative peace *between the great powers* of Europe. During this period (1815-1890), around 26 million km^2 of territory and 400 million people were incorporated into the British Empire through conquest. Britain had no other serious rivals, apart from perhaps Russia in Central Asia. When Russia tried to expand its influence in the Balkans (south-east Europe), Britain fought the Crimean War to preserve the Ottoman Empire and force Russia out of the Balkans. Britain's global dominance was based on the unchallenged sea power of the Royal Navy; its control of world trade; the use of new technologies like the telegraph; and global banking networks which gave it an 'informal empire' across China and South America in addition to its former colonies.

   - **Realists** would say that unipolarity is the ideal system of polarity for international relations. The existence of a global hegemon allows it to act as a *de facto* sovereign and establish a worldwide peace through force of arms. In the absence of challengers, the hegemon can utilise both hard and soft power to achieve a unitary set of objectives. During the 19th century, the British Empire was instrumental in eradicating the Trans-Atlantic slave trade (albeit after doing a great deal to spread it in the first place)

   - **Liberals** would say that unipolarity is dangerous, because the existence of an unconstrained hegemon is equivalent to a global tyranny. For liberals, peace is generated through cooperation, but if the hegemon can do whatever it wants without repercussions, then it will disregard concerns about human rights, the legitimacy of war, poverty, the rights of other states, etc. During the 19th century, there were millions of deaths from famine and colonialism in Britain's Empire across Africa and Asia

2. **The Cold War (bipolarity):** The classic example of a bipolar system was the Cold War between two roughly equal blocs, NATO and the Warsaw Pact, dominated by the USA and the Soviet Union respectively. They were matched militarily,

with combined armed forces of similar strengths and enough nuclear warheads that they if they were to launch them, mutually assured destruction (MAD) would ensue. Although other important states existed, they were largely subordinate to the interests of either the USA or the Soviet Union. Western Europe, for example, was rebuilt by $13.3bn of US aid (the Marshall Plan) after WWII and was financially tied to the USA. The two states also competed politically and economically, embracing opposing ideologies; (sometimes liberal and democratic) capitalism vs (generally authoritarian) communism. In Europe, the two were literally divided by a physical wall running through Berlin, separating Communist East Berlin from pro-capitalist West Berlin.

- **Realists** would argue that bipolarity is a natural tendency in the world order and is stable, like unipolarity. States seek to establish such a balance to curb the hegemonic ambitions of other states. By establishing a balance of power, either major state is less likely to seek hegemony because they anticipate being countered by the other bloc. The ensuing equilibrium generates peace and stability because of rational fear of the costs of conflict. During the Cold War, neither the USA nor the Soviet Union launched direct attacks on each other or dared to use nuclear weapons, keeping the rivalry relatively 'cold'

- **Liberals** would argue that bipolarity is more stable than unipolarity, but still not ideal. This is because unforeseeable circumstances (domestic revolution, natural disaster, economic collapse, etc.) may at some point give one of the dominant states in the bipolar system the ability to emerge as a hegemon. The competition between the two blocs means that more resources are invested into military rivalry and arms races, and there is a lack of proper global integration in terms of trade and common institutions (preventing the emergence of a Kantian peace)

3. **The interwar years, 1920-1939 (multipolarity):** After the end of WWI, there was a relatively multipolar system which many powerful states – principally the UK, France, Italy, Japan, Germany, the USSR and the USA. In the 1920s, no state

really had the capacity to dominate another with ease; any conflict would be at great cost and with an uncertain outcome. Even Germany, the weakest of the powers (after losing WWI) was able to stave off a French invasion and occupation of the Ruhr industrial region. There was an attempt to construct a multinational 'League of Nations' to solve disputes in international relations rather than resorting to force; global trade boomed as a result of the post-war recovery; and there was a concerted effort to tackle poverty, slavery, child labour, and pandemics

- **Realists** would argue that multipolarity is the least stable system of international relations; because states are always self-interested and amoral actors, they will seek an advantage over other states where it can be gained. Because the system is so finely balanced, even a few states building up an alliance bloc to 'pool' their power can upset the balance of power and lead to conflict. As the number of powerful actors increases, so does the number of possible conflicts due to the security dilemma. Realists would argue the breakdown of the multipolar interwar system after the Great Depression (1929 onwards), and the rise of Nazi Germany, Fascist Italy and Imperial Japan were what lead to WWII – there was no strong hegemon to counter them and maintain 'peace' and those states felt that they had a rational chance of achieving global dominance

- **Liberals** would argue that multipolarity is the most preferable system of polarity – it means that states are forced to co-operate with each other, because no one state has sufficient power that it can wield unilaterally. There is no one hegemonic *de facto* sovereign to impose its will and global solutions on other states, so the only way to solve issues like poverty; conflict; human rights; environmental crises, etc. is for states to work together to build some kind of interdependent international architecture. The potential gains of conflict are negligible, whereas the potential gains of cooperation are significant. In the 1920s, France and Germany (despite having been enemies in WWI) collaborated to settle disputes over reparations/payments and their post-war borders, because they recognised neither was powerful enough to 'enforce' a solution on the other

GLOBAL POLITICS SINCE 2000
The End of History?
When the Cold War ended in the late 1980s/early 1990s, the Soviet Union collapsed into a number of successor republics. It was widely accepted that the USA had become the dominant global hegemon or hyperpower and some went so far as to argue that this signalled a 'new world order' and the 'End of History'. The hallmarks of this system were:

- Free trade and reduced barriers/tariffs
- Increased democratisation globally
- Imposition of a 'human rights regime'
- Global rejection of communist policies

Of course, unipolar systems had existed in history before (globally and regionally). What theorists like Fukuyama argued was different about the American-led system was that it relied on *institutions* and *values* to a degree that previous unipolar systems hadn't; this meant that even if the USA itself was to collapse or become less powerful, the enduring institutions that it established would maintain a global consensus on liberalism, democracy and capitalism.

Events since 2000 may suggest that the declaration of American hegemony, permanent unipolarity and the 'end of history' have been somewhat premature.

Current great powers and superpowers
In terms of assessing the polarity of the current global system since 2000, we should consider whether each major state can be considered a 'superpower', a 'great power' or neither.

- If there is only one superpower (the USA), then the global system is by definition unipolar
- If there are two (China or Russia, in addition to the USA), then the global system is bipolar

- If there are three or more superpowers (the USA, China and Russia), or no superpowers and many great powers (the above, and/or Brazil, India, the EU), then the system is multipolar

This discussion inherently includes some degree of speculation about the 'direction' in which the power of states will evolve in the future based on current trends. Although extrapolating from existing data is a core part of politics as an academic discipline, we must be cautious of the limitations of this approach and the fact that existing trends do not necessarily confirm future developments.

The main criteria that we will analyse to determine whether a state is a superpower, a great power or neither are (i) economic power; (ii) military power; (iii) institutional power; and (iv) soft power. It is important to remember that as well as possessing power/ capabilities, a state must be able to *project* them beyond its immediate region or on a global scale to be deemed a great power or superpower. A state with capabilities which lacks the *ability* or the *will* to project its power globally cannot really be deemed a great power or a superpower.

Japan – the superpower that never was
In the late 1980s and early 1990s, Japan's economic growth was tracking along strongly with the USA's and many predicted that it was on course to overtake the USA as the world's largest economy by the early 2000s. Japan had spawned many major corporate giants – Mitsubishi, Toyota, Mizuho, Sumimoto – and had far-reaching cultural and diplomatic influence. Although Japan did not possess nuclear weapons (having disavowed them after WWII), they make extensive use of civilian nuclear power and had the 5th-most powerful military in the world. After the collapse of the Soviet Union, a common view was that a bipolar American-Japanese world was emerging, and some even thought that Japan's growing power would lead to a second Pacific War with the USA.

However, Japan suffered from a significant crash in growth in 1994/95 which it still has not fully recovered from. These two 'Lost Decades' were caused by (i) an asset price bubble and stock market crash; (ii) excessive lending and interference by Japan's central bank; (iii) an ageing population and a declining young workforce.

Japan's failure to live up to its historical superpower potential does not prove that all superpower competitors to the USA are doomed to fail, but it does indicate that we should be careful about predictions that we make about the potential of the BRIC nations (Brazil, Russia, India and China).

Case studies

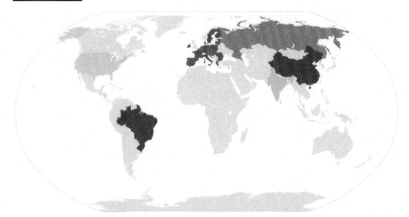

Yellow = USA, Red = China, Orange = Russia, Green = India, Purple = Brazil, Blue = EU

The United States of America

The USA has consistently been at the forefront of global politics since the early 20th century. It increased in power significantly at the end of WWII – when the European powers were decimated and it moved in to fill the global power vacuum along with the Soviet Union. It increased in power again significantly at the end of the Cold War, when the Soviet Union collapsed and the USA was left (at least in the 1990s) as a sole global 'hyperpower'.

Evidence of the USA's superpower status	Limitations of the USA's power/projection
Economic: • As of 2019, the USA's GDP is $21.43 trillion, the highest in	Economic: • The US economy did experience severe difficulties

the world. Its GDP per capita is just over $65,000. The USA's GDP represents about a quarter of the world's total

- The USA's population (over 320 million) is large and relatively highly educated, with more than 80% living in urban areas – these are all indicators of a highly developed economy
- The US dollar is the currency most used in international transactions and is the world's foremost reserve currency, backed by faith in the US economy. The USA's economy is fuelled by abundant natural resources (valued at $45 trillion in total), a well-developed infrastructure, and high productivity
- Silicon Valley in California has been, over the past few decades, the main global hub for digital technology and companies like Apple, Google, Facebook and Visa. Of the world's 500 largest companies, 134 are headquartered in the USA
- The USA is also home to the world's largest financial markets, especially in New

as a result of the 2008 financial crisis but has since recovered

- A potential problem for future economic growth is Trump's damaging trade war with China, which crippled US agriculture and has still not yet been fully resolved – there are many outstanding tariffs which the Biden Administration has not yet removed
- Another problem for future American economic growth is a significant rise in the national debt as a result of Trump's tax cuts for the very wealthy and a reduction in necessary government spending. It remains to be seen whether the Biden Administration will substantially reverse this
- The impact of the covid-19 pandemic, worsened in the USA because of the Trump Administration's lacklustre response, may have serious consequences for the American economy going forwards if people's spending power drops substantially and the country tips into long-term recession

York and Chicago – foreign investments made in the US total almost $2.4 trillion annually	• Finally, it is worth noting that climate change would inflict extreme economic and human costs on some parts of the USA (hurricanes, floods, wildfires)
Military: • The USA possesses the world's most technologically advanced military, with a truly global reach (spending more than the next ten countries *combined* -$732 billion in 2019, representing 38% of global total military spending) • It has made increasing use of UAVs (Unmanned Aerial Vehicle), more commonly known as 'drones', to carry out surveillance and bombing raids abroad with minimal risk to US soldiers • The USA maintains a stockpile of nearly 7000 nuclear warheads, some of which are carried at sea on submarines and others of which are based on land in the USA in missile siloes • The US navy is the largest in the world and has 'blue-water' capability – it is able to operate anywhere in any ocean in the world, even far from US	Military: • Despite the fact that the USA spends more on its military than the next 10 states combined, its military power is not 'invincible' or always effective • The US military is inherently limited against other nuclear powers, which means that it cannot act effectively against Russia and China, or indeed the North Korean dictatorship. It would be difficult to see, for example, how the US military could feasibly counteract a Chinese invasion of Taiwan – which increasingly seems to be on the cards! • Arguably, the US military has not yet fully adapted to the demands of 'modern' forms of war, including controlling insurgencies, countering guerrilla tactics and seeking to suppress more intractable rebellions

shores. This is largely because of the 20 nuclear-powered aircraft carriers operated by the US Navy, which can travel across the ocean for 20 years continuously without refuelling • The USA also maintains over 800 military bases across the planet staffed by 160,000 personnel, with the majority concentrated in the Caribbean, the Middle East, Europe, and Japan/ South Korea (the last two as a counterweight to China and North Korea)	• In particular, the USA was unable to fully excise the Taliban from Afghanistan (Trump caved and signed a peace deal with them in 2020); and intervention in Iraq, although the immediate aim of overthrowing Saddam Hussein's regime was achieved, led to a failed state fractured along ethno-religious lines and the rise of extremist groups like IS when the USA proved unable to suppress the Baathist insurgency and an extension of Iranian influence via militias and proxies
Institutional: • The USA exerts global political influence as the chief architect of international political and economic institutions, many of which are headquartered on American soil (e.g. the UN in New York; the IMF and World Bank in Washington DC) • The USA has a 17% vote share in the IMF, exercising an effective veto; and has an official veto in the P5 of the United Nations Security Council	Institutional: • The USA has somewhat withdrawn from global cooperative projects between 2016-2020 under the Trump Administration, including the Paris Climate Agreement and ceasing funding for the World Health Organisation; and threats to withdraw from NATO, NAFTA and other organisations • Although the Biden Administration has begun to restore these relations, it is

• Given that English is the most widely spoken second-language in the world, the USA has a huge advantage in international activity	unclear whether Trump's presidency has done lasting damage to the USA's foreign alliances and relationships • The USA has less influence in the G20 as an institution of global governance
Soft power: • The USA has achieved global cultural prominence through the products that it exports worldwide – cars, electronics (Apple, Microsoft), digital platforms (Amazon), food (McDonalds, Starbucks) and the entertainment industry (music, Hollywood) • In cultural terms, one could argue that the USA's values of freedom, democracy, capitalism and human rights have become deeply embedded in most systems and institutions of global governance, and have been adopted (sometimes superficially) by most states as governing principles domestically • The US is able to exert soft power to encourage other states to make liberalising reforms, e.g. Saudi Arabia's	Soft power: • One could argue that there has been a serious backlash to the Americanisation of culture and that the USA's attempt to politically reshape parts of the world in its image have failed. In particular, the emergence of groups like Al-Qaeda and ISIS, as well as the (Islamic Republic of) Iran to a much lesser extent, promote a fundamentalist view of Islam and authoritarianism and reject American hegemony • The USA has struggled to extend its soft power influence against effective digital disinformation campaigns waged by China and Russia • The growth of partisan political divisions in the USA, including the threat of white supremacism, may undermine America's soft power

recent freeing of feminist activists	

China

Since 2000, China has made massive strides forwards and many predict that the 21st century will be a 'Chinese century', in which China regains the global predominance that it enjoyed for millennia before the rise of the modern West between the 17th-20th centuries, when the age of European colonialism coincided with stagnation in China under the Qing dynasty. For most of the period 1950-1980, China's internal situation was still very unstable because of Mao Zedong's governance, but reforms under his successor Deng Xiaoping began the process of China's reawakening.

Evidence of China's superpower status	Limitations of China's power/projection
Economic: • China's GDP is currently $14.34 trillion; it overtook Japan as the world's second-largest economy in 2009 and is on track to overtake the USA in less than 15 years if it maintains its growth rates of 8-10% a year (compared to 2-4% for most Western states). The Chinese economy has grown 90-fold since 1978 and lifted 800 million individuals out of poverty (this is the single largest state contribution to global poverty reduction) • China has the largest population in the world at	Economic: • One potential problem with China's economy is that the model is based on cheap labour and manufacturing; if cheaper labour is provided in other states (e.g. India?) this might lead to TNCs outsourcing there instead • The one-child policy (designed to prevent overpopulation) was successful in lowering birth rates but has now led to a rapidly ageing population which might have serious consequences for China's economy similar to those

nearly 1.4 billion (around 1/6 of the global total); this means it maintains a sizeable manufacturing workforce and a growing middle-class consumer market with more disposable income to spend on goods and services • China weathered the 2008 Financial Crisis and 2020 coronavirus pandemic with relative ease, being one of the few countries in the world to consistently run a surplus (spending less than it earns in tax revenue) • China is rich in mineral resources like rare-earth metals (needed for electronic components); China effectively has a controlling stake in the global market for these key minerals and has recently floated the idea of curbing exports to cripple the US defence industry	already being experienced in Japan • The failure to transition to a high-tech 'innovation' economy – a lot of Chinese products are based on imitating foreign technologies, like Huawei – would be damaging to the Chinese economy • Another general issue is that the docility of China's population, despite a lack of political rights, is based on the government's delivery of consistent economic growth and living standards. If this were to slow significantly, it is possible that the authoritarian government would face serious civil unrest and the current political model would break down (conversely it is possible the government would simply crush any democratic protests with force, as with the 1989 Tiananmen Square protests)
Military: • China became a nuclear power in 1964, and has the second-largest military in the world behind the USA	Military: • China's defence spending still lags considerably behind the USA's – in 2019, China spent $261 billion on military-related

- Recently under Xi Jinping's premiership, the Chinese military has been rapidly modernising and building aircraft carriers to better project Chinese power beyond its immediate regional waters. Currently, China has two aircraft carriers (one, Liaoning, was converted from a decommissioned Soviet model in 2012; and a second, domestically-developed carrier, Shandong, deployed in 2020)
- China has increased its military presence in the South China Sea, creating new islands and bases, to reinforce its claims to fishing rights; oil rights; strategic shipping lanes; and to Taiwan, which it maintains is an integral part of Chinese territory instead of a separate state
- China has also begun to develop technologies for advanced warfare; in 2007, using a targeted missile system to shoot down one of its old satellites – this could be used as the basis for missile-interception technology

outlays, whereas the USA spent $732 billion. The USA's navy and air force are more technologically advanced than China's, meaning in any global conflict, the USA would have the upper hand
- The PLA (People's Liberation Army) was 'designed' for large-scale land warfare; indeed, this was its initial role in the Chinese Civil War and in the Korean War of the 1950s. It has engaged in small skirmishes with the Indian army on the Himalayan frontier, but otherwise has not been tested properly in combat. Many observers comment that it is a sizeable, but technologically inferior force to the US
- The PLA currently does not have the global reach of military bases that the US army has – it only has one operational centre in Djibouti, a small East African country bordering the Red Sea. However, it is considering constructing facilities in Myanmar, Pakistan, Sri Lanka,

- China is also a world leader in cyberwarfare and digital technology – between 2010 and 2012, China penetrated the CIA's encoded communication system amongst the CIA's network of Chinese spies and arrested/ killed all 30 (perhaps more) CIA assets in the country

the UAE, Angola, Kenya, Tanzania and Cambodia
- China does not yet have the military force to fulfil certain regional strategic objectives, such as the integration of Taiwan into China. For now, the threat of American intervention is enough to deter the Chinese government from attempting a forceful annexation

Institutional:
- China is a permanent member of the UN Security Council and has often exercised its veto power (in Syria, Xinjiang and Myanmar)
- China has increased its influence in the UN – 4 out of the 15 'specialised' UN agencies are now run by Chinese officials, elected by the General Assembly (often running directly against US-backed candidates)
- China has created alternative institutional models to challenge existing aspects of the 'Western' international order – e.g. the Shanghai Pact (involving Russia, most of Central Asia, India and

Institutional:
- Although China has become much more powerful in recent decades, the core argument that its power will always be constrained is that the systems that it is growing within are systems which were created by the West and the USA – i.e. China has become more powerful by accepting the institutions of capitalist liberal democracy
- Some make the argument (although it is vanishingly unlikely) that China's adoption of liberal capitalist economics to drive its immense economic growth will eventually be accompanied by a democratic transformation, and that

Pakistan) which cooperates to shield member-states from human rights criticisms; and the Asian Infrastructure Investment Bank (AIIB) to rival the World Bank and IMF • China played a key role in the 2015 Paris Agreement and effectively 'kept it alive' during Trump's presidency • China utilises agencies like the WHO to delegitimise Taiwan by pressuring the WHO to not recognise Taiwan's very successful covid-19 response	institutions will change China rather than China changing institutions • China is still outweighed on the P5 of the UN Security Council by the 'liberal Western' alliance bloc of the USA, the UK and France • Western developed countries have a far greater combined vote share in the IMF than China, which restricts its institutional power in global economics • Most institutions of global governance are still based in the West
Soft power: • China is an emerging soft power nation; it has the largest diplomatic network in the world (overtaking the USA in 2019) • China has constructed several hundred 'Confucius Institutes' around the world to teach Chinese language and culture • China is the most popular country in Asia for international students, and the leading destination globally for African students. Increasing	Soft power: • China's current iteration of soft power is more limited than most of the Western world, because it was very closed-off and isolationist during the Mao Zedong years and has only really started 'opening up' since the 1990s • China's soft power strategy has yielded limited results in the West, India and Japan (although it has been successful in Latin America and

ties with Africa have been accompanied by lucrative trade deals (e.g. 1/3 of China's oil supply comes from Angola) • China's extension of humanitarian, health, academic and professional aid programmes to Africa has greatly expanded their presence in the continent, including the funding for the construction of the African Union HQ • China's 'anti liberal' values of Confucianism – order, loyalty and social cohesion – are attractive to many regimes in the Middle East and Africa	Africa), which are concerned with China's wider ambitions • China's increasingly nationalistic focus has limited the universal appeal of the 'Chinese Dream' and the impact of its spread to neighbouring countries – e.g. the Philippines and Vietnam • The scale of censorship in China means that most of China's soft power is generated by the government rather than spontaneously by individuals, the private sector and 'civil society' – this limits the speed at which soft power can be generated compared to the West

Russia

After the fall of the Soviet Union in the early 1990s, the former USSR dissolved into its constituent republics, of which Russia was the largest. In the 1990s, Russia was riven by internal political problems, separatism in southern provinces with majority-Muslim populations, corruption, slow economic growth and other social problems. Collectively, these prevented Russia from projecting its power beyond its immediate region since it was more concerned with dealing with domestic issues. Since 2000, when Vladimir Putin was elected as President (he has ruled ever since despite constitutional term limits), Russia has begun to project its power abroad once more.

Evidence of Russia's superpower status	Limitations of Russia's power/projection

Economic:

- Russia has extensive natural resources, but these remained largely untapped during the communist era. With the advent of a capitalist economy, there is both the incentive to exploit these resources more fully and access foreign investment to do so
- Some estimates hold that Russia possesses about 30% of the world's mineral resources, equivalent to a total value of $75 trillion (obviously this cannot all be extracted all at once). In particular, Russia is abundant in oil, natural gas and precious metals
- Russia's position as an energy superpower gives it great influence, as many countries have increasing energy needs that cannot be met domestically. The Russian state-owned company Gazprom exports natural gas to Europe through a number of subsidiaries, accounting for about 39% of the EU's natural gas imports via 12 pipelines, as well as 30% of the EU's petroleum imports. Eastern

Economic:

- Given Russia's size, population and natural resources, its GDP ($1.7 trillion) is remarkably low. This places it 11th in the global rankings, below Italy, France, South Korea and Canada and only marginally above Brazil and Australia
- There are deep-rooted problems in the Russian economy; it is unusually dependent on natural resources, which constitute 70% of its total exports, and there is relatively little high-tech industry. This makes it very dependent on fluctuations in the world market, and initial projections suggest a significant hit from the covid-19 pandemic
- This also means that sanctions on Russia can be especially damaging when levied on natural resource exports; G7 and EU sanctions in the aftermath of the Russian annexation of Crimea in 2014 triggered a run on the rouble (the Russian currency) and a financial crisis which lasted

Europe is especially dependent – more than 75% of Estonian, Polish and Slovakian oil originates from Russia. Putin has in the past (2015) threatened to cut off gas supplies to the European Union if they intervened in the Ukrainian crisis • It is also worth noting that with global warming and the melting of the permafrost which covers most of Siberia (the vast frozen wastelands that cover most Russian territory), Russia will become the world's foremost agricultural nation, and also be able to access previously untapped reserves of oil, gas and minerals currently trapped in the frozen permafrost ground	from 2014-2017. Inflation peaked at 13% • There is significant corruption in the Russian economy – approximately 15% is unregulated and untaxed as a 'shadow economy' due to tax evasion, mafia activity, bribery, etc. • The dominance of the oligarch class and their tendency to work with law enforcement and the government to secure favourable trade deals and crush competitors discourages foreign investment in Russia and sustainable economic growth in the long term • Wealth inequality in Russia is extreme, with 16% of Russians in poverty despite significant wealth in the capital, Moscow. This is already leading to political instability and protests
Military: • Russia has a large and sophisticated arms industry, capable of designing and manufacturing high-tech military equipment, including a fifth-generation stealth fighter jet (the Sukhoi Su-57), nuclear	Military: • Investment in the Russian military is steadily falling behind NATO and China; although Russia inherited excellent military capacity from the Soviet Union and has built on this, its relative

submarines, firearms, and approximately 7,300 nuclear missiles

- The value of Russian arms exports totalled $15.7 billion in 2013—second only to the US. Top military exports from Russia include combat aircraft, air defence systems, ships and submarines
- Putin's Russia has been increasingly assertive in conflicts abroad, intervening in Georgia (2008), Crimea (2014) and providing ongoing support to Assad's regime in Syria since 2015, in the form of missile strikes, air cover, and some troops on the ground
- Since the US withdrawal from Syria, Russia has taken over many former US bases in Syrian Kurdish territory. In the Syrian conflict, Russia's goals were opposed to those of the USA under Barack Obama; after Russian intervention, the USA was unwilling to meaningfully intervene as they did not wish to risk war with Russia
- Russia, like China, has also invested significantly in

economic underdevelopment prevents it from improving its military at the same speed as other states

- It could be reasonably argued that Russia is not a military superpower, as it no longer has 'global' reach in its military operations as the USSR did. Instead, it focuses on the immediate peripheral regions of Russia (Central Asia; Iran and Syria as Middle Eastern allies; the Caucasus – Armenia and Azerbaijan; and Ukraine). It is a regional, rather than a global power
- Russia only has one aircraft carrier, which limits the capacity of its air force and navy – its naval power has been described as facing a terminal collapse
- It could also be argued that Russia is not a superpower, in that it cannot effectively achieve its own objectives, but is rather a 'spoiler state' – serving as an obstacle to the USA achieving its aims without actively extending Russia's own sphere of influence

cyberwarfare and has pursued 'sharp power' in its use of disinformation (e.g. successful attempts to spread conspiracies denying chemical weapons attacks by Assad against Syrian civilians), propaganda and digital manipulation of foreign elections	• Clashes (some direct, some by proxy) between Turkey and Russia in – Syria; the Nagorno-Karabakh War between Armenia and Azerbaijan; and Libya; have shown that Russia's military capacity is far from unchallengeable and that its military hardware may be outdated and vulnerable
Institutional: • Russia inherited the Soviet seat on the P5 of the Security Council and has exercised the veto a number of times to prevent criticism of its actions in Crimea and Syria, as well as to protect its ally, Bashar Assad • Russia is a member of the G20 and also of Eurasian political associations like the Shanghai Pact and the Commonwealth of Independent States which shield member-states from criticism of human rights abuses	Institutional: • Russia was expelled from the G8 (now the G7) as a result of its intervention and annexation of Crimea from Ukraine in 2014. This has limited its ability to influence top-level economic discussion • Russia has played a limited role in major discussions on climate change and was a reluctant signatory to Paris • The collapse of the Warsaw Pact means that Russia does not have any considerable institutional counterweight to NATO's expansion
Soft power: • Russia has increasingly deployed smart power capabilities through the funding of foreign media	Soft power: • Russia's recent aggression has substantially damaged its soft power. Only 4 countries (Vietnam, Ghana, China and

outlets, and their own broadcasting channels (e.g. RT – Russia Today) to shape global perceptions • Russia's hosting of the 2018 FIFA World Cup boosted its cultural power	Russia) have a positive view (50% or above) of Russia • Russia has been banned from the Olympics for state-sponsored doping

India

India has never been considered a great power or superpower, given that it has never really attempted to project its power beyond the subcontinent. India's foreign policy has traditionally concerned with countering Pakistan as a regional threat and stabilising other nearby states like Sri Lanka. Recently, India has become more assertive on a global level and this is contributing to a perception that it has already or will soon emerge as a 'great power' on the global stage.

Evidence of India's great power status	Limitations of India's power/projection
Economic: • India has become the sixth-largest economy in the world, generally thanks to its limited dependence on exports, high savings rates (and very low budget deficit), fast-growing population of mainly young people (which avoids the dependency issue of an ageing population faced by some other countries), and a thriving middle class in major cities like Mumbai, Delhi, Kolkata and Hyderabad	Economic: • Widespread social inequality, malnutrition and poverty are limiting factors of India's economy, with the majority of the population still engaged in subsistence-level agriculture • Low literacy rates (only 61% nationwide) and poor education, especially in rural areas and amongst women, limit India's human capacity for economic growth and development

• India has become a world leader in high-tech sectors like computer software and biotechnology, somewhat bypassing the 'China-model' of becoming the 'workshop of the world' for cheaply manufactured goods • The fastest-growing part of the Indian economy are Business Process Outsourcing (BOP) and software services, and India is the third-largest start-up hub in the world with over 3,000 technology start-ups per year • As a result, India has achieved briefly overtook China as the fastest-growing economy in the world in 2015 (although China overtook it again in 2018) hovering around 7% growth annually over the last decade	• Poor government policies, such as Modi's demonetisation of high-value notes; inflexible labour laws; and market-distorting subsidies prevent efficient economic growth • Widespread excess bureaucracy and rampant corruption hampers the financial ability of individuals and companies across the country • Rising sectarian tensions as a result of an increasingly vocal Hindu-supremacist nationalist BJP government have led to financially disruptive clashes between the government and citizens, such as (i) Kashmir/Assam, due to the government's Citizenship Act and National Register of Citizens proposals; (ii) in Delhi and Punjab as a result of proposed reforms to farming
Military: • India has the second-largest military in the world, with over 1.4 million active personnel and soldiers • India has invested heavily in missile defence system and	Military: • India has been unable to completely secure control of Kashmir from Pakistan, or Aksai Chin from China • In a 2019 dispute, Pakistan managed to shoot down an

also possesses nuclear weapons, which deters any major invasion by regional competitors • India has comprehensively defeated Pakistan in every major war they have ever fought since independence	Indian fighter jet and capture the pilot alive, showing the limitations of India's air force • India is vulnerable to asymmetric warfare (terrorism), such as the 2008 Mumbai attacks by Lashkar-e-Taiba
Institutional: • India is a member of the G20, giving it a leading role in shaping macroeconomic policies affecting the developed/ middle-income world • India is a founder and leading member of the South Asian Association for Regional Cooperation (SAARC), which gives it a degree of regional power • India has served as a non-permanent member of the UNSC eight times (i.e. a total of 16 years out of 75 years of the UN's existence, over a fifth)	Institutional: • India does not have a seat on the P5 of the UN Security Council, and is not a member of the G7 bloc • India's institutional power in regional and global organisations is blunted by opposition from China, which views India as a major economic competitor • India's role in major negotiations is largely obstructive rather than productive, designed to protect weak domestic sectors (e.g. agriculture – 56% of India's workforce but 18% of GDP)
Soft power: • India has a growing arsenal of soft power globally, largely through the mediums of culture and music (Bollywood,	Soft power: • It is possible that Narendra Modi and the BJP's hardline style of nationalist governance has undermined much of

bhangra, yoga, food etc.) and sport (especially cricket). Many Indian students study abroad in the West, increasing connections between India and the developed world	India's soft power. In particular, the tendency to paint all critics (Rihanna, Greta Thunberg) as secret Muslims, terrorist-sympathisers etc. has damaged perceptions of India's public image

Brazil

Brazil has never been considered a great power or superpower, given that it has never really attempted to project its power beyond South America. Brazil's foreign policy has traditionally been very isolationist, and its internal stability was previously marred by the rule of various military dictatorships. Having established a continuity of relatively stable democratic transitions and beginning to become more assertive on the global stage, some would now argue Brazil is a great power.

Evidence of Brazil's great power status	Limitations of Brazil's power/projection
Economic: <ul><li>Brazil has becoming the leading power in South America. It has the eighth-largest economy in the world, and is rich in natural resources such as iron, gold, uranium and timber. Brazil's estimated reserves of natural resources is around $21.8 trillion</li><li>Brazil also possesses a sizeable agricultural sector, producing foodstuffs that are in high in demand internationally, such</li></ul>	Economic: <ul><li>Brazil's economic growth is not consistent – it decelerated rapidly in 2013 and entered recession in 2014. Coupled with a political crisis that resulted in the impeachment of then-president Dilma Rousseff, Brazil did not recover from the recession until 2017</li><li>Wide social inequality in Brazil and below-average literacy rates limit its economic potential. A large proportion of</li></ul>

as coffee and cocoa, as well as beef. These plantations are generally created in the Amazon • Brazil has a large population of over 200 million, giving it a large domestic market for goods and services	the population live in urban deprivation in *favelas* or slums and the poverty rate has increased recently • Brazil's economic woes mean that its credit rating is only one notch above 'junk', limiting its borrowing capacity
Military: • Brazil has the second-largest military in the Americas behind the USA and Colombia – ahead of Canada/ Mexico • Brazil participates in many UN peacekeeping operations, e.g. it has been active in Haiti since 2004 • Brazil has cooperated with the USA in military terms, allowing the USA to build a base in Brazil in exchange for advanced weapons technology which has boosted Brazil's military capacity • Brazil has the capacity to develop nuclear weapons within a few years if it wanted to do so (it so far hasn't, because it is a signatory of the Non Proliferation Treaty and faces no imminent nuclear threats)	Military: • Facing a lack of regional threats, Brazil's military has struggled to find a role and has never been seriously tested in a combat theatre of war – the last major conflict it was engaged in was the Paraguayan War of 1865 • Brazil's navy is a 'brown-water' rather than a 'green-water' or 'blue-water' navy; it operates primarily in the river zones of the Amazon, and does not have the capacity to conduct operations in Brazil's regional waters or in the global ocean – this limits its power projection • Brazil's most advanced aircraft and weapons are purchased from abroad (primarily the USA and France), limiting the independence of its military

Institutional: • Brazil is a member of the G20, giving it a leading role in shaping macroeconomic policies affecting the developed/ middle-income world • Brazil is a member of MERCOSUR (a South American customs union and trading bloc). As the most powerful member of MERCOSUR, Brazil played a key role in suspending Venezuela's membership after human rights violations by President Maduro's regime; this was made indefinite after a constitutional crisis in Venezuela triggered by Maduro's rigging of the 2018 elections (Brazil supports the opposition leader, Guaido) • Brazil has served as a non-permanent member of the UNSC ten times (i.e. a total of 20 years out of 75 years of the UN's existence, nearly a third)	Institutional: • Brazil has the potential to play a massive role in the implementation of the Paris Agreement, especially since Brazil is home to the majority of the Amazon rainforest. However, the far-right Brazilian President, Jair Bolsonaro, has shown no inclination to adopt environmentalist policies. Indeed, in 2019, there were widespread wildfires across the Amazon – largely as a result of Bolsonaro's expressed desire to open up the Amazon to commercial exploitation, and the subsequent burning down of large tracts of rainforest by cattle ranchers and miners in order to clear the land for 'profitable' activities • Brazil does not have a seat on the P5 of the UN Security Council, and is not a member of the G7 bloc
Soft power: • Brazil has a growing arsenal of soft power globally, largely through the mediums of	Soft power: • It is possible that Jair Bolsonaro's (dubbed the 'Trump of the Tropics') right-

culture and music (samba, Carnival, etc.) and sport (especially football). Brazil recently hosted both the FIFA World Cup (2014) and the Olympics (2016), which gave it a much-increased profile on the world stage	wing government could squander much of the soft power that Brazil has built up over the last few decades by undermining its image as a happy, colourful, exuberant, successful, multiracial democracy

The European Union

The EU is not a singular state, but a regional body which has some state-like characteristics (this is something we will discuss in more depth in the next sub-unit – 3.5 Regionalism and the EU). For the purposes of global politics, some have considered it as a 'pole' when it acts collectively. It has been described as an 'invisible superpower' rivalling the USA and China.

Evidence of the EU's superpower status	Limitations of the EU's power/projection
Economic: • The EU contains many of the world's most prominent and advanced economies (including France, Germany, Italy, Spain, Belgium and the Netherlands). Combined, its economy would be larger than China's and only slightly behind the USA's, with a combined GDP of over $18 trillion • The EU's economy is a single free market with no internal	Economic: • The vast disparity in terms of rates of growth between different national economies in the EU has made the Euro increasingly unstable (e.g. the Greek financial crisis and the austerity measure imposed by the EU to re-stabilise the Euro as a single currency). There is increasing tension between less developed EU countries and Germany, which is

trade barriers, covering over 500 million citizens • 19 member states have joined the Eurozone monetary union which uses the Euro as a single currency, representing 342 million citizens. The Euro is the second largest reserve currency and the second most traded currency in the world • Of the top 500 largest corporations in the world, 161 are headquartered in the EU. The EU has invested in developing poorer regions of the continent (e.g. Romania, Bulgaria and Croatia), and improving infrastructure to provide easier cross-border movement of people, goods and services • The attractiveness of the EU's developed, high-tech economy has led to it concluding numerous free trade deals with other large economies, such as Canada and Japan – the EU is the largest exporter in the world	perceived to 'run' the EU in a dictatorial manner • There are emerging debt crises in Italy and Spain, which may again threaten the integrity of the single-market • The impact shock of Brexit has yet to be fully realised. It is not as bad as the 'hard Brexit' that some feared might happen, but it will still have serious consequences. We can already see tensions arising over the application of the Withdrawal Agreement at the Republic of Ireland – Northern Ireland border, and these will intensify over time. Brexit will not cripple Europe's economic potential entirely, but it may slow growth in the short-term or even lead to other states leaving the EU in the wake of the UK's exit • Because the EU is an inter-state organisation, any decisions on external economic policy (aid, sanctions, etc.) require a high degree of consensus which is not always possible
Military:	Military:

• The EU's constituent member states have some of the world's most technologically advanced militaries, which have been deployed in various conflicts (e.g. Libya and Afghanistan) • The EU has engaged in some collective military action, notably in peacekeeping efforts in North Africa and the suppression of piracy in Somalia • The EU has developed 'Battlegroups' – combined European battalions of 1,500 troops, of which two are operational at any given time, with others on standby. Currently, the two battlegroups are a 'Balkan' BG led by Greece and a 'German' BG (also including many central and northern European states) • France has nuclear weapons, and there are American missiles stationed in many other EU countries, like Germany	• Proposals for a unified EU army have not come to fruition over the past few decades, primarily because of justifiable concerns from states regarding the surrender of a key component of their national sovereignty • Another obstacle to the creation of a European army is the existence of NATO – there is little appetite for creating an institution which would duplicate much of the work of NATO, and it does not make sense for EU states to spend additional money on defence when it is possible to 'pass the burden' onto the USA via NATO • Although EU Battlegroups are a step towards combined operational capacity, full integration is limited by language barriers and differences in the exact type of weaponry used by countries
Institutional:	Institutional:

- Although the EU is not a singular state, it is represented as a singular unified entity (alongside its constituent member states) in the World Trade Organisation, the G20 and the G7
- The political clout of the EU was demonstrated in its negotiations with Iran over the nuclear issue, where it played a key role in convincing Iran to stop enriching uranium in exchange for the lifting of sanctions. Since the USA's re-imposition of sanctions, the EU has collectively maintained a distinct stance and continues to not impose sanctions
- Another example of the EU acting as a unified entity in political negotiations is its membership of the 'Quartet' – the UN, USA, EU and Russia – which has responsibility for mediating the Israeli-Palestinian peace process; it is the largest donor of foreign aid to Palestine
- The EU has other policies of collective action, such as a comprehensive arms embargo
- As with its economic and military power, the key drawback to the EU's exercise of institutional power is not its lack of capabilities but the divisions between the many constituent states of the European Union
- Where states have different aims, it is impossible to get internal consensus to then present a united front in a larger institution of global governance
- For example there are distinct divisions within the EU over nationalism/ how the EU should respond to the Middle Eastern and North African migrant crisis. Some states, especially Italy and Greece, have taken a much more hardline stance than others
- Another division within the EU is the increasing rejection of liberalism and democracy by the 'Visegrad Group' including Hungary and Poland – this damages the EU's wider influence in institutions when it is arguing for a liberal-democratic perspective

to China since the 1989 Tiananmen Square massacre	
Soft power: • The EU exercises soft power as an attractive liberal-democratic, peaceful and successful institution. This encourages other states (e.g. post-Yugoslav Serbia) to change their policies in order to gain admission • Education is another soft power tool in the EU's arsenal – 27 of the world's top 100 universities are in Europe; the EU hosts almost twice as many students from outside the EU than the USA hosts non-Americans, and more than 10-times non-Chinese at Chinese universities • Most of the world's national or second languages are European • EU states dominate soft-power rankings and are globally perceived as happy, clean, lacking in corruption, etc. • EU countries have a great deal of attractive soft power in the case of culture, food, art, music and sports (consider	Soft power: • The attractiveness of the EU's values may be damaged by the recent emergence of far right nationalism in various countries (the Front National in France; the AfD in Germany; Jobbik in Hungary; Golden Dawn in Greece; Law and Justice in Poland; the Brexit project in the UK, etc.). This undermines the perception of the EU as a liberal, tolerant and welcoming place • The EU's soft power does not lead to inevitable outcomes; it was, for example, an ambition of Turkey to join the EU in the early 2000s but it has now clearly decided to carve out its own path under Erdogan and the AKP party, and move away from the liberalising, democratic projects it pursued when trying to gain official candidate status for EU membership • EU soft power has also not been able to successfully rope Russia into a cooperative

how globally dominant Europe's football leagues are compared to the NFL or 'World Series' baseball)	relationship, or to change Russian behaviour in Eastern Europe

An assessment of polarity in 2021

It is important to understand there is no singular, objective 'truth' in response to the question of how global polarity has shifted between 2000 and 2021. A great deal of evidence has been laid out above, but it is possible to draw different conclusions:

- The USA's capabilities and power projection have been weakened since 2000, but they are still the only state with 'superpower' status and so the world remains unipolar

- The rise of China means that the USA is no longer the world's sole superpower – China is also a superpower, and so the global system is now bipolar (Sino-American)

- The resurgence of Russia after a period of post-Cold War weakness, in addition to the rise of China, means that there are now three superpowers in a multipolar system

- The increased unity of the European bloc, in addition to the rise of China, means that there are now three superpowers in a multipolar system

- The USA's power has declined significantly, and with the rise of China, the resurgence of Russia, the increased unity of the European bloc and the gradual emergence of Brazil and India, we are shifting towards what can be described as a *very* distributed multipolar system

Of course, these are also snapshot judgements of the world as it is today; unpredictable events may shift trends in an entirely different direction in a decade's time. As we previously saw, Japan's economic ascendancy did not translate into superpower status. In the mid-2000s, many commentators predicted with confidence that Russia was no longer a military threat to Western interests – this has repeatedly been proved wrong in the Middle East and Eastern Europe.

This is probably the most wide-ranging and expansive part of the course content, because it is inherently concerned with a sweeping assessment of global politics. The more you read, the more you will be able to substantiate your conclusions on the question of contemporary polarity.

Global Politics – Unit 3.5
Regionalism and the European Union

REGIONALISM
Definitions
Regionalism is where three or more states in a particular geographical area form organisations to work together towards a specific goal or to regulate a specific interaction. Regionalism must involve at least three states – a very close relationship between two states would just be described as an 'alliance', 'partnership', etc. Regionalism by definition must be restricted to a particular geographic area which is narrower than the entire globe.

Therefore, whilst **NATO** would be considered an example of regionalism (North America/Europe), the **United Nations** and **WTO** would not.

There are three principal types of regionalism which are classified according to the **motivation** for states pursuing a regionalist project:

1. **Economic regionalism:** Regionalism which is based on the pursuit of integrated financial systems or improved frictionless trade, through common standards on goods/services; reducing tariffs and other barriers to inter-state trade; etc. Nearly every country in the world is now a member of at least one regionalist trade bloc (the UK is a notable exception)

2. **Security regionalism:** Regionalism which is based on the pursuit of peace between former enemies, the enforcement of security within a particular geographical area, or collective security from a common external threat

3. **Political regionalism:** Regionalism which is based on the protection of common values within the bloc of states, the promotion of those common values further afield, and enhancing their political standing, diplomatic weight and status in international politics

THE EUROPEAN UNION
The development of the European Union

There are two principal debates to explore about the development of the European Union. The first is about what type of regionalism the EU best represents (economic, security, political) and how/ whether this has changed over time. The second is about why the EU has developed and evolved over time – as a conscious project of **federalism** or a **functionalist** endeavour for individual states.

Timeline
1951:

- The **European Coal and Steel Community (ECSC)** was created. This was a supranational institution which decided how much coal and steel each member could produce. The founding members were France, West Germany, Italy, Belgium, the Netherlands, and Luxemburg
- The ECSC was created in the aftermath of WWII in order to make another world war impossible. In the century prior to the ECSC's creation, there had been a number of major European wars, three of which had principally arisen as a result of Franco-German rivalry (the Franco-Prussian War; WWI; WWII). At a time where coal and steel were necessary for modern industrial warfare, it was correctly believed that a common system of regulating their production would prevent the onset of another major war

1957:

- France, West Germany, Italy, Belgium, the Netherlands and Luxemburg signed the Treaty of Rome which created the **European Economic Community (EEC)**. By doing this they agreed to work towards the creation of a single market by gradually reducing tariffs between them. It was believed that this would increase trade and prosperity in Western Europe
- The single market would be based on the **'four freedoms'** – free movement of goods, services, capital and persons. This clearly eroded some national sovereignty at borders
- In order to do achieve consensus in these discussions, qualified majority voting (QMV) was introduced for certain issues, which meant that all member-states

gave up a degree of sovereignty. QMV will be discussed in greater depth later, but it essentially means that unanimous consent is not required for a decision – it can be carried by a 'qualified' majority and all states must then implement it, even if they opposed it

1958: The Treaty of Rome came into force after all states ratified it, and the EEC was formally born

1961:

- The UK, suffering from sluggish economic growth, applied to join the EEC, hoping that better access to the EEC market would help to boost its prosperity
- Although all other members were in favour of this, the application was **vetoed** by Charles de Gaulle, the French President. De Gaulle believed that the UK would be insufficiently committed to the EEC and European integration and that its inclusion would obstruct smooth decision-making. He was also fiercely proud of 'European' culture and hated the Americans; he believed that British membership of the EEC was a 'Trojan horse' for American influence

1962:

- The **Common Agricultural Policy (CAP)** was introduced, which introduced generous EEC-wide subsidies for farmers and introduced fixed common price levels in member states for agricultural products, e.g. wheat, wine, meat, butter, etc.
- The CAP was introduced to resolve existing tensions between France and Germany about reducing tariffs between member states. West Germany had a booming industrial sector, and France feared that free trade would 'flood' the French market with manufactured goods of a quality and price could not compete with
- In exchange for opening up the French economy to West German industries, France demanded protection for its large agricultural sector through the CAP

1964: Spain applied to join the EEC and was unanimously rejected, since it was run by a fascist dictatorship under General Franco

1968: After several years of negotiations, the first tariffs were abolished between EEC member states, marking the first step towards the creation of a 'single market'

1973: The UK, Ireland and Denmark were admitted to the EEC, bringing the total membership up to 9. This had been made possible by de Gaulle's resignation (after a decolonisation crisis in Algeria), removing French opposition to British admission to the EEC

1979: Direct elections to the European Parliament were introduced – before this point, a European Parliament had existed but MEPs were nominated by national parliaments. This was introduced to create a greater feeling of connection between *citizens* of EEC member states and the EEC

1981: Greece was admitted to the EEC, bringing total membership to 10. Greece had recently transitioned to a democracy from a military dictatorship and the EEC believed that admitting Greece into the EEC would entrench liberal democracy there

1985: The **Schengen Agreement** was signed by the initial 6 founding members of the EEC, abolishing border controls within the 'Schengen Zone', effectively meaning that it was possible to travel between all of these countries without any kind of visa or passport. In order to do this, they needed to agree common visa arrangements with external countries (since anyone who was allowed to come into one Schengen country could then access all of them)

1986: After recently transitioning away from fascist dictatorships (Salazar in Portugal, and Franco in Spain), Portugal and Spain were admitted to the EEC, bringing total membership to 12. Like Greece, it was believed that liberal democracy would be better entrenched within the EEC

1986:

- The **Single European Act** was agreed between the EEC member states, which provided for the introduction of a genuine **single market** with no tariff barriers by 1992. This was in some ways the culmination of the process of reducing tariffs which had begun in 1968
- To achieve this, QMV was introduced to new areas of economic policy, whereas it had previously been restricted. EEC member states were frustrated at the requirement for unanimous consent, which slowed down the pace of negotiations – QMV would allow a 'qualified majority' to prevail, making it easier to speed up the process of removing the final legislative barriers to a single market

1992:

- The **Maastricht Treaty** was signed, which transformed the EEC into the **European Union (EU)** as a successor organisation. The EU differed from the EEC, in that it also involved cooperation over foreign policy, security policy, justice and home affairs; and it involved the harmonising of the currencies of member states to create a single currency – the **Euro**

- This required harmonising the **fiscal policies** (economic policies) of the member states; the introduction of QMV in more areas; and giving greater powers to the European Parliament. This definitively represented a diminishment of the sovereignty of member states

- One of the main reasons for the Maastricht Treaty's introduction was that the end of the Cold War had led to the recent reunification of West and East Germany. This was genuinely feared by other European states at the time; in a 1989 summit, Thatcher said "We defeated the Germans twice! And now they're back!" and Mitterrand (the French President) said in 1990 "a unified Germany could make more ground than even Adolf had." In one sense, the creation of a European Union and further integration was seen as a way to tie France and Germany so tightly together that a war would be absolutely impossible

- Denmark initially voted against the Treaty in a referendum and discussions over the Treaty nearly collapsed Major's government in the UK. Denmark and the UK were therefore granted exemptions from joining the Euro; and Britain was granted an additional exemption from signing up to the **Social Chapter** which aimed to extend and harmonise rights for workers

1993: The Maastricht Treaty, after having been agreed by all state parliaments/legislatures, came into force and the European Union was formally born

1995:

- Austria, Finland and Sweden joined the EU, bringing total membership to 15
- These states had formerly been neutral buffer zones in the Cold War. Although they had been democracies since the end of WWII, the fear of sparking a conflict with the Soviet Union meant that they did not join NATO or the EEC. The collapse of the Soviet Union and the end of the Cold War meant they were free to join the European Union

1997:

- The **Amsterdam Treaty** was signed, which began the process of 'widening and deepening' the EU (expanding membership eastwards; and providing further levels of integrated decision-making). Member states agreed to sacrifice some sovereign powers on immigration, civil and criminal law to the European Parliament, and to extend the use of QMV in the EU

- It was agreed that every EU member state other than the UK and Ireland would join the Schengen Zone (i.e. passport-free travel)
- The Treaty was signed in anticipation of the formerly-communist, now-democratic Eastern European states, e.g. Poland, Hungary, the Baltics, etc. joining the EU to ensure that they did not 'backslide' into authoritarianism. However, it was feared that they might act with the UK to obstruct further integration once they had joined, so it was seen as necessary to achieve further integration before admitting them

2000:

- The **Treaty of Nice** was signed, which prepared for the 'widening and deepening' of the EU by reforming voting arrangements to take into account how the EU would increase in size and membership. This was done for largely the same reasons as Amsterdam (the EU wanted to admit Eastern European states; but wanted to lay the groundwork for integration first so they couldn't contest it once they had joined)
- Ireland initially voted against the treaty in a referendum; a second referendum was then held, after the EU guaranteed that the treaty would not require Ireland to abandon its long-standing commitment to military neutrality

2002: The Euro became the official currency of participating member states (all EU states at the time, with the exception of Denmark and Britain, which retained the kroner and pound respectively)

2004:

- Cyprus, Malta, Slovenia, Czechia, Slovakia, Hungary, Poland, Estonia, Latvia and Lithuania joined the EU, bringing total membership to 25. With the exception of Malta and Cyprus, all of these were former communist dictatorships in the orbit of the Soviet Union, who wanted to join to entrench democracy and boost the development of their domestic economies
- The **European Constitution** was agreed by EU member states. This would have replaced all previous treaties into one document, given more powers to the European Commission and the European parliament, and confirmed the primacy

of EU law over national law. It was designed to simplify the running of the EU and the process of 'widening and deepening'

- After being rejected in French and Dutch national referendums, the Constitution was abandoned since neither the French or Dutch legislatures were willing to sign it against the fierce opposition of their electorates

2007:

- Romania and Bulgaria joined the EU, bringing total membership to 27. They joined, as former communist dictatorships, to entrench democracy and boost their domestic economies
- The **Treaty of Lisbon** was signed, which gave more powers to the European Commission and European Parliament, increased the use of QMV in the Council of the European Union, and introduced a procedure for leaving the EU (Article 50)
- Like the failed European Constitution, this was designed to simplify the running of the EU, but was necessarily less ambitious and contained more concessions to enable its acceptance by all member states. Article 50 was introduced as a 'get out clause' for states who objected to further integration

2009:

- The **Eurozone debt crisis** began as the governments of Greece, Spain, Portugal, Ireland and Cyprus became unable to pay their debts in the aftermath of the 2008 Financial Crisis. Because all of these countries used the Euro, this had the potential to cripple the entire economy of the EU which also used the Euro, since defaulting on the debt would have led to a collapse in the Euro's value
- A bailout package was negotiated between the European Commission, the European Central Bank, and the IMF (sometimes referred to collectively as 'the troika') to cover their debts

2013: Croatia joined the EU, bringing total membership to 28, for largely the same reasons as other former Communist dictatorships had joined (to entrench democracy and boost the domestic economy)

2016: The UK became the first country to vote to leave the EU

2017: The British government triggered Article 50 of the Lisbon Treaty and began the process of leaving the European Union

2020: The UK became the first country to leave the EU, bringing the number of members back to 27

Map of the EU's territorial development over time

What form of regionalism does the EU represent?

Economic	Security	Political
The ECSC very quickly adopted goals of economic integration, which led to tariff reductions and the creation of the single market in 1992. Since then, there has been further integration of currencies and fiscal policy. The general motivation here has	This was the initial impetus for the creation of the ECSC (1951), and then the further integration of European states into the EU through the Maastricht Treaty (1992). The aim of both of these treaties was to bind European states so tightly together that war would	The expansion of the EU's membership over time has had explicitly political dimensions; to entrench and extend values of liberal democracy. Especially after the conversion from the EEC into the EU in the 1990s, the organisation has done a lot more to try and

been to improve interstate economic relationships in the view that frictionless free trade and freedom of movement for goods, services, people and ideas will enrich all participant member-states. Economic integration and joint prosperity has been a driving force behind much of the EU's development since the 1950s	be inconceivable between them. However, it has not been a driving force for the EU's development other than in these two particular instances (though this is not to say that it is unimportant – EU member states are enjoying the longest uninterrupted period of international peace in the history of the continent)	promote common decision-making, common policies and common approaches to political solutions, e.g. the introduction of the Social Chapter, and various treaties (Amsterdam, Nice, Lisbon) which have deepened the integration between member states and enabled closer foreign policy cooperation

Why has the EU developed and grown over time?

1. **Federalism:** Federalism is the idea that power should be distributed between two 'levels' of government on the basis that they are co-equal and neither is subordinate to the other. This is theoretically how the USA is organised, with state governments (e.g. California, Texas, New York) and a singular federal government. Some people argue that the EU is developing towards a federalist structure in which it becomes a 'United States of Europe' for ideological reasons – i.e. European politicians think it is the right thing to happen and work to achieve that goal. Some prominent EU politicians, e.g. Verhofstadt (Belgian MEP) and Scholz (German Chancellor) have openly advocated for this in the past few years

2. **Functionalism:** Functionalism is the theory that EU membership fulfils a particular function (e.g. security, prosperity, amplification of diplomatic power) and that states have joined in order to fulfil their own national interests instead

of caring about federalism as an ideological project. This is much more of a realist view in terms of perceiving the EU as a collaborative project of self-interested states who have no intention of wholly surrendering sovereignty

3. **Neo-functionalism:** Neo-functionalism is the theory that greater European integration is inevitable because each stage of cooperation opens up the need for further cooperation to make the existing stage 'workable'. In this view, EU integration is a process that will continuously snowball, even if states do not actively push for it. For example, once a single market exists (with totally free movement of goods, services, people and capital) it makes sense to have a single currency (the Euro). Once a single currency is introduced, states probably need to harmonise their fiscal policies (taxation, spending, etc.) to ensure that they maintain the integrity of the Eurozone and prevent economic crises. And so on ad infinitum

The structures and 'organs' of the European Union

The structures and organs of the EU are poorly understood in general, including by many British politicians. This is perhaps one of the reasons that misinformation spread so quickly during the Brexit referendum! It is also perhaps evidence of a **democratic deficit** in the EU – if EU citizens do not understand its structure, can it be a genuinely representative institution?

There are five bodies in the European Union which you need to know for this course:
1. The European Parliament
2. The European Commission
3. The European Council
4. The Council of the EU (also known as the **Council of Ministers**)
5. The European Court of Justice

The European Parliament

The **European Parliament** is a **legislative body** which votes on and amends EU legislation. In order for EU legislation to pass, both the European Parliament and the Council of the European Union (the 'Council of Ministers') have to approve it. Unlike the British Parliament, the European Parliament cannot suggest legislation of its own;

it can only discuss and amend legislation which has been proposed and put before it by the European Commission.

The European Parliament is made up of 705 Members of European Parliament **(MEPs)**, elected by universal suffrage in each state. The voting system is based on proportional representation in 'regions' of each country. Turnout fell consecutively at every EU election since 1994, bottoming out at 42.5% in 2014, but surged to 50.6%, driven by a substantial increase in youth participation. This is still substantially lower than most national elections.

MEPs do not sit in 'national' groupings in the European Parliament building. Instead, they sit in informal interstate 'coalitions' or **'Europarties'** of national parties roughly based on their ideological positions. For example, there is a European Conservative and Reformist group which includes most centre-right parties (e.g. the Conservatives were formerly in this); a Progressive Alliance of Socialists and Democrats which includes most centre-left parties (e.g. Labour was formerly in this); and the Identity and Democracy Party, which is a collection of Eurosceptic far-right national parties (e.g. UKIP and the Brexit Party were formerly in this).

The European Parliament has the following powers:
- It discusses and amends legislation
- It scrutinises members of the European Commission (akin to PMQs)
- It votes to approve the EU Budget
- It votes to approve the nominated European Commission
- It can carry a vote of no confidence (2/3 majority needed) to force the European Commission to resign. This has never happened, but the threat of it compelled the Santer Commission (widely and credibly accused of corruption) to step down in 1999
- *It notably lacks the power to propose legislation*

The European Commission
The **European Commission** is functionally an executive branch of the European Union (although unlike most national executives, it shares this role in a 'dual executive' model

– the European Council also has some executive powers). The European Commission is made up of **27** commissioners, one from each of the 27 member states. Each commissioner is expected to put aside their loyalty to their particular nation-state and for the period of their tenure to represent European interests as a whole.

The President of the European Commission is nominated by the **European Council** (made up of the heads of state of the EU countries). They must then be confirmed by a vote of the **European Parliament**. Proceedings continue until there is a candidate with the support of both institutions. The President of the European Commission is expected to be from a state which is a member of the Eurozone and Schengen Area, fluent in French, and politically experienced. The current President is **Ursula von der Leyen**, the former deputy leader of the CDU (the main centre-right party in Germany). She was preceded by Jean Claude Juncker, a former PM of Luxembourg.

Once the President is approved, the governments of EU states then nominate their candidates for commissioners. Each commissioner is given a 'portfolio' or 'ministry' like members of a national cabinet, e.g. Agriculture. Since the President chooses who gets which portfolio, there is an incentive for member states to choose influential and non-controversial candidates for commissioner, in the hope they will be given a more meaningful portfolio. The European Parliament then gets to vote on the 'completed' Commission of 27 candidates. If they reject the Commission, the President has to pick a new set of candidates. A European Commission sits for a term of **five years.**

The European Commission has the following powers:
- It formulates EU policy and initiates legislation
- It draws up the EU Budget
- It represents the EU in international trade negotiations (e.g. with Canada)
- It enforces EU law across the European Union
- It acts as the 'guardian of the treaties' – it is responsible for bringing proceedings at the European Court of Justice if they are not
- *It notably lacks the power to determine 'constitutional' policy*

The European Council

The **European Council** is the other half of the EU's 'dual executive'. Unlike the Commission, which focuses principally on 'domestic' issues within the EU, the Council generally focuses on external and foreign policy, as well as what might be considered 'constitutional' issues in changing the EU's structure. It consists of the 27 heads of state from the 27 EU member states – e.g. Macron (France).

The Council meets at least every **six months** and more often if there are urgent matters to discuss. The European Council is chaired by a President who is elected by the members of the European Council – the President does not have a vote, is not a head of state, and is there to regulate proceedings (similar to the role of Speaker in the Commons) and represent the Council's views in talks with other powers, for example during the Brexit negotiations with the UK. The current President is **Charles Michel** (former PM of Belgium); he was preceded by **Donald Tusk** (former PM of Poland). The European Council seeks to make decisions through consensus and discussion. When it comes to (i) future treaty changes for the EU, or (ii) admitting new states, the decision must be unanimous (therefore meaning each state effectively has a veto).

The European Council has the following powers:
- It conducts the foreign policy of the EU
- It acts as 'head of state' in negotiations with other powers
- It draws up plans for future treaty changes in the EU
- It resolves issues referred upwards from the Council of Ministers
- It proposes the President of the European Commission

The Council of the European Union (Council of Ministers)

The **Council of the European Union** is confusingly very similar in name to the European Council. To distinguish them more easily, we can refer to the former as the **'Council of Ministers'** which is an accepted way to refer to it. It is a legislative body which votes on and amends EU legislation, alongside the European Parliament. The Council of Ministers does not have a permanent membership; it consists of 27 ministers from each relevant ministry/department in each member state. For example, if the Council of Ministers were to discuss agricultural legislation; it would include ministers for agriculture in each member state. If it were to discuss an issue to do with European health policy, then it would include the health ministers from each state. The Council of Europe uses QMV to make its decisions, rather than requiring unanimous consent or a simple majority.

The Council of Ministers has the following powers:
- It discusses and amends legislation
- It votes on common positions (foreign policy towards individual states) and joint actions (coordinated actions of EU member states)
- *It notably lacks the power to propose legislation*

The Court of Justice of the EU (ECJ)
The **Court of Justice of the EU (ECJ)** consists of one judge proposed by each member state. It conducts proceedings in French and has the following powers:
- It reviews the legal of actions taken by other EU institutions
- It enforces compliance by member states with Treaty obligations
- It interprets contested points of EU law (these decisions are binding)

Summary of EU institutions

Institution	'Branch'	Appointment process	Powers
European Parliament	Legislative	Elected by EU citizens (705 MEPs in total)	Amend legislation; approve and scrutinise the Commission
European Commission	Executive	Nominated by European Council; approved by European Parliament (27 commissioners + 1 President)	Propose legislation + Budget; represent the EU in trade negotiations; enforces law
European Council	Executive	Heads of government of EU states (27 members + 1 President)	Constitutional changes (new members; new treaties) + acts as head of state for 'foreign policy'

Council of Ministers	Legislative	Relevant ministers of EU states (27 ministers at any one time)	Amend legislation; votes on 'common positions'
Court of Justice (EU)	Judicial	Nominated by member-states (27 judges)	Reviews other institutions + interprets EU law (binding)

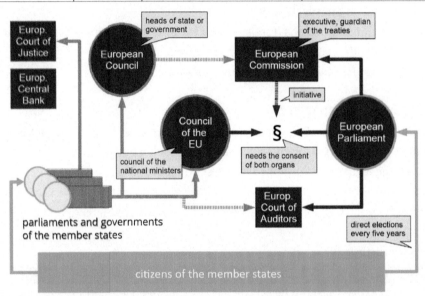

Diagram of the main EU organs and their interrelationship

Debates about EU institutions

Below are some key discussion points to do with the constitutional structure of the EU, followed by an analysis of the central debate – is the European Union a state? It would be difficult to find anyone who argues that the EU is a state in the traditional Montevidian sense (fixed territory; fixed population; sovereign government; international recognition) because the EU institutions are not explicitly **sovereign**. However, the unique constitutional arrangements of the EU mean that some would describe the EU as a **quasi-federal state.** (Quasi = a prefix which means 'resembles/looks like, but isn't technically identical)

234

The primacy of the European Parliament

The European Parliament is considered the "first institution" in all EU treaties, and has ceremonial precedence over all other institutions.

It is indeed unique in that it is the only EU institution which is directly elected by EU citizens – all others are appointed. It has some important powers in its ability to amend and reject legislation, and has a substantial impact on EU policy outcomes. It also has the ability to shape half of the dual executive by voting to approve the Commission President; Commission candidates; and having the power to remove the Commission at any point through a vote of no confidence.

Nevertheless, it lacks some of the features which make national legislatures so powerful – it cannot initiate legislation on its own (it can only react to what has been put forward by the Commission); and it lacks control over substantial areas of policy such as constitutional change, admission of new members, foreign policy, etc.

Supranationalism v intergovernmentalism

Supranationalism is where states give power to a new body which becomes a 'higher authority' than they are. They may have representatives in the supranational body, but its decisions do not have to be unanimous and therefore a state which is part of a supranational body may have to accept decisions that it didn't endorse. This represents an erosion of sovereignty (as long as the state remains part of the supranational body) because decision-making is 'above' the state

Intergovernmentalism is where governments of different sovereign states cooperate in a decision-making process. Each state has its own particular agenda that it advocates for, and reaching a decision requires unanimous consensus between all states involved in the discussion. This does not represent an erosion of sovereignty (a state will never have to accept a binding decision it doesn't want)

Within the European Union;

- European Parliament = supranational
- European Commission = supranational
- Council of Europe = supranational
- European Court of Justice = supranational
- European Council = intergovernmental

All bodies of the EU with the exception of the European Council are supranational. They make decisions through various methods (simple majority, qualified majority) in which not all states or state representatives necessarily must agree in order to reach a decision. These decisions are then binding on all EU member states, so the decision-making process is 'above' states. In the European Council, all 27 heads of government in the body must agree in order for a decision to be reached – e.g. on admitting a new member, or approving a new constitutional Treaty. Here, it is states themselves which are making the decision, and they have full control over it.

This begs the question of why this is the case. The supranational institutions of the EU were created in 1952, in the early years of the ECSC. They were created in this way to encourage deeper integration between former enemies, and to ensure that no one state could obstruct decisions and collapse the negotiating process between them. The European Council was only introduced as a body within the EU in 1975, shortly after the accession of Ireland, Denmark and the UK in 1973.
It was introduced because the UK did not want to belong to an institution which was fully supranational, since this would have been perceived as an unacceptable erosion of state sovereignty. The European Council's creation and specific powers to vote on constitutional changes and admitting new members meant that the UK would never be *forced* to accept further constitutional changes to the EEC which would further undermine UK sovereignty.

Qualified majority voting
Qualified majority voting or **QMV** is the voting mechanism used in the Council of Ministers. For a vote to pass a 'double majority' is necessary:
- 55% of member states must vote for the motion (16 out of 27)
- These member states must represent at least 65% of the total EU population
- =

QMV is used in place of either a simple majority, or unanimous consent. It is used instead of a simple majority, because states would consider it 'unfair' or hazardous to their sovereignty if their ability to block legislation they feel would be harmful could be ignored by a narrow majority. It is used instead of unanimous consent, because a system of unanimous consent amongst ministers would make it very difficult to make much progress at all in legislative agreements.

The double majority serves to protect the interests of both **large** and **small** states, making them both amenable to the 'sacrifice' of their sovereignty to the Council of Ministers.

- Large states are protected by the requirement for votes to represent 65% of the EU population. There are 20 EU states with populations of less than 3% of the EU total – if this requirement did not exist, then those 20 small states would be able to push through votes against the wishes of the larger states (e.g. a demand for greater EU budget funding)

- Smaller states are protected by the requirement for at least 55% of member states to vote for a legislative motion. The five biggest EU states (Germany, France, Italy, Spain and Poland) collectively represent around 66% of the EU total population. If this requirement did not exist, then a few large states would be able to push through votes against the wishes of the smaller states (e.g. a demand for lesser financial support for developing EU economies)

Is the European Union a state?

The EU is a state, or closely resembles one	The EU is not a state in the typical sense
The EU clearly has a fixed population and fixed territorial borders. It is clear who is a citizen of an EU countries, and the EU has external borders with other states. There is also a greater sense of territorial cohesion within the EU because of the prominence of the Schengen Area, in which passport-free travel is possible; this covers the majority of EU states	The EU's representatives and officers generally represent the interests of individual sovereign member states, rather than the EU as a whole. The only genuinely 'European' representatives are MEPs and supposedly commissioners; but elsewhere, it is representatives of sovereign states with their own agendas which dominate the decision-making process

Many of the EU's institutions are supranational. This means that even a state objects to a decision, the decision may still be passed by a simple majority in the European Parliament and QMV in the Council of Ministers	The EU Council is an intergovernmental institution. This means that any state objecting to a decision counts as a veto, and major constitutional decisions about further integration cannot be imposed on states against their will
EU law and EU decisions are binding upon member states. In this sense, the EU has 'pooled' sovereignty from its member states and is then able to exercise control over them and impose decisions, even where they might disagree (e.g. when the UK was part of the EU, they had to accept the Common Fisheries Policy allowing other EU vessels to fish in British waters, despite deep opposition to this)	Some EU decisions cannot be imposed on member states – the individual states of the EU retain sovereign power. For example, additional members can be vetoed by any member state (e.g. France's use of the veto to block Britain's accession in the 1950s and 60s). Furthermore, further constitutional integration can be blocked by dissenting states (e.g. 2005 EU Constitution being blocked by France and the Netherlands)
The EU clearly has the capacity to enter into discussions and negotiations with other sovereign states as a recognised unitary body – e.g. trade negotiations with Canada, Japan and MERCOSUR (the South American free-trade bloc); as well as international diplomatic agreements (e.g. the Iran nuclear deal)	Whilst the EU has specific competence in the area of trade agreements, member states may conduct diverging policy agreements in areas such as security and military policy. For example, EU states are not bound to go to war as a unitary body, as federal states would be compelled to by a federal government

The 'health' of the European Union

Another key debate which we must consider is the 'health' of the EU as a stable and long-lasting institutional structure. Many of the debates discussed below are variations on the primary arguments of the Leave campaign in the 2016 Brexit referendum. They are also put forward by various Eurosceptic politicians and parties across Europe. Whilst the Leave campaign obviously misrepresented many of the facts, there is definitely some truth to many of their criticisms and it is worth exploring these in critical detail with an open mind to determine whether the EU is indeed 'healthy' or whether there are serious problems that may lead to its dissolution.

1. *Democratic deficit*

Perhaps the most significant argument put forward by Eurosceptic politicians is that the EU suffers from a severe democratic deficit, is 'undemocratic' and dictatorial in the way that it makes policy and 'imposes' it on member states. The table below outlines the main arguments for/against this view.

The EU does not have a democratic deficit	The EU has a democratic deficit
Democratic referendums:	Undemocratic referendums:
In some cases, the rejection of EU treaties by referendum (e.g. the 2005 EU constitution being rejected by French and Dutch voters by significant margins), the EU has decided to not pursue that treaty further. This demonstrates that national referendums expressing a clear objection from citizens will lead to responsive action by the European Union	There have been several national referendums to do with further EU constitutional integration in member states. In almost all cases where there were 'no' votes against in national referendums, the referendum was re-run the following year after EU-sponsored campaigns in favour of the new treaty. For example, the Treaty of Nice was rejected in 2001 by Ireland by a 54-46% margin; a new referendum was held in 2002, in which the treaty was approved by a 60-40% margin. The Treaty of Lisbon was rejected in 2008
Furthermore, it could be argued that there is nothing inherently undemocratic about 're-running'	

referendums following educational campaigns, and that there is no requirement for referendums to be 'once in a lifetime'. It is democratic to allow voters to change their minds over time, and the substantially increased margins for 'yes' in Ireland for Nice (2002) and Lisbon (2009) demonstrate this	by Ireland by a 47-53% margin; a new referendum was held in 2009, in which the treaty was approved by 67-33% margin. This practise of 're-running' referendums where they fail to achieve the desired pro-EU result is seen by some as an undemocratic mechanism to pressure states into further integration
Rising turnout: Low turnout in EU Parliamentary elections does not necessarily reflect a democratic deficit. It perhaps rather represents a lack of education about the EU Parliament, its functions, and its powers. Nevertheless this is changing over time and the big youth surge in the 2019 European Parliament elections which increased turnout by approximately 10% demonstrates that democracy in the EU has a bright future. As the EU integrates further and citizens are made more aware of the EU Parliament and what it does, then turnout will increase. There is also low turnout in many national elections – the EU is no more undemocratic than these states	Low turnout: Turnout in EU Parliamentary elections is generally very low, ranging from lows in the low 40% range, rising to a high of just over 50%. This is substantially below turnout in national legislative elections. This is perhaps because people do not really know who their EU representatives/candidates are, what they stand for, and what their powers are. The lack of knowledge and education about the EU Parliament creates a lack of engagement – people feel that the EU Parliament is an irrelevant body. This brings into question the Europe-wide legitimacy of any legislation the EU Parliament approves
Powerful elected representatives:	Lack of elected representatives:

Whilst the European Parliament is the only body directly elected by EU citizens, its proportional voting system allows for accurate representation of voters' wishes. The grouping of MEPs in international 'Eurogroups' allows different and varied ideological views within a country to be properly represented

In addition to this, whilst other bodies in the EU are not directly elected by European citizens, they are drawn from indirectly democratic sources. For example, EU commissioners are nominated by the EU Council, which is made up of the elected heads of government for the different EU countries

The EU Parliament, which has clear democratic legitimacy, also has the power to approve the Commission (the 'appointed executive'), and is ultimately necessary to pass legislation. It is therefore difficult for 'undemocratic' decisions to made that bind all EU member-states

The European Parliament is the only elected body in the European Union. The other major bodies in the EU are either heads of state/government, or appointed/selected by heads of state/government. This creates a further 'level of separation' from the democratic will of the people in determining representatives. For example, in Germany, the Chancellor is the leader of the largest party in the Bundestag – they are not directly elected (similar to the PM in the UK). The Chancellor then has the power to nominate the German commissioner for the EU, the German judge on the ECJ, and the German cabinet (ministers from which will attend the Council of Ministers). There are therefore 'two degrees of separation' from the German public and their EU representatives

N.B. A further statistical observation is that 'representative distance' means that EU legislative policy is therefore further to the economic right than the average EU citizen

2. *Criticisms of Eastern enlargement*

Another criticism of the EU is its enlargement from the 1990s onwards to include the post-Soviet former-Communist states of Eastern Europe. This was arguably one of the main reasons for Euroscepticism in the UK, and is a less important but still relevant argument advanced by continental Eurosceptic politicians.

Eastern enlargement of the EU was sensible	Eastern enlargement of the EU was a mistake
Democratic entrenchment: In the 1990s, the former Communist countries of Eastern Europe were vulnerable to sliding into new forms of authoritarianism (e.g. as Belarus currently has) or civil war (e.g. like the former Yugoslav states). It was thought that EU membership would prevent this and lock them into a democratic system – for some politicians, this was an active 'moral imperative'. Most Eastern European countries have more robust democracies today than they did in the 1990s, e.g. Czechia, Slovakia, Croatia, and do not show any signs of reverting towards authoritarian or semi-authoritarian models	Democratic backsliding: There has been some significant democratic 'backsliding' in several EU countries, most notably Hungary (led by the Fidesz Party – PM Viktor Orban) and Poland (led by the Law and Justice Party – PM Mateusz Morawiecki). The rule of law has been severely eroded by conservative authoritarianism; press freedoms have been curtailed by the closure of media outlets; and the judiciary is not independent. There is no mechanism to suspend or censure EU states for democratic backsliding, which makes this issue more intractable, as there is no way to pressure Hungary/Poland to change
Economic prosperity: In the 1990s, Eastern Europe was in a very poor economic state after decades of Communist rule – it was	Economic downsides: Many Western European Eurosceptics were very critical of the EU Development Fund on the basis

thought that EU membership would give them access to the single market and allow them to grow. Growth in this region would benefit not only those countries, but everyone else in the EU as well. The EU's Regional Development Fund is paid into based on a country's income, which effectively means EU membership for Eastern Europe meant that richer Western European countries were subsidising investment to developing Eastern European economies

There is a lot of evidence to suggest that this has had a clear positive impact – for example in Romania, GDP per capita has risen from approximately $1,700 in 1990 to $13,000 today. This has substantially outstripped economic growth in post-Soviet countries that didn't join the EU, e.g. Ukraine (GDP per capita in 1990 was roughly at the same level as Romania; today it is $3,726 – approximately 1/3 of Romania's GDP/capita). Simultaneously, the freedom of movement principle allowed many Eastern Europeans to travel to Western Europe which drove down labour costs in fields such as agriculture, construction and

that the wealthier EU countries were paying for foreign development and 'contributing more than they were getting back'

There are also migration-related critiques of integrating Eastern Europe into the single market. One critique is that the freedom of movement principle led to mass migration of Eastern Europeans to wealthier Western European countries. For example, the Polish-born population of Britain went up from 94,000 in 2004 to 922,000 in 2017 (nearly 10x!)

This has been criticised by (i) Western European Eurosceptics on the grounds that 'the foreigners are taking over our country and stealing our jobs' and (ii) Eastern European Eurosceptics, on the grounds that mass emigration is draining Eastern Europe of talent, labour and people, making it harder for local Eastern European economies to prosper [this does ignore remittances though, which have led to increased wealth in E. Europe]

Finally, the single market has damaged Eastern European industry

transport, making goods and services generally cheaper	because it has to compete against superior German industry
Security benefits: It was argued that EU expansion into Eastern Europe, combined with NATO expansion into the region, would prevent Russia from reasserting its control over the area and thus make the European Union safer. An EU state has never been a target of war by Russia	Security undermined: Simultaneous EU and NATO expansion (the two now largely go hand-in-hand) could be viewed as having 'provoked' Russia. Current Russian militarism in Ukraine was partially a response to massive Ukrainian demonstrations in favour of joining the EU (2013-2014)

3. *Criticisms of the Eurozone*

A final criticism of the EU is the creation and extension of the Eurozone. This does not apply to all EU member states, but the vast majority of EU member-states are part of the Eurozone or are in the process of adopting the Euro, so it is certainly a salient discussion.

The **Eurozone** is the area of the EU that has adopted a single currency – the 'Euro'. Instead of **monetary policy** (how much money is available in the economy; this can be achieving by changing the money supply, or by increasing/lowering interest rates) being determined by national banks, it is instead determined by the **European Central Bank** (a subsidiary of the EU).

The Eurozone is a good idea	The Eurozone has been a mistake
All Eurozone countries using the same currency means that businesses do not have to exchange large sums of currency and incur currency conversion costs when operating across borders. This	Because German industry is so much more efficient than that of France and southern Europe, the introduction of the Eurozone has led to a boom in German industrial exports, whereas industries in other

enables them to set up supply chains across multiple countries much more cheaply and encourages trade across Europe	countries have suffered in having to compete without the 'protection' of national monetary policy
Since the Euro has the enhanced credibility of being used in a large currency zone (the more widely a currency is used the less likely it is to collapse in value), it is more stable against speculation than the individual currencies that preceded it. The Euro has become the 2nd most-widely used reserve currency after the dollar	Membership of the Euro imposes limitations on the policy choices of member states and therefore infringes of their sovereignty. Because monetary policy is decided by the European Central Bank, individual Eurozone countries cannot choose to devalue their currency to boost exports in a recession, for example
The Euro encourages sensible economic and monetary policies – in order to join the Euro, member-states are required to meet strict criteria in the Stability and Growth Pact, such as: 1. A budget deficit (spending minus 'income') of less than 3% of their GDP 2. A debt ratio of less than 60% of GDP 3. Low inflation over time 4. Interest rates close to the EU average	The Stability and Growth Pact has been applied inconsistently. There are supposed to be sanctions if a country breaches the criteria in the Pact, but the Council of Ministers has not always done this. For example, France and Germany have consistently violated the criteria but are too powerful to challenge; whilst punitive proceedings were started against Portugal and Greece in the late 2000s In addition, the Eurosceptic Italian government was prevented from passing its budget by the European Commission in 2016, even though its

Eurozone states also share the same central bank, which stops irresponsible states solving their problems by printing large amounts of money and generating runaway inflation	proposed budget deficit was below that required by the Stability and Growth Pact
The Euro has made war between participating states absolutely impossible. It was partially responsible for the French government having the confidence to agree to the reunification of West and East Germany in the 1990s	Membership of the Euro limits the policy choices available to Eurozone states in dealing with economic decline; here is a limit to how much they can borrow or how much they can cut tax (because of the budget deficit criteria)

It is worth here also examining a specific case study of Greece in the 2008 Financial Crisis.

- Before Greece joined the Euro (2002), it did not meet the strict 'Stability and Growth Pact' criteria to join the Euro; public spending was very high, and the upcoming 2004 Athens Olympics still had to largely be paid for
- Nevertheless, the EU decided to admit Greece to the euro for reasons of 'political solidarity'
- Greek membership of the Euro allowed them to borrow money at cheaper interest rates than before (generally the 'stronger' an economy, the 'lower' interest rates are – because the Eurozone included economies like Germany and Netherlands, the Eurozone economy was 'strong' and Greece was able to borrow at low interest rates)
- When the Financial Crisis struck in 2008, followed by a global recession, Greece was left stuck with a mountain of debt which it now had to pay at interest rates which the European Central Bank had increased in response to the economic crash
- Greek GDP crashed by 26% between 2008 and 2014

- Greek debt levels became unsustainable, and the country was at risk of defaulting, so they had to rely on loans from the IMF, Eurogroup and European Central Bank (the **'troika'**)
- The conditionalities imposed by the EU and IMF loans required Greece to slash their government spending (austerity) and increase taxation to reduce the public debt. Taxes paid by the poorest Greek households rose by over 300%
- Consequently, youth unemployment in Greece spiked at 60%, there was mass emigration of young Greeks abroad; whole families were left living off the pension payments of grandparents; and cuts to healthcare spending resulted in increased HIV and malaria rates

For critics of the Euro, the Greek situation was brought on and exacerbated by the single currency, which imposed a 'one-size-fits-all' economic and political straitjacket on Greece which prevented them from adopting a more flexible approach to solving their debt crisis. For critics, the Eurozone was poorly-conceived and an accident waiting to happen, given its attempt to enforce an integrated single currency over such a wide range of unsynchronised economies:

1. The Eurozone, because it is built on a single currency, has a single interest rate set by the European Central Bank for the entire group of participating states; this is not sensible for states at different levels of economic development (e.g. strong exporters like Germany and the Netherlands, and weaker exporters like Greece and Spain)

2. Similarly, the cheap interest rates offered by the European Central Bank (relative to Greece's economy) irresponsibly encouraged them to borrow unsustainably and beyond their means

3. A common method to escape economic or debt crisis is to devalue the currency (reduce its exchange rate versus other currencies) to make exports cheaper and more attractive to foreign buyers, thereby kickstarting the economy. Within the Eurozone, this was not a possible strategy for Greece because the European Central Bank controls this policy, so Greece had few opportunities to restore its stagnating economy (which was in any case very dependent on tourism which

collapsed in the immediate aftermath of the crisis)

4. The structure of the EU meant that it would have been very difficult to write off the debt – because (i) taxpayers in wealthier countries would not have stood for it and (ii) it might encourage similarly risky borrowing by other Eurozone members

5. It has also been argued that the structures of the Eurozone's administration have simply punished Greece unfairly. Before the crisis, Greek government expenditure was at the EU average and Greeks worked on average the most days in the EU and had the lowest personal debts. In this view, the standards of living in Greece has been sacrificed to maintain the integrity of the monetary union (this is viewed as particularly unjust, since after WWII – in which Nazi Germany militarily occupied Greece and destroyed most of its industry – the Greek government wrote off 50% of the reparations/repayments owed to it by Germany to allow the German economy to recover)

Nevertheless, others would argue that the Greek debt crisis is not evidence of the Euro's inherent flaws and the overextension of economic integration, but of a need for *further* integration:

1. The creation of the Euro led to the pooling of **monetary policy** (controlling the quantity of currency available and the channels of supplying new money) at the EU-level, but not **fiscal policy** (the use of government spending, borrowing, and tax policies to influence economic conditions), which remained in the hands of individual states

2. This led to a scenario where individual states could pursue fiscal policies that would destabilise their economies, which would in turn destabilise the monetary union and have knock-on impacts on their Eurozone colleagues

3. The solution would be to adopt a supranational **fiscal policy** alongside the existing supranational monetary policy, at the EU level; to ensure that countries could not over-borrow, hide their debts and then expect other countries to bail

them out to protect the Euro

4. This is also true for a banking union; currently each member state is separately responsible for the regulation and **solvency** ('financial health') of its banks. However, in some countries, the banking sector is so large as a proportion of the economy, e.g. in Ireland, that a bank failing might cripple the entire economy and by extension the Eurozone. There is therefore an argument that in addition to the existing monetary union, and a proposed fiscal union, there should also be a banking union, with the same rules and regulations for all banks across the Eurozone (rather than encouraging states to adopt lax regulations to attract banks)

There are three broad perspectives one can take on the Eurozone:
1. The Eurozone could never have worked and is a ticking time-bomb
2. The Eurozone is an excellent idea and has improved the European economy
3. The Eurozone is a good idea, but monetary and banking union must accompany fiscal union [the obvious difficulty in this is that it would require states to pool additional sovereign powers, which might be unpopular and increase the democratic deficit]

The future of Euroscepticism?
Whilst in the UK, Euroscepticism is currently associated with right-wing politics (and this is indeed the norm across the EU), there are also left-wing Eurosceptics.
Right-wing Euroscepticism: The European Union is a bad idea because it undermines national sovereignty and seeks to impose a set of 'European' values which will overshadow the socially and culturally conservative principles of individual nation-states. Examples include:
- The AfD (Alternativ fur Deutschland) in Germany; in the 2017 German federal elections, the AfD won 94 seats (4.7% of the vote), becoming the third largest party in Germany
- The National Rally in France (formerly the 'National Front'), led by Marine le Pen, who came 2nd in the 2017 French Presidential election

- The 'Five Star Movement' (M5S) and 'Lega Nord' in Italy; Matteo Salvini, a dominant figure in the Lega Nord and ex-Deputy PM of Italy described the Euro as a 'crime against humanity'
- The 'Party for Freedom' (PPV) in the Netherlands, led by Geert Wilders, which was the second-largest party in the 2017 Dutch Election

Left-wing Euroscepticism: The European Union, as a single market based on generally neoliberal principles, imposes a capitalist framework which does more harm to workers than good. It has decimated industry in many EU countries and prevented member states from nationalising industries because of its rules on equal competition. Left-wing Eurosceptics tend to be 'soft Eurosceptics' rather than 'hard Eurosceptics' – rather than advocating for a dissolution of the EU, the mainstream Eurosceptic left tends to argue for reforming the EU and undoing the neoliberal-capitalist principles on which they believe it is based (e.g. Syriza, the left-wing party which formed the Greek government between 2015-2019).

There are different perspectives on the future of Euroscepticism in the EU. Some would argue that Euroscepticism is **growing** in significance and will eventually lead to the dissolution of the EU, or at least a significant reduction in its geographical scope. This is because of growing tensions between two 'tiers' of economic development in the Eurozone which make the maintenance of a single currency and interest rate impossible; the 'overreach' of the EU in attempting to create a 'European monoculture', European army and 'European superstate' which will result in a sovereign-nationalist backlash leading to the shattering of the entire regionalist project. Turkey's reorientation towards the Middle East demonstrates the lessening importance of the EU bloc. In this view, Brexit was the harbinger of a more serious wave of Eurosceptisim which will eventually overwhelm the major European countries which are 'net losers' from the EU budget, contributing more than they receive in return and 'subsidising' the development of poorer neighbours.

Others would argue that Euroscepticism is **receding** in significance and is largely reflective of increased tensions and isolationism globally in the wake of the 2008 financial crisis. Since 2008, positive perceptions of the EU have grown in nearly every

EU country, most Eurosceptic parties have lost ground in elections, and there seems to be a clear majority in favour of the EU in every EU country today (bar France). This may be for a number of reasons; the apparent economic chaos generated by Brexit, which makes a similarly 'hard' exit unappealing for other EU members; the success of Merkel's refugee policy in integrating 1 million Syrian migrants, which has dampened the popularity of the AfD in Germany; the increasing threat proposed by Russia which has encouraged greater unity in the EU and led to new applications (Ukraine, Georgia). Even in conservative-nationalist countries like Poland and Hungary, support for the EU is very high because it is clear that membership of the EU is on the whole advantageous. In a world dominated by aggressive 'great powers' – Russia, China, and the USA, European unity is appealing.

EU Parlameter 2018 poll; 'Taking everything into account, would you say that [country] has on balance benefited or not benefited from being a member of the EU?' 91-100%, 81-90%, 71-80%, 61-70%, 51-60%, 41-50%

Most in member nations hold favorable views of EU

% who have a ___ opinion of the European Union

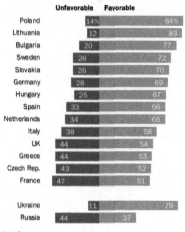

	Unfavorable	Favorable
Poland	14%	84%
Lithuania	12	83
Bulgaria	20	77
Sweden	26	72
Slovakia	26	70
Germany	28	69
Hungary	25	67
Spain	33	66
Netherlands	34	66
Italy	38	58
UK	44	54
Greece	44	53
Czech Rep.	43	52
France	47	51
Ukraine	11	79
Russia	44	37

Note: Don't know responses not shown.
Source: Spring 2019 Global Attitudes Survey. Q8d.

PEW RESEARCH CENTER

Views of the EU in 2019 – they are net-positive in every EU country, although notably close to a 50-50 margin in France. It is worth noting that in the bulk of EU countries, favourable views outweigh unfavourable views by around a 2-1 margin, even in more nationalist states like Hungary

Views of the European Union over time

% who have a favourable opinion of the European Union

	2004 %	2007 %	2009 %	2010 %	2011 %	2012 %	2013 %	2014 %	2015 %	2016 %	2017 %	2018 %	2019 %	'07-'19 Change	'16-'19 Change
Greece	--	--	--	--	--	37	33	34	--	27	34	37	53	--	+26
Germany	58	68	65	62	66	68	60	66	58	50	68	63	69	+1	+19
Spain	--	80	77	77	72	60	46	50	63	47	62	67	66	-14	+19
Sweden	--	59	--	--	--	--	--	--	--	54	65	62	72	+13	+18
Netherlands	--	--	--	--	--	--	--	--	--	51	64	63	66	--	+15
France	69	62	62	64	63	60	41	54	55	38	56	62	51	-11	+13
Poland	--	83	77	81	74	69	68	72	72	72	74	72	84	+1	+12
UK	54	52	50	49	51	45	43	52	51	44	54	48	54	+2	+10
Hungary	--	--	--	--	--	--	--	--	--	61	67	57	67	--	+6
Italy	--	78	--	--	--	59	58	46	64	58	57	58	58	-20	0
Lithuania	--	--	--	--	78	--	--	--	--	--	--	--	83	--	--
Bulgaria	--	81	--	--	--	--	--	--	--	--	--	--	77	-4	--
Slovakia	--	79	--	--	--	--	--	--	--	--	--	--	70	-9	--
Czech Rep.	--	54	--	--	--	34	--	--	--	--	--	--	52	-2	--
Ukraine	--	77	--	--	72	--	--	63	72	--	--	--	79	+2	--
Russia	62	62	69	69	64	59	63	39	31	--	--	--	37	-25	--

Views of the EU from 2004-2019. It is worth noting that since the 'height' of Euroscepticism in 2016 [around the time of Britain's referendum vote to leave], views of the EU have recovered strongly across the bloc by around 15 points on average

The power of the EU on the global stage

When considering the EU's significance as a standard-bearer for regionalism, it is crucial to analyse the EU's relevance and power on the global stage. Before examining the evidence, it is worth briefly clarifying some concepts which appeared in the parts of 3.4 – Power and Developments, which were cut from the Summer 2022 examinations.

Types of power

Power = the ability to compel or influence another (in the context of global politics, other states) to do something they would otherwise not have done

Hard power = Coercive power – ways of forcing or making states doing something, whilst they do not want to do it. This can be achieved through military force (the use, or threat of it), or economic force (such as sanctions or trade embargoes)

Soft power = Persuasive power – ways of convincing states to change their behaviour or policy, or to imitate the values, interests and concerns of the state. This can be achieved through diplomacy, cultural attraction, economic attraction (such as trade deals and improved market access)

Classifications of state power

Great power = A great power is a state (or very integrated collection of states) which is able to project power on a global stage beyond its immediate regional neighbours. China and Russia are commonly cited as 'great powers'; India and Brazil are commonly cited as potential great powers

Superpower = A superpower is a state (or very integrated collection of states) which is able to project power on a global stage in a way which exceeds nearly every other state by orders of magnitude. Other great powers may align themselves to superpowers; and a superpower has few or no equals. The USA is commonly cited as a 'superpower'; China is commonly cited as a potential superpower

We can now analyse the significance of the EU on the global stage, in relation to other major powers such as China, the USA, Russia, and major global institutions.

The EU is a 'hidden superpower'	The EU is not a significant global power
Economic: • The EU contains many of the world's most prominent and advanced economies (including France, Germany, Italy, Spain, Belgium and the Netherlands). Combined, its economy would be larger than China's and only slightly behind the USA's, with a combined GDP of over \$15 trillion in 2020 (1/6 of the global economy) • The EU's economy is a single free market with no internal trade barriers, covering over 500 million citizens • 19 member states have joined the Eurozone monetary union which uses the Euro as a single currency, representing 342 million citizens. The Euro is the second largest reserve currency and the second most traded currency in the world	Economic: • The vast disparity in terms of rates of growth between different national economies in the EU has made the Euro increasingly unstable (e.g. the Greek financial crisis and the austerity measure imposed by the EU to re-stabilise the Euro as a single currency). There is increasing tension between less developed EU countries and Germany, which is perceived to 'run' the EU in a dictatorial manner • There are emerging debt crises in Italy and Spain, which may again threaten the integrity of the single-market • The impact shock of Brexit has yet to be fully realised. It is not as bad as the 'hard Brexit' that some feared might happen, but it will still have serious consequences. We can already see tensions arising over the

• Of the top 500 largest corporations in the world, 161 are headquartered in the EU. The EU has invested in developing poorer regions of the continent (e.g. Romania, Bulgaria and Croatia), and improving infrastructure to provide easier cross-border movement of people, goods and services • The attractiveness of the EU's developed, high-tech economy has led to it concluding numerous free trade deals with other large economies, such as Canada, Japan and MERCOSUR (the South American free trade bloc) – the EU is the largest exporter in the world • The size of the EU's economy means it can impose effective sanctions (e.g. those imposed on Russia in 2014 after the annexation of Crimea, or 2022 after the general invasion of Ukraine)	application of the Withdrawal Agreement at the Republic of Ireland – Northern Ireland border, and these will intensify over time. Brexit will not cripple Europe's economic potential entirely, but it may slow growth in the short-term or even lead to other states leaving the EU in the wake of the UK's exit (if this sets a broader precedent) • Because the EU is an inter-state organisation, any decisions on external economic policy (aid, sanctions, etc.) require a high degree of consensus which is not always possible. For example, EU sanctions on Russia in the wake of Putin's invasion of Ukraine were watered down by Italian (wanted to protect luxury exports), Austrian and Hungarian opposition
Military: • The EU's constituent member states have some of the world's most technologically	Military: • Proposals for a unified EU army have not come to fruition over the past few decades,

advanced militaries, which have been deployed in various conflicts (e.g. Libya and Afghanistan, under the aegis of NATO or other independent operations – such as those of France in Mali against ISIS and Ansar Dine, an Islamist terrorist group)

- The EU has engaged in some collective military action, notably in peacekeeping efforts in North Africa and the suppression of piracy in Somalia
- The EU has developed 'Battlegroups' under the Common Security and Defence Policy (CSDP) – these are combined inter-state European battalions of 1,500 troops, of which two are operational at any given time, with others on standby. E.g. in 2020, the two battlegroups are a 'Balkan' BG led by Greece and a 'German' BG (also including many central and northern European states). EU Battlegroups train in 'wargames' for conflict and security scenarios, e.g. in 2014 practising the suppression of ethnic conflict between the

primarily because of justifiable concerns from states regarding the surrender of a key component of their national sovereignty. The proposal has been on the table since the 1950s, but despite support from state leaders (like Macron and Merkel), there has been little substantive progress

- Another obstacle to the creation of a European army is the existence of NATO – there is little appetite for creating an institution which would duplicate much of the work of NATO (21 of 27 EU states are also NATO members). It does not make sense for EU states to spend additional money on defence when it is possible to 'pass the burden' onto the USA via NATO. Furthermore, some consider that without the USA's participation, Europe could not 'defend itself' and the creation of an independent EU army makes little sense
- Although EU Battlegroups are a step towards combined operational capacity, full integration is limited by

'Greys' and the 'Whites' in the imaginary country of 'Blueland' • France has nuclear weapons, and there are American missiles stationed in many other EU countries, like Germany • In 2022, the EU collectively sent weapons and military aid to Ukraine	language barriers and differences in the exact type of weaponry used by countries. EU Battlegroups have never been deployed, because it is very difficult to get unanimous consent for them in the European Council
Institutional: • Although the EU is not a singular state, it is represented as a singular unified entity (alongside its constituent member states) in the World Trade Organisation, the International Monetary Fund, the World Bank, the G20 and the G7 • The political clout of the EU was demonstrated in its negotiations with Iran over the nuclear issue, where it played a key role in convincing Iran to stop enriching uranium to high levels (highly-enriched uranium can be used to make nuclear weaponry, whereas lower-grade uranium has medical and energy applications) in exchange for	Institutional: • As with its economic and military power, the key drawback to the EU's exercise of institutional power is not its lack of capabilities but the divisions between the many constituent states of the European Union. Where states have different aims, it is impossible to get internal consensus to then present a united front in a larger institution of global governance • For example, there are distinct divisions within the EU over nationalism/ how the EU should respond to the Middle Eastern and North African migrant crisis. Some states, especially Italy and Greece,

the lifting of sanctions (the agreement was called the Joint Comprehensive Plan of Action, or JCPOA). Since the USA's re-imposition of sanctions, the EU has collectively maintained a distinct stance and continues to not impose sanctions

- Another example of the EU acting as a unified entity in political negotiations is its membership of the 'Quartet' – the UN, USA, EU and Russia – which has responsibility for mediating the Israeli-Palestinian peace process; it is the largest donor of foreign aid to Palestine
- The EU has other policies of collective action, such as a comprehensive arms embargo to China since the 1989 Tiananmen Square massacre

have taken a much more hard-line stance than others. States which are closer to the Mediterranean and are faced with the greatest influx of migrants are often those who most oppose EU plans to take in more refugees from conflict zones

- Another division within the EU is the increasing rejection of liberalism and democracy by the 'Visegrad Group' including Hungary and Poland – this damages the EU's wider influence in institutions when it is arguing for a liberal-democratic perspective. There is no formal mechanism to expel or suspend states which experience 'democratic backsliding'

Soft power:

- The EU exercises soft power as an attractive liberal-democratic, peaceful and successful institution. This encourages other states (e.g. post-Yugoslav Serbia) to change their policies in order to gain admission, e.g.

Soft power:

- The attractiveness of the EU's values may be damaged by the recent emergence of far-right nationalism in various countries (the Front National in France; the AfD in Germany; Jobbik in Hungary; Golden Dawn in Greece; Law and

arresting former war criminals for trial	Justice in Poland; the Brexit project in the UK, etc.). This undermines the perception of the EU as a liberal, tolerant and welcoming place
• Many countries want to join the EU, e.g. Ukraine, Macedonia, Serbia, Georgia – it is 'attractive'	
• Education is another soft power tool in the EU's arsenal – 27 of the world's top 100 universities are in Europe; the EU hosts almost twice as many students from outside the EU than the USA hosts non-Americans, and more than 10-times non-Chinese at Chinese universities	• The EU's soft power does not lead to inevitable outcomes; it was, for example, an ambition of Turkey to join the EU in the early 2000s but it has now clearly decided to carve out its own semi-authoritarian, Turkish nationalist path under Erdogan and the AKP party, and move away from the liberalising, democratic projects it pursued when trying to gain official candidate status for EU membership
• Most of the world's national or second languages are European	
• EU countries have a great deal of attractive soft power in the case of culture, food, art, music and sports (consider how globally dominant Europe's football leagues are compared to the NFL or 'World Series' baseball)	• EU soft power has also not been able to successfully rope Russia into a cooperative relationship; nor has it been able to convince China to adopt democratic or human rights principles, despite extensive interactions and many diplomatic summits
• EU states dominate soft-power rankings and are globally perceived as happy, clean, lacking in corruption, etc.	

EUROPEAN UNION
CSDP MISSIONS AND OPERATIONS

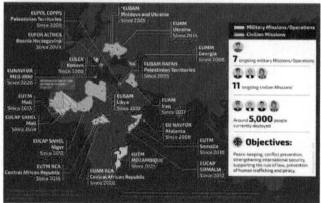

Map of current EU military deployments ('military missions' are active conflicts, 'civilian missions' are to support security and stability outside of ongoing conflict)

Regionalism beyond the European Union

There are many institutions of regional governance beyond the EU, but the specification requires us to look at four in particular:

- The Arab League (AL)
- The African Union (AU)
- The Association of South East Asian Nations (ASEAN)
- The North American Free Trade Agreement (NAFTA)
    - N.B. Although the specification says 'NAFTA', this has been superseded since July 2020 by the US-Mexico-Canada Agreement (USMCA)

In the table below, a brief overview of the membership; role; objectives; activities; successes and failures of each institution is outlined.

Arab League	African Union	ASEAN	NAFTA/USMCA
MEMBERSHIP:	MEMBERSHIP:	MEMBERSHIP:	MEMBERSHIP:

Founded with 7 members in 1945 (Egypt, Lebanon, Jordan, Iraq, Yemen, Saudi Arabia, Syria); it has since expanded to 22 members across the 'Arab world', including Palestine as a non-state member. Syria's membership has been suspended since 2011 because of the civil war	Founded in 2002, now representing a total of 55 member states across Africa. South Sudan joined in 2011 upon independence from Sudan; and Morocco in 2017. The memberships of Mali, Burkina Faso, Guinea and Sudan are currently suspended because of military coups	Founded in 1967 by Indonesia, Malaysia, Singapore, Thailand and the Philippines. It was updated with a 2008 charter for further integration. Now comprises of all 10 states in South-East Asia (above, plus Laos, Vietnam, Myanmar, Brunei, Cambodia)	Signed in 1994 between the USA, Mexico and Canada - the 3 major North American economies. It was renegotiated during Donald Trump's presidency as the USMCA, which was drafted in 2018, signed in 2019, and came into effect in July 2020
ROLE/ OBJECTIVES: The stated aim of the Arab League is to 'draw closer the relations between member states and coordinate collaboration between them, to safeguard their	ROLE/ OBJECTIVES: The aims of ASEAN are to encourage social, cultural, economic, technological and educational development; to promote peace and stability in	ROLE/ OBJECTIVES: The African Union was designed to replace the earlier Organisation of African Unity. Its objectives are to achieve greater unity, peace, stability and economic	ROLE/ OBJECTIVES: NAFTA/USMCA is designed to eliminate tariff and trade barriers across North America in order to engender greater international

independence and sovereignty, and to consider in a general way the affairs and interests of the Arab countries.' In other words, it is a very loose form of security and economic regionalism, and has few 'political' dimensions or 'common values'	the region; and to promote adherence to the UN Charter and the rule of law. ASEAN's initial formulation was as an anti-Communist alliance, but it has since moved on from this stance It primarily represents ideas of economic/ security regionalism	integration in Africa; to promote democratic principles; health and economic development; and African interests on the global stage. It therefore represents all three dimensions of regionalism – security, economic and political (democratic values)	trade on the continent, and therefore reduced prices for goods and a wider availability of goods, both of which will benefit consumers
STRUCTURE: The structures of the Arab League are entirely intergovernmental – there is no supranational decision-making. Each member state has one vote in the League Council, and decisions are	STRUCTURE: ASEAN does not have a legislative body; heads of government/state of members meet at least annually to discuss policy based on the principles of 'The ASEAN Way' – compromise, consensus and	STRUCTURE: The African Union's highest decision-making body is the Assembly of the African Union, which consists of heads of state/government; decisions here must be unanimous to be	STRUCTURE: NAFTA/UMSCA is not strictly speaking a regionalist 'organisation' – it is just a treaty or framework involving a set of rules that member states must implement.

binding only for those states that have voted for them	consultation whilst avoiding conflict	binding. Other institutions include the Pan-African Parliament (appointed)	Therefore, there is no permanent structure for negotiations/ discussions
SUCCESSES: In 2011, the Arab League Council agreed to suspend Syria because of Assad's war crimes and crimes against humanity in suppressing protests by the Syrian people In 1997, the Arab League created the Greater Arab Free Trade Area (GAFTA). This is a pan-Arab free-trade zone which enables the progressive reduction of tariffs; as of today, must tariffs have been eliminated. The 'Agadir	SUCCESSES: ASEAN agreed the creation of a free trade area (the AFTA) in 1992. This provides for low-tariff trade within ASEAN countries, with tariffs at a maximum of 5%. There are plans in place to create a true single market with a single currency – this would be larger in terms of population (500m+) than the Eurozone ASEAN works together to encourage tourism and has	SUCCESSES: The African Union has been somewhat effective at combating the AIDS pandemic, pushing for the recruitment, funding and training of 2 million community health workers continent-wide The African Union has a significant presence in peacekeeping operations and carries out some 'collective foreign policy'. For example, there have been AU peacekeeping	SUCCESSES: NAFTA immediately eliminated most tariffs between the US, Mexico and Canada when it was introduced; and the remaining ones were gradually phased out. Now, only a few minor agricultural tariffs remain between the USA and Mexico NAFTA has increased trade volumes, clearly benefiting Mexico and

Agreement' (2004) seeks to convert this into a true free trade area, and to combine this with the EU's free trade zone All member states are part of GAFTA (with the exception of Mauritania, Somalia, Djibouti and Comoros, which are all currently in the process of applying to join)	been very successful in doing so; this is perhaps clearest in the cases of Thailand, Vietnam and Cambodia, for whom tourism is now a major economic sector In 1995, ASEAN states negotiated the Southeast Asian Nuclear-Weapons-Free Zone Treaty to ban nuclear weapons from being stationed in the region by any other country. All member states have signed it	operations in Somalia and Darfur (Sudan), as well as in Mali against local Al-Qaeda and MNLA forces The African Union has been able to coordinate effective joint sanctions, e.g. imposing travel bans and asset freezes against the leaders of the rebellion in Comoros	Canada. It has also benefited the US in terms of reduced prices NAFTA's replacement, the USMCA, preserves much of the trade architecture of the original treaty but also opens up the Canadian dairy market to US farmers, and ensures that at least 30% of all cars are made by workers earning at least $16/day
FAILURES: The Arab League's first exercise of collective action was to fight the 1948 Arab-Israeli War. In this it was	FAILURES: ASEAN is firmly committed to the principle of state sovereignty, which makes it difficult to	FAILURES: Economic integration between AU members has been very slow. The AU has long	FAILURES: The original NAFTA framework broke down under the presidency of

decisively beaten, and has generally been unable to 'solve' the Palestine issue because of internal divisions between states

The Arab League has also been split over the Gulf War in 1991; the Saudi intervention in Yemen; and Qatar-Saudi tensions. It has been unable to mediate a resolution to the civil war in Syria | advance integration at a faster rate. Most ASEAN countries would not support supranational governance

It also makes it very difficult for ASEAN to deal effectively with 'internal' state issues, e.g. the crisis in Myanmar (both the Rohingya genocide, the 2021 military coup and the ongoing civil war) | discussed the creation of a single market with a central bank and common currency (possibly called 'the Afro') and initially set a deadline of 2023. This is almost certain to be missed by the AU, and would be rife with the same problems as the Euro (difficulty of applying a blanket fiscal policy to states at different levels of development), on a magnified scale | Donald Trump, because he felt that the terms of trade with Canada and Mexico were damaging US manufacturing. This led to the USMCA re-negotiation to secure terms more favourable to the US economy (e.g. 30% of cars to be made by workers earning at least $16/day – this would shift automobile manufacturing jobs from Mexico to the US, since most Mexican factories do not meet this wage) |

Most of these regionalist institutions are nowhere near as effective as the EU, because the EU has uniquely integrated supranational mechanisms of governance. In the intergovernmental structures of the AU, Arab League and ASEAN, it is much more difficult to reach consensus and implement joint policy. One view is that these other regional blocs will move in the direction of the EU over time. Another view is that they will never be as successful as the EU in the short-term because:

- Democracy is less entrenched (and, with the exception of the AU, there is no bloc-wide commitment to democracy), which makes inter-state cooperation more difficult
- The EU was born out of the unique circumstances of a brutal continent-wide war, which made the commitment to supranational regionalism much more appealing to member states

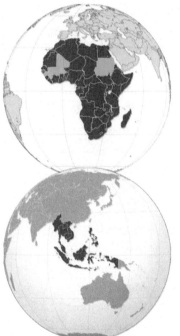

Top-left going clockwise; the African Union, NAFTA/ USMCA, the Arab League, ASEAN

Regionalism and contemporary global issues

Conflict

Regionalism has helped to solve the issue	Regionalism hasn't helped to solve the issue
The EU has done very well in resolving conflict amongst participating member states – there have been no major wars in Western Europe since the creation of the EU. The EU has engaged in peacekeeping efforts in North Africa and Somalia. Arguably, the raft of EU sanctions deployed against Russia in the wake of the 2022 invasion of Ukraine will have a notable impact in crippling the Russian economy and reducing the appetite for war in the Kremlin The EU's negotiations with Iran (as part of the P5+1) helped to defuse Middle Eastern nuclear tensions and prevent an open war between Saudi Arabia/Israel and Iran The African Union (AU) has engaged in peacekeeping efforts across the continent; in Mali, Western Sahara, the Congo, South Sudan, and the Central African Republic; some of these have been very important in restoring stability in post-conflict zones	The EU has been unable to prevent Russian expansion in Eastern Europe; and in any case, does not have a unified military that could help to resolve conflicts. Many EU negotiating efforts have been unsuccessful, e.g. attempts to mediate the Israel-Palestine conflict as part of the 'Quartet'. The EU was unable to prevent the outbreak of serious violence in Yugoslavia during the 1990s The African Union has failed to resolve many conflicts, including the Morocco-Western Sahara territorial dispute The Arab League and ASEAN have been unsuccessful in preventing conflict, because of their strict stance on the preservation of state sovereignty – this is why little has been done about the Saudi intervention in Yemen, despite the ongoing humanitarian catastrophe; or in the Myanmar military's genocide against the Rohingya Muslim minority

Poverty

Regionalism has helped to solve the issue	Regionalism hasn't helped to solve the issue
Both ASEAN and the EU are good examples of regional blocs which have reduced tariffs and increased interstate trade, consequently significantly improving poverty rates in the bloc. For example, both Cambodia and Laos are expected to have cut the percentage of the population in extreme poverty to 1% by 2026/7; this is a remarkable achievement for countries that had poverty rates of 30% a few decades ago The EU also contributes funds to institutions of global economic governance like the World Bank; between 2015-2019, the EU contributed €2.07 billion to support development projects in developing countries around the world	Corruption in many African governments has crippled efforts by the African Union to implement continent-wide poverty reduction initiatives; a lot of money is lost to embezzlement. The AU's main focus so far has been conflict resolution, and there are few specific initiatives for poverty reduction High poverty rates persist across the Arab League, and some ASEAN countries, e.g. Indonesia; there are few centralised initiatives for poverty reduction, as most economic discussions centre on trade (which does definitely improve GDP, but not necessarily wealth for all citizens)

Human rights

Regionalism has helped to solve the issue	Regionalism hasn't helped to solve the issue
The EU and African Union both adhere to democracy as a fundamental principle and do a lot to entrench this in their respective	Because most regionalist organisations adopt a 'non-interventionist' principle with a strong focus on state sovereignty, it

continents. The EU in particular has advanced a wide array of rights and liberties in its legislation

In 2015, the European Commission proposed a scheme to redistribute 120,000 arriving refugees from Syria, Eritrea and Iraq (fleeing civil wars and widespread persecution) across EU states based on their GDP/population. The plan was approved by QMV and was partially implemented, despite legal challenges

The EU's response to the Russian invasion of Ukraine has been largely positive in human rights terms; the EU has invoked the 'Temporary Protection Directive' to take in Ukrainian refugees and instantly give them rights to live and work in the bloc, as well as accessing social service benefits

All EU states align with the ECHR and are party to the European Court of Human Rights, helping to uphold rights across the continent

is difficult to uphold human rights in the bloc. For example, it has not been possible for ASEAN to deal with President Duterte's abuse of human rights in his 'War on Drugs' in the Philippines

The Arab League consistently overlooks issues of rights for women, religious minorities, and LGBT groups as 'state matters'

Furthermore, one could argue that the EU's refugee and migration policy has been actively detrimental to human rights. 'Fortress Europe' militarised responses to push back asylum seekers and refugees at the EU's peripheral borders; for example in Greece, and Poland, are contradictory to international law. This is especially true for migrants/refugees from the 'developing world' in a racist manner. Because of opposition from Slovakia, Hungary, Romania and Czechia, the 'Migrant Redistribution Scheme' was generally abandoned by the Commission in 2020

Environmental issues

Regionalism has helped to solve the issue	Regionalism hasn't helped to solve the issue
The EU has contributed as a collective bloc to environmental negotiations (it sits as a separate observer without voting rights in major treaty discussions under the UNFCCC framework). Ambitious targets are set by the EU collectively, in addition to the individual targets set by member states. Current EU targets are to reduce GHG emissions by 55% by 2030; and to be carbon neutral by 2050. Other key proposals in the EU's climate plan are tighter emissions limits for cars; a tax on aviation fuel; a 'carbon border' tariff for importing materials like steel and concrete; and a requirement to renovate buildings for energy efficiency	Only the EU has really put forwards meaningful climate change policies, out of all the major institutions of regional governance. Indeed, it may actually be argued that by pursuing economic regionalism and an increase in trade as the primary goal, most regionalist institutions are undermining climate change goals. The Arab League in particular, which has several major oil-producers as members, is reluctant to take serious action on decarbonisation

In addition, the EU's 2021 Climate Plan has not yet been fully approved in the European Commission and current targets are insufficient |

Regionalism and globalisation
Another key debate in the academic study of regionalism is the relationship of this process to that of globalisation; is regional integration something which leads to globalisation, or something which counteracts and undermines it?

Regionalism leads to globalisation	Regionalism counteracts globalisation
Trade deals: Single market and customs union deals struck in	Trade deals: Regional institutions prevent states from being

regionalist blocs are generally the precursor for further global integration. They make it easier for free-trade zones to be created, because two large blocs or economic can negotiate with each other, and automatically bring all of their states directly into an economic relationship with each other (instead of each state having to negotiate accession separately).

This can be seen through the recent trade deals that the EU has struck with Canada, Japan and MERCOSUR (at various stages of ratification and implementation). In this view, economic regionalism is inevitably a building block for economic globalisation

overwhelmed by the power of larger states when negotiating trade deals, preventing the maximal outcome of economic globalisation (total integration with almost no barriers). For example, in trade negotiations with the USA over the Transatlantic Trade and Investment Partnership (TTIP), the EU was able to secure terms such as not allowing growth hormones in meat or chlorine-washed chicken; and protecting 'DOP' products like champagne, which can only be described as such if produced in the Champagne region of France. It is hard to imagine a lone state negotiating so effectively (indeed the UK caved on food standards when negotiating post-Brexit deals with the USA)

Sovereignty: State sovereignty is fundamentally undermined by regionalism, especially forms of regionalism which rely on supranational governance. The ability of people to make and implement their own democratic laws is eroded – for example, the ECJ ruled that temporary and agency workers are entitled to the same holiday rights as full-time workers. EU member states do not have a choice over whether or

Sovereignty: States can increase their negotiating leverage through membership of regionalist organisations; this provides the means to resist the worst effects of globalisation and to interact with more powerful states on an even footing. For example, in the negotiations over the border between the Republic of Ireland and the United Kingdom, the UK was clearly more powerful and would

not to implement this. In this way, we could argue that regionalism is a step towards political globalisation and the full integration of political decision-making in such a way that individual states have lost or sacrificed part of their *de jure* sovereignty through membership of a regional institution like the EU	have dominated a bilateral discussion. However, Ireland was not negotiating as a lone state but as part of the broader EU bloc, which allowed it to resist the imposition of a 'hard border'. Regionalism preserves and enhances the *de facto* sovereignty of all states in the organisation, and enables them to resist globalisation
Relationship with TNCs: Some would argue that regional organisations pursue integrated trade, and therefore prioritise the needs of 'big corporations' and TNCs like Coca-Cola, GlaxoSmithKline and Unilever, rather than ordinary people. This accelerates the process of economic globalisation as corporations with a larger turnover and a sharper competitive edge push out smaller companies. States find it difficult to protect their own industries through subsidies, tariffs or nationalisation, because the terms of economic regionalism tend to limit these practises as 'anti-integration'	Relationship with TNCs: Some would argue that regional organisations can adopt joint policies and approaches to prevent TNCs from 'shopping around' for the lowest taxes and laxest regulations. If all states in a bloc set a common standard, then TNCs have no choice but to play by those rules if they want to operate in that market. In the EU, a company like Apple (with a value slightly less than the GDP of Ireland) cannot escape environmental regulations by setting up in another EU country because these are standardised. Therefore, regionalism is a barrier to globalisation

Future prospects for regionalism

The final debate with regards to regionalism is the degree to which regional organisations have a bright future. Will they survive and prosper; or wither away?

Some of the main arguments are outlined below, although this is not an exhaustive list.

Regionalism has a bright future	Regionalism does not have a bright future
Many countries are queuing up to join the EU (there are 5 recognised candidates – Turkey, Macedonia, Montenegro, Albania and Serbia); and several potential candidates (Bosnia, Kosovo, Ukraine, Georgia and Moldova). This demonstrates the attractiveness and long-term durability of the bloc	In 2016, the UK voted to leave the EU and in 2020 became the first country to leave. This was unprecedented for an institution of such integrated supranational governance and might signify the growing strength of Eurosceptic sentiment across the EU (especially in Italy, Austria, and France)
ASEAN is continuing to integrate not just in economic areas, but has formally begun the process of unifying 'political-security' and 'socio-cultural' pillars	ASEAN is a cautious and conservative bloc, which prevents bold steps forward. There are fundamental disagreements over democracy, human rights and governing practises
The Arab League has shown signs of strength, cohesion and effectiveness in its suspension of Syria over Assad's reaction to 2011 protests and the ensuing Syrian Civil War	The Arab League has achieved nothing substantive in the Syrian conflict, and it is likely that relations with Damascus will be normalised if Assad 'wins' (survives) the civil war
Even with the UK voting to leave the EU, it is obvious that the UK and EU must continue to economically cooperate. Nearly every country is part of a regional trade bloc, and the UK is coming to realise the same	There is significant opposition to economic regionalism (e.g. opposition to the UK rejoining the single market; as well as strong opposition in the USA from Trump and Sanders against the TPP (Trans-Pacific Partnership) trade bloc

The problems that led to the formation of regional organisations have not gone away, e.g. immigration, climate change. These issues are likely to get worse, which will catalyse further integration of regional organisations in order to deal with these mounting challenges	There is real democratic support for the 'taking back control' argument in much of the Western world. Many people view regional blocs as undemocratic, and favour the state 'taking control' of matters itself (e.g. peripheral EU states' stance on refugees)
Security fears are mounting in Europe as a result of Russia's expansionism; and in Asia as a result of China's growing power and assertiveness. This may strengthen regional blocs as a bulwark against 'great power' threats – e.g. Finland/Sweden considering NATO membership in light of the 2022 Ukraine war	Some would argue that co-operation is necessary in the face of security challenges, but that this can be achieved without formal institutional structures and organisations, and instead simply by multilateral negotiations and partnerships (e.g. UK/US/EU coordinating on sanctions against Russia in 2022)

Global Politics – Unit 3.6
Comparative theories of international relations

THE STATE
Definition of the state
A **state** is defined by Max Weber as "a human community that successfully claims the monopoly on the legitimate use of physical force within a given territory." In other words, it is a defined area in which there is a sovereign political authority.
The **Montevideo Convention (1933)** defines a state as a political entity possessing all of the following qualities:
1. A permanent population
2. Clearly defined borders and territory
3. A functioning sovereign government
4. Majority recognition from other states (and the capacity to interact with them)

To illustrate this with examples:
1. **Palestine** would not be a state, because the Palestinian Authority is not sovereign; in many instances, it must defer to the Israeli government or the IDF (Israeli military). Palestinian territory is also poorly defined and fractured by a multitude of illegal Israeli settlements, so it is in practise unclear what the legal boundaries/ borders of Palestine are

2. **Antarctica** would not be a state because it does not have a political sovereign; the Antarctic Treaty System (established in 1961) designates Antarctica as a natural reservation for scientific research and investigation, and bars any country from military activity there

3. **Syria** in the midst of its civil war might not be considered a functioning state because the 'official' governments do not have a monopoly on the legitimate use of physical force. Different people believe different groups (the Kurds, the Turks, ISIS, Syrian rebel forces, Iran, etc.) should have the right to exercise physical power in the territory and the 'right' of Assad's government to utilise physical power is not universally recognised

4. **Abkhazia** is a territory which broke away from Georgia with Russian assistance (along with South Ossetia). It survives only by Russian military and economic assistance and is recognised as a state by only 5 other UN member states. In practise, this means it is not a state because it does not have established political relations with other states and doesn't have the capacity to interact with them, precluding it from involvement in global trade. It also doesn't have a strictly sovereign government and is heavily reliant on Russia. The **Turkish Republic of Northern Cyprus** is in a similar situation, vis-à-vis Cyprus and Turkey

5. **Cosa Nostra** (the Sicilian Mafia) are paid protection money by roughly 70% of Sicilian businesses. However, they would probably not qualify as a state, because they are not recognised as a 'legitimate' actor, even though they do exercise physical power. Large criminal syndicates in general (the triads, yakuza, Mob, etc.) all fall into this category – they utilise power but are not seen as the sovereign power in the territory. The Italian government can prosecute the Cosa Nostra, but the Cosa Nostra cannot prosecute the Italian government. It is clearly recognised by everyone who the 'superior power' is

Points 1-3 of the Montevideo Convention closely reflect Weber's definition. Point 4 is different, as it doesn't rely on any *internal* characteristic of the state, but on *external* recognition from other established states. This is generally a sensible part of the definition, because without an ability to interact with other states, it is difficult for a governed territory to survive and prosper. However, in certain circumstances, a state may fulfil points 1-3 (population, territory, sovereignty) but lack full international recognition and/or membership of the UN, yet still be a viable political unit. Examples of this would include **Taiwan** (not a member of the UN or recognised by most states, but still heavily involved in global trade and very wealthy) and **Kosovo** (not recognised by Serbia or its allies, but recognised by 51% of UN member states, including most of North America, Europe and the Middle East). It is perhaps not necessary for a state to have 'official' diplomatic recognition, but it definitely needs to have the ability to interact with other states, and/or to have recognition from enough powerful states that it can be viable in the international arena. Point 4 of the Montevideo Convention is therefore more ambiguous and less clear-cut.

The Westphalian state system

The current model of international politics is based on something developed in the 17th century called the 'Peace of Westphalia'. The Peace of Westphalia was designed to put an end to the religious conflicts that had plagued Europe for centuries, fought between different denominations of Christianity, as Catholic polities tried to overthrow Protestant ones and vice-versa. There were overlapping loyalties to kings, local rulers, and religious authorities. The Peace of Westphalia redrew the map of Europe 'neatly' into organised nation-states, and asserted that each nation-state (with a singular sovereign) would have the right to determine which kind of Christianity it wanted to practise within its own borders, and that this right should not be infringed by other nation-states.

This reflects the key principles of Weber's definition:
- A state must have a well-defined **territory**, with a population and clear borders
- A state must be **sovereign** (have the full legitimate ability to make decisions in that territory)

The controversy in the Westphalian model of statehood and international relations (reflected in concerns today about humanitarian intervention, climate change policy and so on) is that it seems to suggest that a state has the absolute right to carry out any policies it wants to within its own borders – including genocide, suppression of civil liberties, environmental desecration, etc. It suggests that anyone living within the boundaries of the state must conform to the state's legislation.

The dilemma of the nation-state

The model of 'nation-states' is problematic for international relations in several ways.

1. **Nations without a state:** E.g. the Palestinians (effectively under Israeli sovereignty) or the Uighurs (under Chinese sovereignty); or national groups which cross state boundaries, e.g. the Kurds (spread across Syria, Iraq and Turkey) or the Basques (spread across northern Spain and south-western France). In these cases, national groups may turn to violence to 'liberate' themselves and create their own nation-states. The existing states controlling

those groups may instigate violence to suppress those national identities in favour of the state's main national group to maintain the cohesion of the state. In these scenarios, should other states intervene? Is there an absolute sovereign right for states to suppress national minorities?

2. **States not recognising other self-defined nation-states:** E.g. the general lack of recognition from the international community of the Turkish Republic of Northern Cyprus (except Turkey). This may lead to tensions between two established states over whether a territory should be recognised as an independent state and threaten to escalate into wider conflict. As mentioned above, a national territory without diplomatic recognition as a state will struggle to engage in international relations. However, it is possible over time that a self-defined nation-state, though initially rejected by the international community, will gradually come to be recognised as a legitimate state because of the changing realities of the situation (e.g. Communist China was initially not recognised as a state by the West, but now is)

3. **Nation-states with competing claims to the same territory:** E.g. Kashmir being disputed between India and Pakistan; the Falkland Islands being disputed between the UK and Argentina; disputes in the South China Sea between China, Vietnam, Brunei and the Philippines. Since the definition of statehood requires a singular sovereign in a territory, this means that war or general diplomatic hostility is a likely consequence of nation-states both claiming a territory is inhabited by people of 'their nation'

Reconsidering national sovereignty

A very basic definition of sovereignty is 'absolute or supreme power'. Within its defined territory, a state is deemed to be sovereign – both over its citizens and anyone else who resides within its **jurisdiction** (the area in which laws apply). It can make and unmake any laws, and take any action that it deems appropriate.

However, developments in global politics have called the strict definition of sovereignty into question. Globalisation means that states are, especially in economic and ecological terms, interdependent.

1. **Economic interdependence:** States fundamentally do not have complete control over economic activity/impacts/processes within their territory once they are tied up in the network of international trade. Policies made in one state can affect the economy of another. We can see this in the economic fallout from Brexit, and the economic fallout from the US-China trade war instigated by President Trump against Xi Jinping's China

2. **Climate change:** States fundamentally do not have complete control over ecological impacts/processes within their territory, since the climate is inherently a global phenomenon – storms, air flows, the water cycle, temperature, etc. do not 'respect' state borders. Policies made in one state can affect the environment of another. We can see this in the phenomenon of climate change – the largest total polluters in the world are the USA, the EU, India, China and Russia. Yet countries with limited carbon emissions in the developing world are still impacted by droughts and floods. A state cannot adopt an 'isolationist' climate change policy

3. **Pandemics/global health:** States fundamentally do not have complete control over public health within their territory, since pandemics (AIDS/HIV; swine flu; coronavirus) do not 'respect' state borders. Policies made in one state can affect the public health of another. Unless a state completely cuts itself off from the global flow of people and goods, it cannot really stop a pandemic from spreading into its territory

All of this suggests that nation-states are not really 'sovereign' in the strict sense of the word. They do not have absolute or supreme power within their territories because things happening in other states affect them deeply. Instead, it might be more useful to think about a new model of sovereignty in a globalised world, which acknowledges that states do not have **absolute** power, and that the effective ability to exercise power within a state requires cooperation with other states.

However, it would not be appropriate to say that nation-states are 'pointless' in a globalised world. For example (data graph below accurate as of 1st November 2020), coronavirus cases are highest in Europe and the Americas, whereas they are significantly lower in the rest of the world. The reason this is the case is because different states have adopted different domestic policies regarding lockdowns, masks, social distancing, testing and tracking, quarantines, etc., and these have meant different outcomes. Even though the global spread of the virus calls into question the strict definition of national sovereignty, the differing rates of the virus across states proves that the concept of nation-state sovereignty is not entirely meaningless.

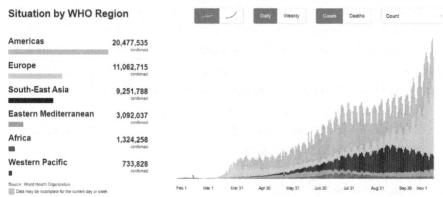

THEORY 1: REALISM

Realism is a **positivist** theory of global politics. Positivists believe that it is possible to distinguish between 'facts' and 'values', and claims to provide an **amoral** (not concerned with morals at all – neither 'moral' nor 'immoral') explanation of the world 'as it is' and offer practical solutions based on this understanding. Realism claims to be 'realistic' and devoid of wishful utopianism or moralising. **Hans Morgenthau** neatly summarised realism in claiming:

"Politics is a struggle for power over men, and whatever its ultimate aim may be, power is its immediate goal; and the modes of acquiring, maintaining and demonstrating it determine the technique of political action."

The principles of realism

As a starting point, realism focuses on nation-states, arguing that they are the most important **actors** (entities/bodies which perform actions) in the global system. They believe that the following are **axiomatic** (self-evident) features of human and state behaviour:

1. Human nature is **selfish**, and so states as conglomerations of humans, are also selfish
2. States are **rational** (i.e. they will act in their immediate self-interest)
3. States are **amoral** (i.e. they do not pursue abstract concepts of 'good' or 'morality')
4. States seek **power** (i.e. they seek the ability to compel and influence other states)
5. States are **unitary actors** (i.e. a state, though it has many citizens, acts with a singular will)

Many of the realist beliefs about state behaviour are similar to traditional conservative beliefs about human nature, particularly those of **Hobbes.** In the work of Hobbes, unconstrained human beings exist in a brutal "state of nature", competing for their own self-interest and harming others in order to achieve this. Only by establishing a **sovereign**, which implements law and acts as an overarching authority, can this anarchy be escaped. What realists propose is that the international arena is effectively a "state of nature", with a multitude of competing state actors but no overarching sovereign actor to keep states in line and enforce peace (because states themselves are sovereigns). This is a condition known as **international anarchy.**

In a system of international anarchy, concepts such as **rights** and **justice** would be meaningless, since states would act only to preserve and extend their own interest (the acquisition of power) and would not care about whether something is 'good' or 'ethical' or 'moral'.

It is important to note that there is a distinction between two schools of thought in realism:

- **Classical realism:** States are selfish because human beings are selfish; states are conglomerations of human beings, and so naturally reflect this
- **Structural realism:** States must be selfish because it is the only rational way to survive in a system of international anarchy (the 'Prisoners' Dilemma')

Realism and international relations

The way in which realists understand state interactions can be explained through the thought experiment of the **Prisoners' Dilemma.** In this hypothetical, the police have captured two criminals (A and B). They have enough evidence to charge both with a lesser offence (1 year in prison), but want to get them for a more serious charge. The police separate A and B into different cells where they cannot communicate and offer both a separate plea deal:
- If A betrays B on the more serious charge but B stays loyal and doesn't snitch on A, then A will be set free and B will serve 20 years in prison (and vice versa)
- If both stay silent, then they will both be imprisoned for 1 year on the existing lesser charge
- If both A and B betray each other simultaneously, they both serve 5 years

Clearly the optimal overall outcome would be for both A and B to stay silent; but this relies on mutual trust and confidence, and on the ability to communicate effectively. Absent these things, the best option is betrayal (because you can never be sure about the intentions of the other person!), and the likely outcome is that both betray each other and reach a sub-optimal equilibrium.

In the case of international relations, realists believe that power is a limited resource and therefore that the pursuit of power is a **zero-sum game** (i.e. for someone to win, someone else must lose – like chess or football, for example). If the following are true:
1. Power is a zero-sum game
2. States rationally seek to maximise their interest (acquire power)
3. States are amoral and do not act based on 'ethics' or 'morality
: then it seems an inescapable conclusion that war and conflict are inevitable and permanent features of international relations. Power cannot be acquired without

harming another state's interests (because there is a limited amount of it), so naturally states will fight in order to gain power.

This is what realists call the **security dilemma**, which is re-summarised below:
1. States seek power in order to make themselves secure and maintain their interests
2. Other states see this as a threat, since power is zero-sum
3. So they themselves try to make themselves more powerful and maintain *their* interests
4. Conflict is inevitable because there is no way for states to peacefully 'expand' their power

Realists would generally argue that the security dilemma is **intractable** (unsolvable).

Solutions to the security dilemma?
Realists acknowledge there are some apparent solutions to the security dilemma, but that these are all temporary and will eventually break down.

Cooperation:
One potential solution is cooperation in global institutions and organisations, such as the United Nations (UN), European Union (EU), North Atlantic Treaty Organisation (NATO), etc. Realists would argue that:
1. These institutions are **not genuinely cooperative**; states use them to further their own national interests, rather than to pursue a common global good (e.g. Putin's Russia using their position on the Permanent 5 (P5) of the UN Security Council to veto interventions against their ally, Bashar Assad, in Syria)

2. Global institutions only 'work' because a **dominant power** exercises overall control and forces them to conform to their vision, not because states are *truly* cooperating (e.g. the allegation that Merkel's Germany is the dominant force in creating EU policy)

3. Temporary cooperation is possible, but permanent institutionalised cooperation is doomed to fail because states' selfish pursuit of power will lead to the

disintegration of cooperation, and allies cannot be indefinitely trusted (e.g. Brexit; Hitler backstabbing the Soviets and invading them despite signing a Neutrality Pact; Trump's attempt to withdraw the USA from NAFTA)

Balance of power:

Another apparent solution is a 'balance of power'. This is where no one state has enough power to dominate all others. If this looks likely, then weaker states would ally or **bandwagon** together to balance out the power of the stronger state. Or, weaker states would cluster around two larger states as alliances. This fits with the realist notion of states being rational actors and acting in their self-interest (for protection). Theoretically, this would dissuade actual conflict from breaking out, since both sides would be 'evenly' matched and the outcome of the conflict would be uncertain. In conflict, there would be much more to lose than to gain for a rational state.

However, a state could always **upset** the balance of power by becoming more powerful (more industrialised; a larger military; etc.) In this case, the process of 'balancing' only makes conflict worse in the long-term because instead of war between individual states, you instead get much more destructive wars between alliance systems. An example of this would be WWI breaking out between the Entente (Britain, France, Russia) and the Central Powers (Germany, Austria, Ottomans). In the years building up to WWI, many people thought war would be impossible because the two alliance systems had successfully 'balanced' each other to the point war would be futile. Even though the initial 'spark' for the war was just a relatively minor dispute between Austria and Serbia, it exploded into a continental war because of the alliances that had been built around Britain and Germany.

Some realists argue that the development of **nuclear weapons** has allowed for a genuine, permanent 'balance of power' to exist between nuclear-armed states. This is because the unquestionable outcome of a nuclear war would be **mutually assured destruction.** This seems to have prevented direct large-scale wars between any nuclear power (including during the Cold War between the Soviet Union and the USA; and today between India and Pakistan). Nevertheless, it has not prevented smaller skirmishes (e.g. between India or Pakistan) or indirect **proxy wars,** where both states back different sides in a third country (e.g. between Russia and the USA in Syria). Again, the balance of power is an imperfect and unsustainable solution to the security dilemma.

Global hegemony:

According to most realist thinkers, periods of 'peace' which represent a solution to the security dilemma are best seen when a single state establishes a **global hegemony**. This is when, through acquisition of immense power, one state dominates all others and is able to bend everyone else to its will. This has been seen historically ('Pax' meaning 'Peace' in Latin) in:

- *Pax Romana* [1st-3rd centuries]
- *Pax Mongolica* [13th-14th centuries]
- *Pax Britannica* [19th century]
- *Pax Americana* [late 20th century]

This does not contradict realist beliefs about the inevitability of war, because it is not arguing that war has become inherently impossible; merely that whilst there is a global **hegemon**, they have accrued enough power to make themselves temporarily unchallengeable and arbitrate all other conflicts – effectively acting as a sovereign for the duration of their dominance. Nevertheless, this is not permanent – all global hegemons have eventually collapsed due to a combination of internal and external pressures. Today, we are perhaps seeing the collapse of the *Pax Americana* because of the USA's internal socio-political difficulties and over-extension in the 'War on Terror' in the Middle East, which has greatly damaged American credibility. Once the global hegemony collapses, international anarchy returns in full measure.

Like a balance of power and cooperative institutions, global hegemony is again only a temporary solution for realists to the security dilemma.

Case study: Saudi Arabia

Saudi Arabian foreign policy under the Crown Prince Mohammad bin Salman (MBS) seems to fit the realist framework quite well. MBS has cultivated close relations with Trump's USA and Netanyahu's Israel. This is because he sees them as valuable political, economic and military counterweights to Iran, with whom Saudi Arabia has an intense regional rivalry. A realist would argue that Saudi Arabia is facing a security dilemma vis-à-vis Iran.

In 2017, MBS negotiated a £110bn arms deal with the USA and shares military intelligence extensively with Mossad (the Israeli secret service). MBS has been willing to use violence abroad to achieve the extension of Saudi power and regional security, including funding extremist Sunni militias in Syria and Iraq (to counter Iranian-funded militias); conducting a massive war in Yemen to reinstate a pro-Saudi government, resulting in nearly 3 million refugees and 17 million at risk of severe famine; murdering a critical journalist (Jamal Khashoggi); and kidnapping the Lebanese PM, Said Hariri, in 2017 when it appeared that Lebanon was drifting into the Iranian sphere of influence. In the realist framework, Saudi Arabia's commitment to Islam is superficial and used only to give it a veneer of legitimacy in its actions. In other words, the Saudi state doesn't act according to a particular moral or ethical framework but in order to achieve amoral strategic aims.

THEORY 2: LIBERALISM
Liberalism generally developed as a school of International Relations as a reaction to deficiencies in realism that became apparent in the latter half of the 20th century (following WWII).

1. **Decline in conflict:** In 1951, there were 600,000 battle-related deaths in war; in 2006, there were only 10,000. This seems to undermine the realist argument that conflict is inevitable. In addition, most conflicts today are **intra-state** (within different factions of a state) rather than **inter-state** (between states), challenging the realist tenet that states are unitary actors, and that conflict is generated by a security dilemma between states

2. **Growth in world trade:** The total value of world trade was $629,000,000 ($629m) in 1960; in 2010, it was $30,000,000,000,000 ($30tn). State economies are becoming increasingly interdependent and most economic activity now takes places *between* states rather than *within* states. The realist conception of states as sovereign, selfish, uncooperative actors pursuing a zero-sum game cannot seem to explain why states have established increasingly close economic

links from which they all mutually benefit

3. **Growth in democracy:** More states are moving towards 'peaceful' liberal-democratic models, which disfavour war as a method to pursue power and instead endorse diplomacy and political debate as a means to achieve their goals. Like the decline in conflict, this undercuts the realist assumption that states always act amorally and have no aversion to the use of violence if this helps them to secure their aims

The principles of liberalism
Liberals believe that human nature is fundamentally **altruistic** and **co-operative** and that we can achieve more power working in concert than fighting over a (wrongly-perceived) limited amount of power. This has been classically illustrated in the **'Stag Hunt'** scenario by **Rousseau**:

"Two hunters lie in wait for a stag, which will feed them both amply. If they make a lot of noise, the stag will escape. The hunters are reasonably sure that the stag will eventually cross the path of their hiding place. Meanwhile, a rabbit appears on the path. If one hunter leaps out and kills the rabbit, he will eat; but the noise will scare off the stag and the other hunter will starve. The rabbit is guaranteed but the fear is the stag will never come. Both hunters would agree to wait for the stag, because they will both have more than enough food from it, but the rabbit is a paltry prize."

The **Stag Hunt** is similar to the **Prisoners' Dilemma** in that it acknowledges there is an inherent risk in cooperation (what if the other actor betrays you?), but that since the benefits of cooperation far outweigh the risk, that most rational actors would choose to cooperate. This more closely reflects **liberal** and **socialist** principles of human nature than the conservatism of realism.

The philosopher **Hume** presented a further hypothetical scenarios which also illustrates the conceptual basis of liberalism as a theory of IR (even though Hume was not writing in this context); rowing a boat down the river with the two boatmen holding an oar on opposite sides. In this instance, only by cooperating can individuals achieve a scenario which is in their mutual benefit. If only one individual rows, the boat will veer into the riverbank; if neither rows, then the boat will not move. Other liberals have referenced cooperative animal behaviours (e.g. killer whales swimming together at speed to generate waves that will knock seals off ice floes) to argue that cooperation is natural.

In general, liberals would argue that human nature is **inherently** altruistic, and therefore that states also have the **capacity** to act in a moral, rational and altruistic way. Like realism, liberalism claims to be a **positivist** theory – describing the world empirically 'as it is'.

The Kantian Triangle

The foundation of modern liberal theory in International Relations is not that conflict is *impossible*, but that it can be made *less likely* or avoided by pursuing certain cooperative mechanisms. In other words, peace is **not the default,** but it is **achievable**.

The three mechanisms referenced frequently by liberals are the 'Kantian Triangle', adapted from the philosopher **Immanuel Kant**, of:
1. Democracy
2. International organisations
3. Economic interdependence

Democracy:

Liberals claim that the 'nature' of a state is **not fixed**, and that the state is **not a unitary actor.** A state's interest reflects the plurality of interests in a state, and the interests of a state may therefore differ according to which political groups control the government, to public opinion, or even pressure-group activity. For example, the Vietnam War was brought to an end partially by massive anti-government protests in America from the working class, civil rights activists and students.

Liberals believe that the **constitutional** and **political** organisation of a state affects its behaviour towards other states:
- **Constitutional organisation:** Whether a state has mechanisms that uphold human rights or provide for judicial oversight of the executive government
- **Political organisation:** Whether a state is a democracy or an autocracy; whether internal differences and disputes are settled via the bullet or the ballot

Human beings, in the liberal sense, are generally rational, altruistic and cooperative. If all humans in a state have a say in political decisions through democracy, then it is overwhelmingly likely the state will act in the same way. If the political decisions of the state are made by a small group of individuals, then hostile and non-cooperative behaviour becomes more likely.

The liberal perspective on **'democratic peace theory'** is that states have a **choice**, and that adopting liberal-democratic models of government make a state more inclined towards cooperation, harmony and balance in the international arena, e.g. Canada; or Germany; or Japan. Liberal theory on state behaviour is not necessarily **utopian**, but it is **optimistic.**

International organisations:
The second major pillar of liberalism is the importance of intergovernmental organisations **(IGOs)** and non-governmental organisations **(NGOs)**. It is difficult to specify precise statistics, but the number of international organisations has certainly grown exponentially since the Second World War.

Clearly, without international organisations, many modern challenges – such as climate change – are unsolvable. As the **'Stag Hunt'** scenario demonstrates, power and gains are not zero-sum, and there is far more to be gained by cooperating. International organisations reflect and hold the principles of liberal internationalism – the first attempt at this was the League of Nations, followed later by the United Nations and its sub-bodies, e.g. the World Health Organisation, and a multiplicity of regional organisations; ASEAN, the African Union, NAFTA, the EU, the Arab League, etc.

Liberals believe in international organisations because they believe in the inherent rationality and cooperativity of human nature; international organisations reflect this on the global stage.

Economic interdependence:

Drawing on the classical liberal economic models of Cobden, IR liberals argue that states can be tied together through **commerce**, which reduces the likelihood of war and conflict. If states are economically integrated, then it is much less likely they would go to war since this would be mutually destructive to their economic interests. This would be the case regardless of ideological differences or other disagreements, as can be seen by the reluctance of the USA and China to engage militarily. It was also the driving precept underpinning the creation of the European Coal and Steel Community (forerunner of the EU) centred on France and Germany, who had fought three wars in the previous half-century. The reasoning was that by tying the two economies together, it would make war impossible (this has so far proved true!)

In the view of liberals, trade and economic interdependence is also the best way to spread cultures and ideas which will lead to **'bonds of eternal peace'**, and can also lead to cooperation on issues like development, poverty reduction, and tackling climate change across the planet.

Complex interdependence
If the elements of the 'Kantian Triangle' are fulfilled, then **complex interdependence** (Keohane & Nye) is established internationally. In this model, states are so thoroughly interlinked through economic relations; international organisations; and democratic fraternity, that trade and diplomacy become much more attractive options. States begin to develop a common **ethical code** and are networked together, rather than acting as discrete, **atomistic** units.

International relations to global governance?
Given that states want to and *can* act cooperatively, **global governance** (political integration of states) can be achieved to some extent. This has also been driven by other factors though, and states are not necessarily the only important actors on the global stage. Other key actors may include:
- **Religious groups:** E.g. the Catholic Church
- **Social movements:** E.g. environmentalism, BLM, #MeToo
- **Transnational corporations (TNCs):** E.g. Apple, Facebook, Alphabet, Amazon
- **Terrorist groups:** E.g. IS, Al-Qaeda

We are perhaps moving past a world of independent nation-states, who are the only meaningful actors interacting with each other **(international relations)** to a world in which states *and* other actors have a stake in politics and governance **(global politics).**

Case study: The European Union
The European Union was established as the 'European Coal and Steel Community' in 1950, with the aim of uniting European states economically and politically to secure lasting peace. The six founding countries were Belgium, France, West Germany, Italy, Luxembourg and the Netherlands. Over time, the ECSC underwent many developments. Some key milestones were:
-   **1957:** The Treaty of Rome creating the 'European Economic Community' and a common market, with an aim to minimise tariffs and trade barriers
-   **1973:** The accession of Denmark, Ireland and the UK
-   **1986:** The accession of Spain and Portugal, after the collapse of the right-wing dictatorships of Franco and Salazar respectively in the 1970s and the implementation of democracy
-   **1990:** The end of the Cold War and the integration of East Germany into West Germany
-   **1993:** The creation of the Single Market and the conversion of the EEC into the EU
-   **1995:** The accession of Austria, Finland and Sweden; and the introduction of the 'Schengen Agreement', allowing people to travel across much of the EU without a passport
-   **2002:** The full implementation of the Euro as a single currency across most of the EU
-   **2004-2007:** The accession of ten former Communist, Eastern European states

In this way, the European Union broadly reflects key aspects of the liberal framework of international relations. It is a model for how commerce and trade can create closer ties between countries and prevent conflict; and of how a bloc of democratised states can serve as an inspiration for other states to disavow autocratic models (right-wing fascism in Portugal, Greece and Spain; Communist dictatorship in Eastern Europe), and to adopt more democratic models themselves.

The continued existence of the EU suggests that institutionalised international cooperation is a real possibility and that it can serve as the basis for lasting peace. Over time, the central structures of the EU have become more developed, efficient and systematic – with a well-formed dual executive, dual legislature and judiciary. Clearly, the fact that so many states have joined the EU (expanding the original 6 to 27) demonstrates the attraction of complex interdependence and that given the opportunity, rational democratic states will band together for a greater mutual good than could be achieved alone, disregarding conflict as a way to achieve power.

THEORY 3: ANARCHICAL SOCIETY

A third theory of international relations which attempts to synthesise realism and liberalism is the **anarchical society** or the **'English School'.** This is somewhat misleading, since many founders of the theoretical tradition are not English but South African, Italian, Japanese and American. It is also sometimes referred to as **liberal realism.**

Neo-realism + neo-liberalism, liberal realism (anarchical society)
N.B. 'Neoliberalism' here is not the same as that of Rand, Nozick, Thatcher, etc.

Neo-realism (structural realism)
The classical realist argument is that:
Human beings are aggressive, states reflect the nature of their constituent human beings ▢ states are aggressive, security dilemma, conflict

The structural or neo-realist argument is that:
International anarchy, states seek (at least regional) power for security, power is zero-sum, security dilemma, conflict

Both variants of realism ultimately conclude that conflict is a key feature of international relations, but differ as to its fundamental cause. Classical realists focus on the inherent nature of humans and states; whereas structural realists (such as **John Mearsheimer**) focus on the way that the international structure forces states to act. In the classical realist model, therefore, conflict is totally unavoidable because it is an axiomatic part of human and state behaviour. In the structural realist model, conflict could hypothetically be avoided if states could find a non-violent way to achieve security.

Neo-liberalism
The classical liberal argument is that:
Human nature is altruistic and rational, states <u>can</u> be rational and cooperative, states will serve a moral-ethical interest rather than pure self-interest, states will cooperate (and sovereignty will be ceded to international organisations)

The neo-liberal argument (e.g. **Robert Keohane**) is that:
Human nature is rational, states will rationally cooperate if a policy can lead to mutual gains in power, states will cooperate (sovereignty will be pooled into international organisations), this cooperation will intensify somewhat over time and states will stick to cooperation even if it is not in their immediate self-interest

Both variants of liberalism conclude that states will cooperate, but whereas classical liberals focus more on cooperation as something that instantly consolidates around a moral-ethical shared framework, neo-liberals believe that the strength of cooperation is something that develops slowly over time and only if it serves a mutual and material interest.

The 'international anarchy' synthesis
As a first principle, **Hedley Bull** (the founder of the English School) accepts the **neo-realist** premise that the international stage is anarchic – i.e. there is no overall sovereign to enforce order. However, he disagrees with neo-realists that this will inevitably lead to a struggle for power and conflict; and disagrees with the conclusion that only a balance of power or global hegemon can stave off disorder. Bull posits that even though there is no global sovereign, states can still construct a set of rules, norms and values within which they can cooperate; this is a **neo-liberal** premise. Instead of an anarchical free-for-all, what we can achieve is an anarchical society or a society of states.

Bull points out that states will not always cooperate, because they are not selfless and will not be altruistic if it excessively damages their self-interest. But states *will* cooperate if there are mutual gains. States can identify **universally common interests** which do not really advantage one state over another, but benefit all states collectively. These can form the basis of common values/rules. E.g.:
- Not engaging in unprovoked or purposefully destructive wars
- Not attacking diplomats, ambassadors or political representatives
- Trade in resources in which both countries have respective comparative advantage

Over time, these common **interests and values** can be codified into a set of **norms and rules.** These are not 'laws' in the formal sense, in that there is no sovereign authority to compel states to follow them by the use of force. Yet, states would generally follow them anyway, because they benefit everyone and don't really disadvantage anyone. **Diplomatic immunity** is a good example of this. Diplomatic immunity means that a diplomat (a permanent political representative from one state to another) can be expelled back to their home state, but cannot be prosecuted and punished in their host state for a crime. On one level, this might seem ridiculous as a diplomat could theoretically get away with any crime – up to and including murder (e.g. PC Yvonne Fletcher, shot by an unknown gunman who fired from inside the Libyan Embassy in London, 1984). However, most diplomats would not commit flagrant crimes, so as not to upset this norm; and most states would respect diplomatic immunity, because if they didn't, then they would be at risk of *their* diplomats being expelled in an act of retaliation.

An **anarchical society** therefore emerges, in which there is still no overall sovereign **(anarchy)** but there is a common understanding of the 'rules of the game' between states **(society)** which prevents constant conflict. States *can* cooperate in an institutional way, but only when it is in their interests.
Over time, *"...a group of states (or, more generally, a group of independent political communities) which not merely form a system, in the sense that the behaviour of each is a necessary factor in the calculations of the others, but also have established by*

dialogue and consent common rules and institutions for the conduct of their relations, and recognise their common interest in maintaining these arrangements." (Bull, 1977)
Rules and norms will therefore evolve into **inter-state** institutions. However, states are still **sovereign** and participate voluntarily and of their own free will – and will ignore the institution temporarily if it goes against their self-interest. A good example of this is the **United Nations.**

The English School is therefore a synthesis between **realism** and **liberalism. International anarchy** exists, but states can **avoid the security dilemma** by upholding **common norms** which are mutually beneficial for all states' security. This will lead to **limited institutional cooperation**. Although states will temporarily act in their **self-interest** if it clashes with the institution, they will not totally destroy the '**anarchical society**' because this is fundamentally against their self-interest.

COMPARING LIBERALISM AND REALISM

Feature	Realism	Liberalism
Human nature	Human nature is selfish, imperfect and irrational in the long-term even though it rational in the seeking of immediate utility and of perceived security	Human nature can be altruistic, rational and cooperative and is generally so on the whole; although this is not guaranteed for all individuals
Power	Power is a finite resource and the pursuit of power is a 'zero-sum' game for states – a 'winner' requires a 'loser'. Power is necessary for security	Power is unlimited and all states can gain power simultaneously; it is not a game of 'winners' and 'losers'. Cooperation = multiple winners

Order and security	The international system is anarchic, so states can act with impunity. Because states don't trust each other, an intractable 'security dilemma' emerges. Peace can only be maintained temporarily by a global hegemon or a balance of power	The international system is characterised by co-operation and complex interdependence, which can provide states with mutual security. States do not *have* to feel threatened by each other and can establish a stable international order
Likelihood of conflict	For classical realists, conflict is inevitable because states reflect aggressive human nature. For structural realists, conflict is inevitable because the security dilemma means states must pursue power to feel 'safe', which creates conflict with other states	It is in the rational long-term interests of states to cooperate and avoid conflict, because this is mutually destructive and based on a mistaken perception of zero-sum gains. States will prefer to solve disputes via diplomacy and debate
International organisations	International organisations can exist, but will be ineffective or eventually fail. Lack of trust and the pursuit of national interests means that institutional cooperation is difficult,	International institutions (both economic and political, governmental and non-governmental) reflect the cooperative ability of states, and are growing in number. Over time, they have gained

	and organisations will be dominated by great powers/a global hegemon	greater influence and powers
Significance of states	States are the key and only meaningful actors in the international system; pursue a national interest defined by power; are unitary; and are not guided by morality or justice	States are no longer the only actors in the international system – there are also non-state actors. They are not unitary and may sometimes act according to ethical principles
Links to Ideologies	**Conservatism** Authority ⊇ stability; the "state of nature"; the condition of human nature (psychological and moral imperfection) **Nationalism** Conservative nationalism; chauvinistic nationalism	**Liberalism** Developmental individualism; rationality; constitutionalism; liberal democracy; social contract/ govt by consent **Socialism** Collectivism; sociable and cooperative human nature **Nationalism** Liberal nationalism

Printed in Great Britain
by Amazon

37381413R00165